Play Blackjack Like the Pros

D1019487

ALSO BY KEVIN BLACKWOOD

The Counter

PLAY BLACKJACK LIKE THE PROS

Kevin Blackwood

HARPER

NEW YORK • LONDON • TORONTO • SYDNEY

HARPER

The material in this book is for information purposes only.
Following the methods and strategies will not guarantee success.

PLAY BLACKJACK LIKE THE PROS. Copyright © 2005 by Kevin Blackwood.
All rights reserved. Printed in the United States of America. No part
of this book may be used or reproduced in any manner whatsoever
without written permission except in the case of brief quotations
embodied in critical articles and reviews. For information address
HarperCollins Publishers Inc., 10 East 53rd Street,
New York, NY 10022.

HarperCollins books may be purchased for educational, business,
or sales promotional use. For information please write: Special
Markets Department, HarperCollins Publishers Inc.,
10 East 53rd Street, New York, NY 10022.

FIRST EDITION

Designed by Debbie Glasserman

Library of Congress Cataloging-in-Publication Data

Blackwood, Kevin.
    Play blackjack like the pros / Kevin Blackwood.—1st ed.
        p.   cm.
    ISBN 0-06-073112-5
    1. Blackjack (Game)   I. Title.
GV1295.B55B57   2005
795.4'23—dc22

                                                        2004054182

11   12   13   WBC/RRD   10   9   8   7   6   5

This book is dedicated to two legends of the game:

Allan Brown, one of the classiest players ever to sit at a blackjack table. Few gamblers anywhere in the world have matched your success or skill. I'm honored to be your friend.

Stanford Wong, the pioneer and trailblazer for many card counters like me. Your astute insights paved the way and showed us all how to win at blackjack.

CONTENTS

Contents

by Stanford Wong

Games and puzzles have always fascinated me. I especially enjoy figuring out solutions to complex problems. When I was about twelve I started unlocking the secrets of blackjack. I used an office calculator (personal computers did not exist then) to work out the odds. I removed the dealer's upcard and two player cards, and figured out what the player's expectation was for standing, hitting, or doubling down. Unfortunately, before I finished, Dr. Edward Thorp beat me to the punch with *Beat the Dealer*, the first book on card counting. Some people doubted that blackjack could be beaten, but I was convinced that Thorp presented a valid winning system. I learned his Ten-Count System, and then had to wait until I turned twenty-one before I could use my new skill in Nevada.

The game keeps changing, so there is always a need for new books with the most current information. Casinos develop countermeasures to try to thwart card counters, and skilled players in turn figure out new ways to get an edge. Since I published *Professional Blackjack* in 1974, many other books on card counting have appeared. Kevin Blackwood is the latest author to make a contribution to this science. His *Play Blackjack Like the Pros* does a good job of explaining how to win under today's rules and playing conditions. It's also written in a fun style that makes for an entertaining and enjoyable read.

Blackwood is a high-stakes pro who spent years in the trenches. He claims to have won over a million dollars at the game, and I have no reason to doubt that he has. Can you do that, too? Well, yes, you can, if you really want to. You don't need a computer brain to play winning blackjack. Use Blackwood's textbook and win your own million.

There are no shortcuts to magically transform you from zero to hero at the blackjack tables, so be prepared to work hard—the casinos don't simply mail checks to people who learn to count cards. Yet the game definitely can be beaten, and *Play Blackjack Like the Pros* provides all the necessary tools to make you the favorite every time you walk through the doors of a casino.

So good luck, and may you make the casinos pay for this book many times over!

INTRODUCTION

Can You Become a Pro?

For the last two decades, I've lived what many would consider the American dream, earning big bucks while working only part-time. My profession? Card counter. My office? Blackjack tables all over the world. Incredible perks accompanied my vocation—ringside boxing tickets for the big fights, offers to play golf with celebrities, front-row seats to sold-out shows, and gourmet dinners at the finest restaurants. Though I enjoyed these lavish experiences, the comps were strictly a side benefit. I chose this unusual line of work for only one reason—to make money. *Easy money.* And I succeeded, becoming one of the top blackjack players in the country.

How did I win in a game where everyone is expected to lose? More important, is it possible for you to follow in my footsteps and routinely withdraw money from casinos? Contrary to what some people believe, you don't need to be a mathematical genius or play on some highly capitalized team to become the predator instead of the prey in blackjack. I'll show how my career refutes these two common misconceptions, and how discipline, drive, and persistence were the keys to my success. These qualities ultimately separate the few who actually make a living at blackjack from those who frequent the glitzy temples of chance only to help pay the light bill.

MOVIES AND MISCONCEPTIONS

The typical Hollywood myth portrays professional blackjack players as walking data banks—"Rain Man" clones with incredible photographic memories. But you don't have to be a brilliant autistic savant like Dustin Hoffman's character to succeed at the tables (although I've had many sessions where I felt like Tom Cruise after some big wins at Caesars Palace). The truth is that anyone with reasonable intelligence can learn to count cards and win at blackjack. Determination is far more important than aptitude, and my main strength is a dogged tenacity.

Finding the hottest clubs takes hard work and extra effort. In my pursuit of profitable games, I traveled all over the world to places like the Dominican Republic, where I played private tables in small, dirty, and dangerous casinos. I flew to the Orient when casinos there instituted rare bonuses for five-card hands. I made only one gambling trip to Europe, but it was profitable, as I pounded several clubs in Belgium offering an advantageous early *surrender* rule.

It wasn't in search of frequent-flier miles that I journeyed to these distant destinations. Like other card counters, I still made periodic pilgrimages to the gambling Mecca known as Sin City, but to beat blackjack on a consistent basis required hard work and a willingness to boldly go where few had gone before.

REALITY

My gambling philosophy could be summed up in two words— aggressive and selective. I always sought to maximize my wins by spreading aggressively whenever I had the edge. Also, I was extremely selective in choosing casinos, absolutely refusing to play marginal games. It takes a great deal of perseverance to overcome the many obstacles facing card counters, and far too many settle for mediocre blackjack conditions.

The result is most players never reach the highest levels. They view professional gambling as the ideal lifestyle, since it combines high profits with the ultimate in flexible hours. These people gravitate to card counting because they want the kind of job in which, when everyone else rolls out of bed in the morning, they just roll over. However, trading in your paycheck for casino chips is anything but easy, and not for the faint of heart.

It might be fun to daydream about how you're going to win enough on your next trip to buy that new Porsche, but it's a whole different world when you've sat through twelve draining hours of the worst cards imaginable. It takes steel nerves and thick skin to remain unaffected by the kaleidoscope of emotions bombarding you at the tables.

Yet there are few legal jobs anywhere in the world that offer the potential of clearing ten grand a month from just a few days of work. So the reward is great, and I know it can be done. I started out with only a small amount of cash and have won over a million dollars at the blackjack tables.

Very few individual players in the world can make that claim, and I will share many anecdotes from my career to help you learn from my experience. But my life has been far from a picture-perfect fairy tale. I've also made my share of mistakes, and I'll recount a few of those boneheaded blunders to show you *what not to do* as well as *what to do*.

BECOMING A WINNER

My card-counting career refutes many of the common myths people believe about gambling, but I certainly wasn't the only person consistently crushing blackjack. Thousands of other skilled players learned the same winning principles and attacked casinos all over the globe. To add a little spice to this book, I'll sprinkle in a few anecdotes and biographical vignettes from some of the more interesting characters I've met in blackjack, such as:

Allan Brown—one of the best all-around blackjack players and winner of several big money tournaments.

Anthony Curtis—probably the most visible face of anyone today in the gambling world because of his frequent TV appearances.

Mickey Weinberg—perhaps the brainiest card counter of all time and developer of shuffle-tracking computer chips.

Rick Blaine—a seasoned pro who has led some of the biggest blackjack teams.

Howard Grossman—sharp, fast-talking, and controversial, he has done virtually everything there is to do on both sides of the blackjack tables and ran the first card-counting school in Las Vegas.

Every chart, graph, story, or example in this book is written to help answer the one central question in the minds of most readers: *can you become a pro?*

The good news is that the skills and techniques needed to become a winning blackjack player can be mastered by nearly anyone and are easier to learn than poker, where you also need to read your opponents in addition to learning the correct strategies. Almost everyone can improve their game and win more often, and I will offer several different levels of playing ability, from beginner to expert.

Play Blackjack Like the Pros is more practical than theoretical, and I want to paint the big picture of how to succeed at the tables rather than overwhelm you with superfluous details. And don't expect to understand everything the first time through. Many of the exercises will take practice and patience, but don't let the mathematical part of card counting or the barrage of new terms scare you. I'll outline the basics of the game for the novice, and an extensive glossary in the back covers blackjack jargon and lingo.

Every story in this book is true and none of the numbers (wins and losses) have been embellished, exaggerated, or inflated. However, some of the names and places have been changed or are composites to protect the identities of the innocent (or in some cases, the guilty).

Now it is true that many of the highly profitable single-deck games have disappeared in the last few years. But as long as the game of blackjack has been dealt, there have been legal ways to reverse the odds and beat the house. I believe that creative and disciplined players will continue to find chinks in the casinos' armor. *Play Blackjack Like the Pros* will give you the knowledge to exploit those weaknesses and become a consistent winner.

CHAPTER ONE

The Myths of Blackjack

THE TYPICAL TOURIST

One of the biggest obstacles keeping most blackjack players from improving their game is that they aren't realistic about their current skill level. It is human nature to overrate ourselves and few of us are very objective in analyzing our flaws. A large number of tourists think they play basic strategy accurately. They may even have read a book or bought a laminated card intended to teach them the correct method.

Yet in the fast-paced environment of the casino, what little they learned often melts away in the heat of battle. They never quite embedded proper strategy into their brain so it became second nature. Instead, they use some combination of correct plays and hunches. For example, they are told to always hit 16 against the dealer's *face card*, so they dutifully comply, only to *bust* out three times in a row. Inevitably, the next time the tourist receives the dreaded 16, he gives up on basic strategy and stands.

This time the *dealer* draws the *paint* and pays the table. The tourist is pleased and elated that he could outsmart the experts. He becomes convinced there's a better future in consulting an ouija board for his decisions than in relying on basic strategy.

This is one of the more common gambler's fallacies and is called *selective memory*. I will discuss a few of these misconceptions in this chapter to illuminate why blackjack is different from other casino games, and show the *real* reasons why it can be beaten.

SELECTIVE MEMORY

Like some mythical monsters, selective memory rears its ugly head in many shapes and forms. The above illustration of hitting stiffs is fairly common, as players tend to remember big hands or jackpots they won. They often give themselves the credit for wins and blame outside sources for their losses. When you don't hit a stiff, it is more temporarily gratifying since you do stay alive longer. But over the long run you are paying a high price for that short-term pleasure.

The best example of selective memory comes from huge wins. Often when I'm introduced as a high-stakes blackjack player to someone new, the first question I get asked is "What was the most you ever won in one day?" A much better question would be "What is the most you ever lost in one day?" This is because experienced pros vividly remember the days when everything came unglued much more than the great trips. These disasters can even be beneficial since they temper one's outlook and help to keep a sober perspective of the overall picture.

However, tourists typically display much more selective memory of their ups and downs in gambling. After I politely decline to answer their question about my biggest wins I am often subjected to their highly detailed story of some big slot jackpot they hit or that one magic evening at the table where all the cards fell perfectly and they couldn't lose.

The point here is not that I'm a magnet for attracting the most boring and long-winded people at every cocktail party I attend. It's that usually the big wins stand out to people. I'm always slightly amused by these tales, and I often follow up with an innocent question of how they have done overall. Most invariably look me straight in the eye and say they are ahead.

This obviously cannot be the case, or Donald Trump would have to get a real job. Possibly the worst thing that happens to these players is when they have that one big killer day at the tables. The absolute worst thing is to win big on your first trip. Then you feel bulletproof. You always remember how easy it was and tend to overlook all the losing trips. But even huge jackpots can be squandered away if you play long enough.

Yet many don't realize that truth. They sincerely believe they're up overall because of that one royal flush they hit three years ago. The best way to counter this fallacy is to keep good records. Only if you maintain an accurate log can you get a true appraisal of what your hobby is costing you. Otherwise, you are just guessing. Most people fail to face up to reality.

Don Henley sang that there are three sides to every story—yours, mine, and the cold hard truth. Keeping track of your gambling finances might provide information you don't want to hear, but is the only way to find that truth.

STREAKS

Another common myth revolves around hot or cold dealers—nearly sacred words you'll routinely hear to describe the incredible swings that occur at blackjack. Even some card counters aren't immune from this type of thinking—the leader of the first team I joined refused to play at any table where the dealer was excessively hot (which was an absurd superstition).

It's easy to understand the source of such logic. Dealers do have streaks, and some days it seems like they never bust. However, unless you happen to be Nostradamus, there is absolutely no way to determine the future. The cards don't care and don't know how many hands the house has won over the last hour. You can perceive with your own eyes that the dealer is riding a hot or cold streak—

that is reality. Yet there is absolutely no way to know when it will end.

Past results never affect future results. I could cite several mathematical reasons for this, but let me give you a practical example. Say you are *heads-up* at a six-deck shoe playing flawless basic strategy. Unfortunately, the house is crushing you and it seems like the bald guy sweeping in your chips hasn't busted since Nixon was president. Suppose at this moment in time (when ol' cue ball is simply on fire) he is replaced by a pleasant and shapely female dealer (fortunately with hair). If the cards remain unchanged as she takes over (no *burn card*), what will happen over the rest of the shoe? Exactly the same thing that would have happened if the bald dealer had stayed at the table. Dealers (unless they are cheating) have absolutely no control over the cards. They cannot influence whether they win or lose.

So the only thing that would be different in our illustration is that playing the rest of the shoe might become more pleasant, since you at least had a nicer-looking adversary across the table. Most don't understand this concept and tend to blame dealers for bad cards, or curse out the numbskull sitting next to them for taking the dealer's *bust card*, or steam over the moron who split tens and cost them a big bet.

BLACKJACK IDIOTS

Bad players and bad decisions even out over time. Again, selective memory is at work here because we tend to remember the time it hurt us when that stupid punch-drunk sailor at *third base* accidentally hit his hard 18 and caused everyone at the table to lose. These "mistakes" help just as often, but we forget those or attribute them to luck, as in "You really screwed up, but we got off easy that time." The flip side is like Pavlov's dog. Whenever one of these dimwits makes a truly horrendous play and it works, he *always* remembers that one wonderful moment of success and is encouraged to keep doing it.

CHEATING

Another question I often hear is "Don't the casinos cheat?" The short answer is no. It might have been different back in the mob-run era of Las Vegas, and some early blackjack authors were overly paranoid about cheating and spread this legend. But today the chance of getting cheated is virtually nil.

So you have no reason to get angry at dealers. They have no control over the outcome. My suggestion is to be polite to them in either circumstance. And if you tip, it only makes sense to tip the same amount whether you win or lose. The dealer is giving the same level of service and cannot influence the cards in any way. However, not all dealers understand this principle, either, and think they deserve more when you finally get lucky and pull that *snapper* (casino slang for a black-jack). I will leave it up to you whether to respond at that moment with a tip equaling a generous portion of your winnings or with a mathematical discourse on the erroneous theory of hot dealers.

HOUSE MONEY

Another well-known saying is "I'm playing on house money." Many gamblers fall into this trap and take greater risks when playing with winnings (house money) rather than their own cash (crinkled bills they brought with them from under the mattress). The fallacy in this thinking is blatantly obvious—money is money. Whether you obtained it by working in the factory for forty hours or found it on the sidewalk, it still has the same value.

However, the distinction comes in how it is appreciated by the holder. Money you slaved over to earn is less likely to be wasted than a big jackpot you won on a whim at the slot carousel. True professionals purge themselves of this mentality. They know that if someone feels compelled to buy a new boat after a nice fat win, they might also have to sell it after a big loss on their next trip. Adopting a long-run mentality is important if you want to keep your newfound loot rather than squander it.

BETTING SYSTEMS

The next windmill I'd like to take a shot at is progressive betting systems. If someone asks me whether to use one, I give a short answer—they simply don't work. One of the best known is the *Martingale system*. The basic theory is to double your bet after each loss until you finally win, then drop back down to one unit. For example, if you started with $5, you'd go to $10, $20, $40, $80, $160, $320, $640, and so on until you win a hand, netting you a whopping $5 profit overall.

For the sake of brevity, I will not give a detailed explanation of the flaws of progressive betting, but the bottom line is this—you will have a lot of small wins punctuated by bone-rattling losses. It is commonly assumed that you will never lose too many hands in a row, but it does happen. For example, if you were to lose ten hands in a row, you'd need to risk over $2,500 just to win back your original $5 loss. Gamblers either don't have unlimited bankrolls to continually double up their losses until they win or the casinos' maximum bets (often $500 or $1,000) prevent them from pushing that much out on the felt. Casino veteran Mark Pilarski calls the Martingale system "the worst money management system you can use. You would think this form of betting is foolproof and logical because you have to win sooner or later. But after spending 18 years on the casino floor, permit me to declare one given. Six, seven or eight losses in a row are not unusual; it's actually quite common. A quick string of losses and you'll be tapped out in mere minutes and trying to score free drinks in the keno lounge."

I could cite much more evidence, but that is not the purpose of this book. Every mathematical simulation done on blackjack will tell you the same thing—progressive betting will *never* make you a winner over the long haul. If the house has a 1 percent edge on a given game, then you will lose approximately 1 percent of your money regardless of how often you change your bets. In the short run, you might get lucky and push out the big guns at the right time. But unless you're counting, there's no reason to ever jump your bets and expect to gain any advantage by doing so. If progressive betting makes you happy and gives you a more pleasurable gaming experience, then feel free to continue frolicking. However, if your concept of fun involves winning rather than losing, then let me explain how card counting works.

CARD COUNTING 101

This section is markedly different from the earlier part of the chapter because card counting is not just another false system. Indeed, the casinos would like people to dismiss card counting as just another one of the myths of gambling—one that is impossible to do without a photographic memory—or is an outdated technique that no longer exists because of six-deck shoes. If becoming a winning card counter were truly unattainable for us mortals, then my writing and you reading this book would be a complete waste of time. Yet it can be done—by people like me and by readers like you.

Later chapters will cover the how of card counting. At this juncture all I will cover is the why. It's important this concept is fully understood before you try to improve your blackjack skills, because if you truly believe it can be done, then you will be far more motivated. It is only natural that some people are skeptical of card counting. Almost every game of chance has its share of quacks selling books with a secret system guaranteed to beat the house. Unfortunately, they forgot to put the truth in the blurbs—that the only way they got rich was by selling suckers their book, not by using their anniversary date to beat the lottery. I suggest you check out the credentials of anyone who wants to sell you a book showing how to win easy money. My guess is few of their tax returns would measure up to their claims.

MEMORY

I consistently won because blackjack is different from other casino games. This quirk that allows people to exploit the game is best illustrated by two key words—dependent and independent. Those terms aren't used just to explain the status of your relationship after you return home from an all-night gambling bender. They also have some applications in mathematics and show why the game of twenty-one differs markedly from other table games.

Craps and roulette are the best models to illustrate the concept of independent trial processes. Simply put, it means each new roll or spin is totally independent of any previous results. This is intuitive to most people, yet commonly ignored.

For example, a shooter may be hot as a pistol at the craps table. Yet the odds against him throwing another seven on his next roll is exactly the same as when he started—5 to 1. The dice have absolutely no memory, and the past does not affect the future.

The flip side of that example can be found in roulette. A tourist may be monitoring the sequence of numbers that have hit over the last few hours at the wheel. He has noticed that his favorite number (22) hasn't come up once, so he assumes it is due and starts betting it heavily. However, the odds again remain unchanged. The chance of hitting 22 remains fixed, no matter what has transpired earlier in the day, since the little ivory ball has no memory.

However, blackjack is different because the *past* does impact the *future*. This happens because as cards are played, they are removed and placed into the *discard rack*, never to be seen again (at least until the shuffle). So the starting composition and ratios between high and low cards is constantly changing as cards are removed.

The easiest way to illustrate this principle is with aces, which give the player about a 50 percent starting advantage to begin his hand. The main reason for this monster edge is because every snapper you pull pays an extra bonus. But the odds of receiving a blackjack can change dramatically each round. For example, if half the cards are removed from a single deck and all four aces remain, your chances for starting a hand with an ace would now be about 1 in 7 rather than 1 in 13. However, if all four aces are gone, then your odds of getting that coveted blackjack would be very easy to calculate—zero.

So here we have a game that offers astute players useful information from previous hands. Blackjack is different from craps and roulette because it does have *memory*. Skillful observers can track the subtle changes in deck compositions and jump their bets when there is an excess of tens and aces in the remaining cards.

Sharp readers might question this concept since the dealer has the same chance of receiving great cards as the players. That is true, but there are three main reasons why high counts tip the odds against the house in these situations. First, the player gets paid 3 to 2 ($15 for every $10 bet) for his snappers, while the dealer in essence only receives even money for her blackjack. (I will normally use feminine terms to refer to dealers and masculine terms for players, not for any sexist reasons, but simply to make it clearer to follow.) Second, players have the ability to *double down* on their bets—an especially attractive option in *positive counts* (when the remaining deck composition has a greater percentage of tens than normal) while the dealer can only hit. This surplus of face cards makes a huge difference when you're pushing out another stack of chips to double down on your 11. Last, the dealer is required to hit all her stiffs (12–16) and tends to bust those hands much more frequently in high counts (because the deck is rich in big cards). The player doesn't have this restriction and can choose wisely to change his play and stand at those times.

This should help explain why counting can create an edge over the house for smart players who pay close attention to what cards have been played. The advantage primarily comes from correctly raising your bets during the high counts, since the remaining decks are loaded with more face cards and aces than normal.

CHAPTER TWO

Beating the House

The fact that I ended up making my living in casinos was in itself a long shot. While growing up in Maine, no one I knew considered professional gambling as a possible vocation. At that time few casinos even existed outside Nevada. So first of all, there were no opportunities anywhere near Maine. Second, most frugal New Englanders frowned upon any conspicuous waste of their hard-earned cash. The concept of losing one's money, but having a good time, seemed as silly as asking Mrs. Lincoln, "So other than your husband getting shot, how did you like the play?"

And last came the morality issue. Though gambling no longer carried the same stigma previous generations attached to it, I had grown up in a church that frowned upon playing cards of any type, let alone gambling. So I started out as one of the most unlikely candidates for a future career in card counting.

All that changed a few years later when I was finishing up my master's degree at grad school. One day in the library, I took a break from some stimulating studies on ancient Near Eastern archaeology and browsed the magazine rack. A story about gamblers in an old

Sports Illustrated article caught my attention. One of the high rollers profiled was a blackjack player named Ken Uston. He had masterminded several card-counting teams that won millions from the casinos. Their astounding profits ignited a chain reaction in my head and I immediately felt like I'd found my calling in life.

FALSE START

Some of the smaller casinos in Nevada used to operate a lot of junket flights to bring traffic into out-of-the-way towns like Wendover and Elko. These obscure destinations were so desperate for business that I found an overnight flight to Carson City for free if you showed at least $300. This was pretty much all the money I had at that time, but I expected my pauper days to end soon, so the trip seemed well worth the risk.

I learned a simple counting system on the plane, then mastered basic strategy on the boring ride from Reno to the state capital. I was the first one out of the bus and started betting $5 a pop at the table nearest the front door. I didn't know how to size my bets (an optimal form of wagering in relation to your advantage on each given hand) when the cards favored me, so I simply jumped up to $25 on any high count.

I started out on fire and after two hours was up $600. It all seemed so easy, and I couldn't understand why everyone wasn't doing this for a living. I fantasized about the changes my newfound riches would bring, and at the current win rate of $300 an hour, many things seemed within my grasp.

However, none of those dreams of the future included the next sequence of events. As quickly as the pile of chips had grown in front of me, they vanished. Soon, I not only lost all my winnings, but all my money. I spent the last few hours of my first casino experience sitting outside on a bench waiting for the sun to rise and my miserable red-eye gambling junket to end.

It was embarrassing, to say the least. I had foolishly told several of my friends how I intended to make my mark in the blackjack world. Instead, I had to show up for work the next day tired, beat, and broke—just another bozo with "loser" stamped in capital letters across my forehead.

HISTORICAL PERSPECTIVE

I wasn't the first, nor would I be the last chump to think I could beat the casinos with some clandestine strategy. Historically, gambling clubs have welcomed system players to their tables with open arms. The casinos know that most schemes devised to beat the house are flawed, and eventually the dealer will take away whatever money and hopes the player brought on the flight down.

Dreams usually die slowly for most people, but Las Vegas has a way of speeding up that process. Some players might get lucky, but casinos rest assured that no one will win over the long run. This conviction comes from the simple fact that most games offer a fixed percentage of advantage for the house. This edge measures 1.4 percent for players in craps and soars much higher for roulette or keno. Yet blackjack is different in that it offers no fixed edge—it changes depending on how people play their cards.

This peculiarity made blackjack popular, and a big part of the game's appeal lies in its myriad of choices. There are many decisions to make, and to a great extent you control your own destiny depending on whether you correctly decide to hit or stand. Yet back in the days of the abacus, no one could be certain how each hand should be played. Many gamblers before 1960 simply mimicked the dealer by hitting all hands until they reached a total of 17. This technique sliced through a bankroll faster than a machete through a pineapple, and put players at a very stiff 5.5 percent disadvantage.

The game of twenty-one appeared to be a never-ending cash cow for the casinos, but those pillars of confidence came crashing down from a most unlikely source—the pen of a meek-looking, bespectacled mathematics professor. Dr. Edward Thorp saw that blackjack was different from other games in that the past could affect the future. This unique characteristic sparked a revolution in the gambling industry.

THE DARK AGES

No one knows for sure who the first card counter was. Previously, the only sure way of beating the house was by cheating, until some players figured out that they could obtain an advantage in certain situations by carefully watching the cards. There were rumors of a few intuitive individuals who deduced that the odds changed as cards were played. These forerunners used no real system, but were able to find some profitable situations in the deeply dealt single-deck blackjack games prevalent in the earliest casinos. Perhaps they just estimated how many face cards and aces remained near the end of a deck.

Whatever edge these early "prehistoric" counters obtained must have been diluted greatly by the lack of a commonly known basic strategy. The best published playing strategy available at that time recommended splitting only aces and never doubling down, a very ill-advised tactic that placed players at a 3.6 percent disadvantage against the house. A group of four mathematicians changed all that in the 1950s, starting a chain of events that eventually rocked the entire gambling world.

THE COMPUTER AGE

Roger Baldwin, Wilbert Cantey, Herbert Maisel, and James Mc-Dermott were four bright minds that fate brought together at the U.S. Army's research laboratory at Aberdeen Proving Grounds in Maryland. All of them shared a passionate interest in the game of blackjack. Evidently, they also shared a lot of free time, because over a three-year period, they painstakingly analyzed and dissected the nuances of their favorite card game. This was before the advent of computers, and all their calculations had to be tediously worked out on desk calculators.

Their findings were published in the *Journal of the American Statistical Association* in 1956. The article was titled "The Optimum Strategy in Blackjack," and it represented a quantum leap forward for gamblers. Their calculations showed an incredible improvement and reduced the hefty disadvantage from nearly 4 percent (for those using what was previously considered to be the best-known strategy) to only 0.6, creating a close to break-even game for players willing to learn the correct decision for each hand. However, their message fell on deaf ears, even though later studies showed their strategy was far stronger than they thought and actually made players a slight favorite (+0.1) in the standard single-deck games commonly used by casinos.

It took a few years, but finally a man came along who didn't overlook the groundbreaking work done by these four pioneers. Dr. Edward Thorp recognized the importance of their findings and quickly realized there were more nuggets to discover. Their article had concluded players wouldn't be able to utilize information from previous hands. Thorp disagreed. He saw how the odds might fluctuate as cards were removed from play. He then set out to devise a way to isolate those swings and turn them into lucrative betting opportunities.

Thorp's research held a distinct advantage over Baldwin's group since the world had entered the computer age. He used a high-speed (for that era) IBM computer at MIT to prove his theory. He then took his theories out of the classroom and tested them at the blackjack tables.

THORP'S THEORY WORKS

The overwhelmingly positive results from his first blackjack trips convinced Thorp that skilled players could indeed beat the game. He published his conclusions, along with a few accounts of his casino adventures, in 1962. *Beat the Dealer* quickly became a best seller. The quiet, respectable professor had unlocked Pandora's box and casinos hastily changed the rules of blackjack, fearing the imminent onslaught from hordes of card counters.

Ironically, just the opposite happened. Very few players were capable of mastering the complex Ten-Count system Thorp offered in his book. Yet the public now knew that smart players could win, and many mistakenly judged themselves capable of beating the game. The end result saw blackjack shoot past craps to become the most popular table game, and profits soared for casinos. The rules soon returned to normal as *pit bosses* realized how few would-be card counters could actually beat them in the long run. The foundation for the tremendous growth of today's Las Vegas was poured by the masses who read just enough to try, but far too little to win.

Edward Thorp fired the first shot in the revolution. Then he quietly moved on to more scholarly pursuits. He had unlocked the key to the casino vaults by proving that blackjack could be beaten, but he felt no desire to go any further. Instead, Thorp left those riches for future followers to chase. However, the easy money most envisioned never materialized.

OVERCOMING SKEPTICISM

You don't have to be a rocket scientist to do the math. Around a quarter of a million people read Thorp's book, yet only a handful of his disciples could actually beat the dealer. My blackjack career seemed just as likely to end up in the toilet. After my initial disastrous foray into the blackjack world, there wasn't even one reason to believe I would be any different from all the other suckers, who came, saw, and got their butts kicked. I didn't even want to think about blackjack again, and vowed to never pursue such foolish fantasies in the future.

But fate hadn't quite finished dealing its cards to me.

It's likely that my story of losing everything has been played out thousands of times by novice card counters who got destroyed on their first trip to the big city. Most at that point either gave up on card counting or quit blackjack altogether.

Yet I hated losing. I was highly competitive, and it upset me to walk away like a spanked puppy. So I tried to analyze where I might have gone wrong. My first reaction was to think that the casino had cheated me. Perhaps its management recognized how powerful a threat my $25 bets posed to their bankroll, and they decided to launch a preemptive strike against me. Eventually, I realized how comical that scenario sounded.

Next, it crossed my mind that card counting didn't actually work— it was just another scam. I was tempted to latch onto this excuse since I'd always been a skeptic at heart, but the math did make sense. The odds had to change as cards were removed from the deck. That simple fact elevated blackjack over any other game of chance.

Although I had no intention of going back to the lion's den for more humiliation, I was curious to discover the real reason for my downfall, so I decided to do further research on blackjack. All it took was one good book by Ken Uston to get me back in the game. The previous text I had read painted too simplistic a portrait of how to beat blackjack. But Uston's *Million Dollar Blackjack* renewed my faith in the numbers and removed any nagging doubts over whether card counting was legit. More important, it clearly showed why I had failed. I made the classic error of rushing in unprepared.

After gleaning wisdom from a few other authors, I decided to plunge back into the waters. I rarely backed down from challenges; but I didn't want to repeat my previous mistake. This time I knew I had to master correct strategy *before* I entered the casino. Once you are inside, it is too late.

So for my second bite of the cherry I got very serious. I wanted to be the favorite. I wanted to win. This time I practiced at home rather than at the school of hard knocks. Experience taught me that casinos were expensive places to learn how to count.

TESTING ONE, TWO, THREE

It is impossible to overstate how important proper preparation is. Without it, your gambling adventures may end up like mine started. Over the next month, I drilled the rudiments of blackjack into my brain and systematically counted down thousands of decks. This task is accomplished by taking a freshly shuffled deck, starting off with a count of zero, and then adding or subtracting each individual card's count value as fast as possible throughout the deck while maintaining an accurate count. My first efforts clocked in at a snail-like fifty seconds. Yet within a few days I had broken through the magic twenty-five-second barrier. By the end of the month it seemed like I could fly through the cards, and routinely clocked in at fifteen to twenty seconds.

I also learned basic strategy flawlessly, rather than trying to memorize it over a short and bumpy bus ride. Perhaps the most important part of the process occurred every evening when I converted the dinette set into a blackjack table and dealt myself hands for a couple of hours. I used chips to bet and meticulously recorded the results from each session. This log served as a great building block of confidence, since it confirmed what the books said—that I could beat the game if I played correctly and bet the right amounts in relation to my bankroll. That is exactly what happened. My results showed two out of every three nights on average were winners. So I knew it could be done—at least in the comfort of my own kitchen.

After I'd reached a certain level of proficiency, I mixed in additional degrees of difficulty, and blasted either rock music into the room or had the television blaring. Many distractions bombard your senses in the casinos and I wanted to shield myself from their subtle attacks. I figured if I could flawlessly count down a deck with the thumping sound of Pink Floyd assaulting my ears, I'd be ready for the tables.

I also made the difficult decision of moving up to an advanced count. Most beginners are wisest in starting out with a one-level count (where the individual card values are never higher than plus or minus 1), but I wanted to get every available edge. Also, I planned to play mostly single deck initially, and the more advanced counting systems are much stronger for those games.

One trick I could do at home was to always check my count at the end of the deck. In a casino you may think you are counting correctly, but there is no way to know for sure since only a portion of the cards are ever seen. However, on my kitchen table, I could flip through the remainder of the deck and then dutifully record my results. I eventually got to the point where I rarely made a mistake.

BACK IN THE SADDLE

Despite my newfound confidence, I was still slightly hesitant to risk real money. I knew I could beat blackjack at home, but worried that my abilities might still come up short in the real world. So, for my first trip of act two in my blackjack career, I only took forty bucks. Two thin twenties folded neatly into my wallet. That way I wouldn't have much at risk until I found out if I had the talent.

At that time I lived in Oregon, and many towns had legalized social gaming in their taverns. I went to a small coastal community with a friend and found a single-deck game that amazingly dealt out nearly all fifty-two cards. I bet only $2 to $10 that first night and surprised myself by how easily I kept up with the count and flow of the game. I hit a lucky fluctuation and finished the evening seventy bucks ahead. Encouraged, I decided to make a couple trips a week over the next few months.

My practice paid off this time and I continued winning. Usually, bankrolls go up and down, but I never had to dip beyond that initial forty bucks. That was all I started with and, despite being seriously undercapitalized, was surprisingly all I ever needed. Besides receiving far more than my fair share of luck, I was also extremely fortunate to have numerous single-deck games within a short drive to play with no heat. Living close kept my expenses down, and avoiding the scrutiny of pit bosses gave me an ideal transition into my new career. I quickly decided this was my new vocation and not just a hobby. I won enough to rapidly move my bets up, first to a max of $25 a hand and then $50. At that point my bankroll had risen to over five grand, and I felt ready to take on Nevada.

LEARNING CURVE

I've included this lengthy account of my humble beginnings to illustrate the most fundamental point in this book: success can only be obtained with discipline and preparation. My first bumbling attempts almost certainly mirrored the failures of many others who skimmed through the basic concepts of blackjack and deemed themselves ready to get rich. I still made mistakes, even on my second go-round. For example, I didn't understand the concepts of optimal betting (sizing my bets in relation to my advantage), which caused far more excessive risk to my bankroll than necessary. But I'd studied enough to make myself a winner and was realistic enough to see how much I still needed to learn.

No book can turn you into a winner unless you are willing to master the material. *Play Blackjack Like the Pros* will lay out the proper steps for you to get there, but it's not easy. It does take a lot of hard work and tenacity. Yet blackjack can be beaten, and anyone with an average aptitude and good discipline can become a winning player.

I have taught many players how to win at blackjack, so I know what works. One of my earliest pupils was Alex Strickland, and I will use him as a model to show how beginning players should approach the game. A couple other students later joined us to form what was certainly the world's fastest card-counting team of all time. I will tell you more about that group later on, but first let's find out what steps can be taken to improve your game.

CHAPTER THREE
The Rules of Blackjack

You can probably only imagine what an incredible lifestyle I have led as a high-stakes card counter—moving confidently from table to table while admiring supermodels coo over how smoothly I handle my chips. After many years of blackjack, I am very polished in the way I play, but, unfortunately, I also can only imagine the part about the supermodels.

However, I didn't begin my blackjack career as an expert—I was easily the most clueless player at the table the first time I played. We all have to start somewhere, and I vividly remember my first nervous foray into a casino—I felt as out of place as a Ku Klux Klan recruiter at a reggae concert. But the rules and etiquette of blackjack are actually fairly easy to learn. This chapter will lay out the basics for those of you who want to avoid looking stupid like I did on my first trip.

If you are not a novice and are already familiar with these terms, then I suggest you skip this chapter entirely and move right on to chapter 4.

1. Getting Started

The first step is to select a seat. Blackjack tables vary in size, from five to seven players. Find an open spot, and then lay your cash on the felt. The dealer will slide an equal amount of chips back across the felt to you. It's wisest to start off with a small amount, as you can always buy more chips later if needed.

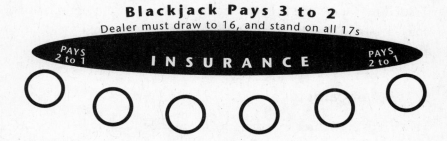

2. Procedure

After the dealer has shuffled, someone at the table will cut the cards and play will proceed. If the game is one- or two-deck, the dealer will hold the cards in her hand and deal every player two cards face down. However, the majority of blackjack games today are six or eight decks dealt face-up from a shoe, located to the dealer's left. It doesn't matter whether your cards are faceup or facedown, since the dealer has strict rules to follow and isn't influenced by seeing the values of your cards. Her hand will always start off with one card exposed and one card hidden, regardless of the number of decks.

3. Betting

Every table will have fixed minimum and maximum betting limits. On the felt in front of your chair is a betting circle or box. All bets have to be made before you receive your first two cards. You can change your bets from hand to hand, but you can never alter your wager once it is placed in the betting box.

4. Rules

Blackjack rules are fairly standardized worldwide, with a few minor variations. One variation is whether the casino hits on soft 17 (a *soft hand* is any hand that counts an ace as 11 rather than 1). This is usually spelled out right on the felt. However, other rule changes are harder to ascertain, such as when you can double down. In Vegas it is typically on any two cards, but in Reno, it might be restricted to just 10 or 11. If you are not sure what your options are, don't be afraid to ask the dealer. As a teacher once told me, there are no stupid questions, just a lot of inquisitive idiots.

5. Value of Cards

Most cards are valued exactly the same as their pip number. For example, a 7 is always worth 7 points. Face cards (jack, queen, and king) all have the same value as a 10 (10 points), and individual suits (clubs, hearts, spades, or diamonds) make no difference whatsoever. The ace is the only tricky card since it can be used either as 1 or 11, depending on the hand. It's also the most important card in the deck since the combination of an ace and any ten on your original two cards is called a *natural* (or blackjack) and pays 3 to 2. A winning hand normally pays even money ($10 for every $10 bet, but a natural pays $15 for every $10 bet).

6. Decisions, Decisions

The great appeal of blackjack lies in the many decisions available to players. Each hand presents a wide range of choices. You can *hit* (take another card to improve your hand) or *stand* (if you are happy with the total you already have). Other options are doubling down (doubling your original bet and receiving only one more card), *splitting* (making two separate hands out of a pair by matching the original bet), surrendering (forfeiting one-half of your original bet and throwing in your hand), and *insurance* (a hedge bet available when the dealer shows an ace as her upcard).

7. Resolving the Hands

After everyone has finished playing their hands, including the dealer, the dealer will go around the table and resolve the outcome for each player. If you win, she pays even money on your bet. If you have a lower total than the dealer or bust out (exceed a point total of 21), you lose and she takes your chips. In the event of a tie, called a *push*, nobody wins and no money changes hands. The object of the game is to have a higher total than the dealer without busting.

8. Examples

You are playing at a table with two other gentlemen. You receive a pair of 7s and the dealer flips over an 8 for her upcard. After a moment of hesitation, you decide to hit the 14. This is done by scratching the cards on the felt (in a handheld game) or scratching with your finger behind your cards (in a faceup shoe game). In this case you and the two other players all draw face cards and bust (exceed 21) and the dealer wins all bets without even having to play her cards. Surprisingly, the main advantage for the house in blackjack lies in the simple fact that the dealer always acts last.

Your next hand is a 13. The dealer now shows a 9 as her upcard. You choose to stand this time, thus making sure you are still alive at the end. Standing is signaled by waving over the top of your cards (in a faceup game) or tucking the cards under your chips (in a handheld game). Unfortunately, the dealer has a king in the hole and her 19 makes you a loser again. Trying to outguess the dealer like this is ultimately a losing proposition. Only by learning correct basic strategy can you have any realistic chance of moving from novice to expert.

Other options like doubling down and splitting involve putting more money into play, so it is critical to learn the correct strategy. On a double down, you match your original bet (that is, you push out another $10 next to the $10 bet already in the box), and receive only one additional card. A good time to double down is when you have totals of 10 or 11 for your starting two cards. This is because nearly a third of the time you will receive a 10 (that includes all face cards) for your double down (giving a strong total of 20 or 21). Pair splits are similar in that you also match your original bet, but here your first two cards are split apart and two separate hands are played out. Each one of these (unless starting with a pair of aces) can be hit more than once (unlike the double down).

CHAPTER FOUR
Basic Strategy

Gambling is a zero-sum game. Someone always wins and someone always loses. In blackjack, you can decide which you want to be—the victor or the vanquished. In every casino there is a massive redistribution of wealth going on with the rich (the house) usually getting richer. It's up to the poor (the players) to be proactive if they want to get a piece of the pie.

Basic strategy for blackjack is the foundation for any future exploits in the world of card counting. Unless you master basic strategy, you are unlikely to ever beat blackjack in the long run. It is that important, so don't leave home without it.

We all tend to be creatures of habit, and it's often difficult to learn new tricks. The longer you've been playing, the more likely you are to misjudge your own blackjack IQ. It is very common for seasoned gamblers to assume they already play their hands correctly and to think they know the answers to all the questions. Many people's motto in life is "Don't confuse me with the facts, my mind is already made up."

Some remain skeptical of any strategy that conflicts with their own battle-hardened version of hunches and guesses. Yet there is an exact and correct way to play each and every hand. This is not some secret I have conjured up or just my opinion—it is a fact beyond a shadow of a doubt. Basic strategy was determined from years of research and by running literally billions of hands through computer simulators. There really is no debate over the optimal way to play blackjack if you want to achieve the highest return for your gambling dollar. For instance, it is a mathematical certainty that hitting 16 is far better than standing against any dealer's big upcard.

However, some superstitious gamblers still play their hands differently, depending on how hot or cold the table is running. In the short run, going by your gut may seem to work; but over the long run, every time that you deviate from established basic strategy will cost you money.

Perhaps the idea of memorizing basic strategy still seems a little intimidating. You're worried that the next few pages will be packed with complex formulas and graphs that will take weeks to master. Maybe that wasn't what you had in mind when you bought this book, and you aren't too thrilled about jumping back into advanced math decades after your last algebra class. But it doesn't have to be frightening or overwhelming. There's no need to call up your old high school teacher and beg for help.

Basic strategy is actually just that—fairly basic. I honestly think that almost anyone can learn the optimal way to play each and every hand within a short period of time—some have within a few hours. The gain for that one afternoon of memorization is immense, as I will show shortly.

However, if you are still apprehensive and looking for something less demanding, let me start with a stripped-down version. This will reduce the house advantage to less than 1 percent and can be mastered in a minimal amount of time. I call this the *Microwave* strategy for those twenty-first-century guys who don't have the time or patience to cook a real meal and instead want to get their dinner hot and ready within minutes.

Microwave Strategy

Hard Hands

■ 17 or more, always stand.

■ 12 through 16, hit against a 7–ace, otherwise stand.

Double Downs

■ On 11, double against a 2–10, otherwise hit.

■ On 10, double against a 2–9, otherwise hit.

■ On 9, double against a 3–6, otherwise hit.

■ 8 or less, always hit.

Pair Splits

■ Always split aces and 8s.

■ Never split 5s or 10s.

Soft Hands

■ Soft 18 or more, always stand.

■ Soft 17 or less, always hit.

(Soft hands are any combinations where the total is calculated by counting the ace as 11, while *hard hands* either don't have any aces or count the ace as 1.)

Now, let's break down the abbreviated strategy into smaller, bite-size chunks. There are three simple rules that will cover a majority of the hands you will be dealt. Number one is always standing on hard 17 or above (*pat* hands). This is rather obvious, and if anyone has trouble understanding this one, I suggest you lay off the Jack Daniel's while you are at the tables.

The second rule is always hit on hard 12 through 16 (*stiff* hands) when the dealer's upcard is 7 or higher.

And last, you should always stand on hard 12 through 16 (stiff hands) against the dealer's 2–6.

These three rules can be mastered by anyone during a TV commercial and cover the majority of your playing decisions. The terms "pat" and "stiff" are used to differentiate between pat hands (17–21) that do not have to be hit, and ugly stiff hands (12–16) that could potentially bust out with one hit card. Approximately 43 percent of the hands you'll receive will total 12–17, so if you can play these correctly, you will be cutting the house edge down to a much more manageable number.

Next come the nerve-racking double downs. With the Microwave strategy, you double on totals of 10 or 11 when your total exceeds the dealer's upcard (as in double 10 against 9, but not 10 against 10). The only other double is 9 against 3–6 (when the dealer is weak and most likely to bust). For hard totals of 8 or less, you simply hit.

Pair splits tend to disconcert some casino patrons. When dealt a pair of 7s, they often feel like they're in a Dirty Harry movie and the dealer is asking, "Well punk, what is it? Do you feel *lucky*?" So here is an uncomplicated condensed version—always split aces and 8s and never split 5s or 10s.

There are a couple of easy tricks to help you remember these two groups. Aces and 8s are often called "the dead man's hand" from their fatal association with Wild Bill Hickok. Fives and 10s can be recalled easily by thinking of the old five-and-ten Woolworth stores. The rationale for not splitting these two combos is that a pair of 5s gives you a total of 10, which is better to double or hit than to split. And a pair of face cards is a solid starting hand of 20. Close to 70 percent of your gain in blackjack comes from being dealt either a pair of face cards or a snapper, so don't be too quick to part with your gift horse.

The strategy for soft hands, though often confusing to many, is reduced to a very simple form here. If you have soft 18 or more, you stand; otherwise you hit.

That's it—a detailed strategy boiled down to a few rudimentary principles. Yet even this shortened version will make you a stronger player than almost everyone else in the casino. You will be playing a game that will return more money to your pocket than craps, baccarat, and most slot machines.

However, I still think it is worth the effort to take the next step and learn the complete version of basic strategy. You are giving up a lot if you only eat frozen turkey potpies nuked in the microwave every night for dinner rather than gourmet meals prepared leisurely over a hot stove. The extra gain will be worth the effort, and I highly recommend you take the time to progress to the next level.

With that in mind, here is a generic basic strategy. ("Otherwise" will be abbreviated as "O/W" and "versus" as "vs" in the following chart.)

Basic Strategy

Hard Hands	Playing Strategy
8 or less	Always hit.
9	Double vs 3–6. O/W hit.
10	Double vs 2–9. O/W hit.
11	Double vs 2–10. O/W hit.
12	Stand vs 4–6. O/W hit.
13	Stand vs 2–6. O/W hit.
14	Stand vs 2–6. O/W hit.
15	Stand vs 2–6. O/W hit.
16	Stand vs 2–6. O/W hit.
17 through 21	Always stand.

Pair Splits	Playing Strategy
A-A	Always split.
2-2	Split vs 2–7. O/W hit.
3-3	Split vs 2–7. O/W hit.
4-4	Split vs 5–6. O/W hit.
5-5	Never split.
6-6	Split vs 2–6. O/W hit.
7-7	Split vs 2–7. O/W hit.
8-8	Always split.
9-9	Split vs 2–6, 8–9. Stand vs 7, 10, A.
10-10	Always stand.

Soft Hands	Playing Strategy
A-2	Double vs 5–6. O/W hit.
A-3	Double vs 5–6. O/W hit.
A-4	Double vs 4–6. O/W hit.
A-5	Double vs 4–6. O/W hit.
A-6	Double vs 3–6. O/W hit.
A-7	Double vs 3–6. Stand vs 2, 7, 8. Hit vs 9, 10, A.
A-8 or A-9	Always stand.
A-10	Celebrate!
	Never take insurance.

INSURANCE

The last addition to basic strategy is also one of the most important—insurance. Despite the sincere advice of most dealers, pit bosses, and seasoned gamblers, you *never* make the insurance bet if you are a basic strategy player. They will implore and maybe even beg you to take even money when you have a blackjack and are nervously staring at the dealer's ace.

Many will swear this is the best bet in the entire casino—the only sure thing. Once again the flaw comes in its shortsightedness. It does guarantee that you will receive at least some payoff for your snapper. But you are paying a high price for that instant gratification. If you took insurance thirteen times at fifty bucks a pop, on average you'd win the bet four times (since there are four face cards for every thirteen cards) and lose the other nine times (all the non-face cards). Your wins would net you an extra $400, but your losses would total $450. This $50 loss (or one bet out of thirteen) makes insurance a whooping 7 percent favorite for the house, and it's actually one of the worst casino bets.

SURRENDER

Surrender is one of those rare options that benefit players rather than the house. It is not all that common a rule, but is offered at many of the bigger casinos around the world. It allows players to throw in (or surrender) their first two cards (in exchange for losing half their bet). This helps immensely on those nights when it seems like every other hand is a stiff.

Though it is a good rule, it's often bungled by most of the goofballs who have no idea when to throw in their hand. The mathematics are actually quite simple—you surrender when you expect to win *less* than one out of four hands. It's possible some people misunderstand the principle of giving up 50 percent of your bet and think they need to apply it to any hand that has less than a 50 percent chance of winning. This certainly is far from the case.

Here is the correct strategy for surrender in a six-deck shoe. The code for all basic strategy charts is as follows:

H = hit, S = stand, D = double down, P = split, and SR = surrender

Player's Hand	DEALER'S UPCARD		
	9	10	A
15		SR/H	
16	SR/H	SR/H	SR/H

There are two options listed because surrender takes precedence. If the rules allow it, you would surrender *first*. If not, then you would hit. Also on some hands, the correct play might be to double or surrender on your *original* two cards, but the correct play becomes hit when you have a three-card (or more) hand since those other options are no longer available.

The actual gain from surrender is fairly small (about 0.06 percent), so it doesn't seem like adding this knowledge to your growing arsenal is very important. But surrender has other benefits. It can greatly reduce fluctuation, especially on those days when bust is your middle name. Also, it goes from being a marginal rule to a tremendous one when card counting is added to the equation. A skilled player who knows the rough composition of the remaining cards can utilize the full power of the surrender rule and add immensely to his bottom line.

HARD HANDS

Whether to hit or stand is the most common decision confronting blackjack players. The vast majority of hands fall into this category. Approximately 85 percent of the money you lose at the table comes from being dealt hard 12–17 as your starting hands. So it is critical that these frequently occurring combinations are played correctly. Yet some gamblers play as if they're in Disney's theme park ride

Pirates of the Caribbean—every hand is an adventure. They pick up their cards, hesitate for a moment, then grit their teeth and hang on for the ride.

It doesn't have to be like this. Ignorance and incompetence don't need to go hand in hand with gambling. The chart on page 29 shows the exact way to play each and every blackjack hand you will ever receive, and most of it is not that different from the Microwave strategy.

For example, playing the hard hands is nearly identical. You still stand anytime your total is 17 or above and hit all your stiffs (12–16) whenever you find yourself facing 7–ace. The general theory here is that the dealer is often pat (has a total of 17 or greater) when showing a big upcard and the best course of action is to hit or surrender stiffs to reduce your losses.

However, remember to distinguish between hard hands and pairs. For example, two 7s should be played differently than a hard 14, and the correct strategy for splitting will be explained shortly.

Here is a summary of the hard-hand strategy in chart form.

Hard-Hand Strategy

Player's Hand	DEALER'S UPCARD									
	2	3	4	5	6	7	8	9	10	A
17–21	S	S	S	S	S	S	S	S	S	S
16	S	S	S	S	S	H	H	SR/H	SR/H	SR/H
15	S	S	S	S	S	H	H	H	SR/H	H
14	S	S	S	S	S	H	H	H	H	H
13	S	S	S	S	S	H	H	H	H	H
12	H	H	S	S	S	H	H	H	H	H

When the dealer is a little kinder and shows a 2–6 as her upcard, the philosophy is reversed. It's almost always best to tuck your sorry-looking stiff under your chips and hope the dealer busts out. The only difference here comes when you have a 12 and the dealer has a 2 or a 3 showing. The correct play is to hit on totals of hard 12 or less and stand on hard 13 or more, which is a minor change from the Microwave version.

Here's a chart of the bust-out rates for the dealer depending on her upcard. It's important to examine these so you can see the importance of standing on stiff versus stiff. Remember, you've got to be alive at the end of the hand if you want to have any chance of winning because "Dead men don't get paid."

DEALER'S UPCARD	2	3	4	5	6	7	8	9	10	A
% Bust	35	37	40	42	42	26	24	23	23	17

DOUBLE DOWNS

The next block to tackle is the hard double downs. These can be real moneymakers, and the entire trip often comes down to whether you win or lose these big hands. The strategy for them is actually fairly elementary, especially for multiple decks. (The reason some boxes have D/H is that you can only double down on your *original* two cards, so if you have a three-card 11 versus a 7, then you would hit rather than double.)

Player's Hand	DEALER'S UPCARD									
	2	3	4	5	6	7	8	9	10	A
11	D/H	D/H	D/H	D/H	D/H	D/H	D/H	D/H	D/H	H
10	D/H	D/H	D/H	D/H	D/H	D/H	D/H	D/H	H	H
9	H	D/H	D/H	D/H	D/H	H	H	H	H	H
8 or less	H	H	H	H	H	H	H	H	H	H

Anytime you have a hard eight or less you always hit. This is so simple even a dog could learn it without going to obedience school. There are three hard hands (9, 10, or 11) where you double down, and the correct time to do this is exactly the same as in the Microwave strategy. However, one of the hardest plays to make is pushing out a couple more chips to double on your 11 when the dealer shows a face card. What scares most players away from this venture is the fear that the dealer might already have 20. But the odds favor the brave in this scenario, and you will make more money over the long run by taking the extra risk and doubling down against her 10.

SPLITS

Basic strategy is simply a determination of the most cost-efficient play in each situation. It never means you will win if you hit rather than stand. It just gives you the optimal play to make. Sometimes it prompts you to be aggressive by instructing you to double down rather than hit. Other times it takes on a defensive posture and minimizes your losses with the weaker hands.

Both the offensive and the defensive components of basic strategy are displayed in pair splits. A pair of 7s best illustrates this. When you're dealt a hard 14, you're an underdog against even the dealer's worst cards (5 or 6). However, if the 14 consists of two 7s, then you also have the option of splitting rather than just standing or hitting. And splitting the 7s turns a big underdog (approximately 17 percent) into a heavy favorite against a 5 or 6.

You also split for defensive reasons. Getting dealt 16 against a face card is your worst starting hand. You are dead in the water no matter how you play it. Yet if the 16 is two 8s, splitting reduces your overall loss considerably from either of the normal choices of hitting versus standing. It is the lesser of two evils, but easily the smartest way to salvage some money from a losing position.

Most hands, however, are split when the dealer is weakest. This is also true for double downs—when you are fortunate enough to be playing against a 4, 5, or 6 upcard you typically want to go gangbusters, and get as much money into play as possible. Against the bigger upcards (7–A) you tend to split and double down much less often. These are extremely important principles to keep in mind and will greatly aid your comprehension of basic strategy.

Player's Hand	DEALER'S UPCARD									
	2	3	4	5	6	7	8	9	10	A
A-A	P	P	P	P	P	P	P	P	P	P
10-10	S	S	S	S	S	S	S	S	S	S
9-9	P	P	P	P	P	S	P	P	S	S
8-8	P	P	P	P	P	P	P	P	P	P
7-7	P	P	P	P	P	P	H	H	H	H
6-6	P	P	P	P	P	H	H	H	H	H
5-5	D	D	D	D	D	D	D	D	H	H
4-4	H	H	H	P	P	H	H	H	H	H
3-3	P	P	P	P	P	P	H	H	H	H
2-2	P	P	P	P	P	P	H	H	H	H

You probably noticed there are several differences in pair splitting from the Microwave strategy. This might be a little more confusing to memorize, but you can divide them into more manageable groups.

You still always split aces and 8s and never split 5s and 10s.

The way you play any of the following pairs—2, 3, 6, or 7—is virtually identical: all will get split against any dealer upcard of 2–7 (except for 6-6 versus 7, which is hit).

So that only leaves two hands—4s and 9s. A pair of 4s is actually fairly simple to play and is split just against a 5 or 6 (and only when the rules allow you to double down after you split).

Figuring out how to play a pair of 9s is a little trickier—you are supposed to split against 2–6 (when the dealer is in trouble), and also against an 8 or 9. The logic here is that when the dealer has a 7 up they often have 17, and your two 9s already total 18 and will usually beat her. Splitting the 9s against another 9 is a cost-saving defensive play, while standing against a face card or an ace is wisest because you will lose even more money by splitting against such power.

SOFT HANDS

Add an ace to the equation and the scale of difficulty shoots up rapidly. Many people don't have a clue whether to double, hit, or stand on many of their soft hands. They act totally mystified and take so much time to make up their minds that they ought to bring an eight-ball with them to the table to speed up the process. But there is no reason to be intimidated or any need to consult higher powers. The correct strategy can easily be learned, although mastering the soft hands is definitely more difficult than the hard hands.

The main rule from the Microwave strategy stated that you always hit soft 17 or less. Now this dictum is modified—in some cases the correct play is to double down rather than hit, but it is still extremely important you never stand on these totals (soft 17 or less). In other words, if you can't remember whether to double down, at least make sure you hit. Staying on your A–5 is not going to win for you very often or make you many friends at the tables.

Player's Hand	DEALER'S UPCARD									
	2	3	4	5	6	7	8	9	10	A
Soft 19 or more	S	S	S	S	S	S	S	S	S	S
Soft 18	S	D/S	D/S	D/S	D/S	S	S	H	H	H
Soft 17	H	D/H	D/H	D/H	D/H	H	H	H	H	H
Soft 16	H	H	D/H	D/H	D/H	H	H	H	H	H
Soft 15	H	H	D/H	D/H	D/H	H	H	H	H	H
Soft 14	H	H	H	D/H	D/H	H	H	H	H	H
Soft 13	H	H	H	D/H	D/H	H	H	H	H	H

Let's start with the soft doubles. Again, the principle is to get more money out when there is the greatest chance the dealer will bust (4, 5, or 6). Also, you might notice that you *never* double a soft hand against a deuce.

The A-7 is certainly the most difficult play for experienced gamblers to grasp. Doubling down with soft hands often will cause someone in the casino to raise their eyebrows. But hitting your soft 18 may bring a look of disbelief from a fellow player or a sincere question from the dealer over whether your cigarette contains only tobacco.

The reason you hit A-7 is to cut your losses. Though many players are happy as a clam when they reach a total of 18, it is still a losing hand against a 9, 10, or ace. Remember that there is no way to bust a soft hand and many ways to improve it.

PERFECT PLAY

So that's it—the entire basic strategy packaged into convenient groups and ready to be incorporated into your game. Some early blackjack authors like Lawrence Revere made a big deal about precision and the importance of never making mistakes. His impeccable high standards scared many students into thinking they could never win at blackjack if they made any errors.

I totally agree with Revere that everyone should strive for the highest degree of accuracy possible in his play. But the truth is that some miscues are really not very important. There are several plays that are nearly toss-ups—it hardly matters what you do. For example, 12 versus 4 will yield almost the same result whether you hit or stand. However, hitting a 14 against the same 4 would be a big mistake. Hitting a 16 versus 4 is a colossal blunder, and hitting an 18 against the same 4 a total disaster. So not all aspects of basic strategy are created equal. Just like in *Animal Farm*, some are more equal than others.

That is why the Microwave strategy is so brief on pair splits and soft hands. These combinations tend to come up much less frequently than the hard hands, and how you play them will have a smaller impact on your overall edge. However, don't get me wrong, I don't advocate laziness. Future profits hinge on how strong a base you start with.

The strategy outlined in the previous pages is a generic basic strategy based on the most common casino conditions (where six-deck shoes are used and where the dealer stands on soft 17). There is actually only one correct strategy for each different set of rules. If the number of decks·change or if you can't double down after splits, several decisions would need to be revised to play optimally. Fortunately, there is little lost by playing a one-size-fits-all strategy. You typically only give up 0.03 percent by not fine-tuning your play for the most common rule changes. This translates to less than a hundred bucks a year for most recreational players.

However, if you do want to play as accurately as possible (and I do), it is not that hard to adjust your strategy for new games. Kenneth Smith runs a great Web site at www.blackjackinfo.com that allows free downloads of the correct basic strategy for any set of rules.

LEARNING TECHNIQUES

Assuming you're ready to take on the full-fledged form of basic strategy, what is the best way to master it? Fortunately, there are different educational techniques since all of us don't learn in the same way. I am much better at remembering what I read or see visually. If it is auditory, I often miss key components. (For confirmation of this, just ask my wife.) So I used rote memorization and flash cards to drill the strategy into my head.

However, the only important thing is that you find the style that works best for you. A lot of good intentions crumble when you get thrown into the fast-paced casino environment. For this reason, it's important that the principles are second nature before you venture into their lair.

There are several ways to learn this entire strategy. You can do it by rows, such as the matrix charts starting on page 31, or you can condense it into a written version, like the chart on page 29. Perhaps computers are your forte and you'd prefer having a program beep whenever you make a mistake. Today there are very sophisticated modern methods of learning from computer software. The industry standard is Casino Vérité Blackjack, a truly amazing program that has a myriad of tools for both beginners and pros.

Regardless of your process, it's important to find a way to work on the unusual and difficult hands. Simply dealing cards to yourself on the kitchen table will not aid you in memorizing some of the obscure situations that rarely come up (such as A-A versus A). Therefore, the next chapter will contain a practice chart that incorporates every hand, no matter how remote.

I cannot overemphasize how critical it is to master the fundamentals before you step inside the doors of the casino. The last thing you want to do is guess at the tables, and "Lost Wages" is a terrible and expensive place to learn the basics.

Having said all that, I do want to reiterate an earlier point. It is okay to make mistakes. We all do. Don't be discouraged because you think only an unemotional robot with perfect recall can succeed at this game. I made my share of boneheaded plays over the years and still was extremely successful. This is exactly why I included the details of my first disastrous attempt to learn the game.

Speaking of mistakes, here's another *colorful* story. In kindergarten I happily colored Santa Claus with a green crayon, completely unaware that I was color-blind. My teacher thought she had another backwoods moron on her hands and demoted me to the remedial reading class.

Many years later this same infirmity affected my blackjack play. Usually, it's easy to tell all the chips apart even when you're color-blind. But once I accidentally pushed out a big chip on a minus count (a negative situation that favored the house). The colors of the tokens in that casino were very unusual, and I thought I was making a small bet. Imagine my surprise when the dealer yelled out to the pit boss, "Checks play, one thousand dollars!"

Fortunately, God is often merciful to the stupid, and I won the big bet despite the bad odds. The rest of the day I was especially careful to grab the correct denomination before I made my bets.

The moral of the story is you don't have to play perfectly to prevail over the casinos at blackjack.

Anyone can become a winning player. You don't need to be a machine to be successful, just someone who is willing to learn what it takes to be a winner. And deep down, I think all of us want to win rather than lose.

So don't let a few mistakes deter you from achieving the ultimate goal. Despite my inauspicious start with crayons in public school, I didn't flunk out of kindergarten and went on to enjoy many years of higher education. Likewise, learning to win consistently at blackjack may be overwhelming at first, but if you stay disciplined it can be done.

CHAPTER FIVE

The Intermediate Player

Gambling fever is sweeping across our country like a wildfire after a drought. Yet the majority of Americans stoically accept the unwritten first commandment of casinos: *the house is always supposed to win*.

This doesn't have to be the case. Instead of being the victim, there is a way to turn the tables. Blackjack offers everyone that opportunity if they are willing to put in a little work. When I first started consistently beating the house, I felt like a kid who found free money on the sidewalk. I told all my friends about card counting, expecting them to join me on the road to wealth.

However, most of them failed to share my zeal for the game, and their halfhearted attempts to become winners soon died out. Eventually, I quit trying to spread my newfound gospel and decided to keep my rather unique vocation to myself.

Yet occasionally some people still discovered my secretive life. Once, an old college friend, Alex Strickland, approached me to teach him the tricks of the trade. He'd saved over ten grand working on an Alaskan fishing boat and wanted to make some quick cash gambling. I pictured Alex as the type hell-bent on finding shortcuts in life—

someone who considered traffic lights mere suggestions. So I didn't think he'd be willing or disciplined enough to succeed in blackjack.

Nevertheless, I gave him a copy of basic strategy and some practice charts to learn the obscure and unusual hands. These charts are important tools because many card combinations will rarely come up in normal play and are easy to forget. (Lawrence Revere was the first blackjack author to point out the advantage of this type of training.)

Following are some practice charts I devised for Alex. The first two numbers correspond to the player's hand, and the third number is the dealer's upcard (T stands for all 10s and face cards). In the first example, the player's hand totals 15 (a ten and a five) and the dealer is showing an 8 upcard. The correct action in this example is for the player to hit. If you cannot remember the right play, simply refer back to the basic strategy table on page 29 to find the answer. The proper way to use a practice chart is by mentally or verbally giving the correct response for each problem as quickly as possible.

Practice Chart

T-5 8	6-4 9	4-4 5	3-3 7	A-A A	A-3 6	A-6 4	T-4 3	A-7 3
9-4 7	T-2 6	8-3 9	2-2 4	T-4 4	9-5 T	T-2 A	7-7 9	A-7 2
8-8 T	A-4 4	T-5 5	A-6 6	9-3 3	8-3 T	8-8 9	T-6 9	9-6 4
T-4 2	5-5 7	3-3 5	3-3 2	A-A 8	T-6 T	3-3 4	9-2 8	A-2 5
9-7 A	9-9 4	6-6 4	T-4 6	T-3 A	8-8 A	9-9 7	T-6 3	8-7 7
T-2 5	T-2 T	9-9 T	A-4 3	8-7 3	4-4 4	A-8 4	A-5 5	A-2 6
7-4 5	8-5 6	T-6 5	8-2 4	9-9 5	A-A T	2-2 5	T-5 9	A-7 T
5-3 6	A-7 5	3-3 3	7-4 A	2-2 2	T-4 A	9-9 3	7-7 2	A-3 5
9-9 6	T-3 5	9-7 2	9-2 6	A-7 9	9-9 A	A-4 5	6-4 T	7-7 6
A-7 A	A-4 6	T-3 4	T-3 3	A-6 5	T-3 2	9-3 4	T-2 7	T-4 5
7-2 7	A-2 3	9-9 2	7-3 3	A-4 2	A-8 6	A-8 3	8-7 6	7-7 5
T-6 8	A-5 4	7-2 6	2-2 7	6-2 5	7-7 8	T-2 2	A-2 4	A-3 4
8-2 6	T-5 2	A-A 9	T-6 4	7-3 A	6-6 7	A-6 3	T-5 A	7-2 3
A-3 3	A-5 6	T-3 2	5-4 8	2-2 8	3-3 6	2-2 3	9-7 6	5-4 2
4-4 7	T-4 7	6-3 4	T-3 8	7-7 3	A-6 2	6-6 5	T-5 7	9-7 7
A-7 6	5-5 2	T-4 8	6-6 3	4-4 6	6-6 2	6-3 5	7-3 8	6-2 6

This chart is a valuable tool after you've committed basic strategy to memory. Some people can readily recite all the rules by rote memory, but have difficulty recalling each particular hand when they are pressured in the trenches. A random chart like this mixes up the situations and is more similar to actual casino conditions. Hopefully, after many repetitions with this chart, basic strategy will become much more automatic.

This practice chart can also be divided into three groups (hit/stand, pair splits, and soft doubling) for easier learning.

Hit, Stand, or Surrender?

T-3 4	9-7 T	T-3 7	8-4 5	T-6 7	9-7 A	T-4 T	8-7 2
9-5 7	T-4 6	9-6 7	T-3 8	8-6 5	T-2 9	9-7 3	T-3 2
T-6 6	8-5 A	T-2 3	9-3 4	T-5 8	9-5 8	T-4 5	8-6 9
8-7 T	T-2 6	9-4 5	T-5 5	9-7 9	T-5 A	8-5 T	T-6 2
T-6 5	9-7 8	T-5 9	8-5 6	T-2 8	8-6 4	T-2 2	9-5 2

Split, Hit, or Stand?

6-6 6	9-9 4	4-4 3	8-8 8	6-6 2	9-9 9	2-2 7	9-9 6
4-4 5	9-9 7	7-7 2	9-9 A	9-9 3	A-A A	7-7 3	4-4 6
3-3 7	A-A T	7-7 7	9-9 5	4-4 4	9-9 8	8-8 T	4-4 7
3-3 4	6-6 4	8-8 A	2-2 5	3-3 2	2-2 4	3-3 9	T-T 5
6-6 7	2-2 8	2-2 2	9-9 2	7-7 8	9-9 T	3-3 8	2-2 3

Double Down or Hit?

A-2 6	A-7 T	A-3 5	A-4 4	A-3 3	A-7 A	A-3 2	A-8 6
A-4 6	A-6 2	A-5 5	A-2 4	A-5 3	A-6 7	A-2 3	A-7 9
A-5 7	A-3 6	A-7 8	A-2 5	A-6 5	A-3 4	A-7 2	A-6 8
A-8 5	A-6 6	A-5 6	A-5 4	A-7 5	A-6 3	A-7 4	A-4 3
A-7 6	A-4 5	A-7 3	A-8 3	A-6 4	A-7 7	A-8 T	A-5 2

FLOWCHARTS

Separating the practice chart into these three main groups also helps to explain the thought process or flowchart necessary to become a skilled player. Many hands offer several choices, and some options take precedence over others. It's important to learn this hierarchy in the decision-making process. Sixteen versus 9 is a good example to show the sequence of thinking. The first option would be whether to surrender (the answer is yes). If that rule were not offered or if you had a multiple-card 16 (rather than the original two cards), then the first decision would be whether to hit or stand (hit).

Likewise for A-3 versus 6. The initial decision here is whether to double (yes). If doubling isn't an option, then the proper play for the hand drops down the flowchart to whether you should hit or stand (hit).

Pairs can be more complicated, as first you need to choose whether they should be split; if not, you then need to move on to the hit or stand decisions.

These practice charts are also very useful for later, when you're learning matrix numbers for your count system. Then, instead of reciting the correct basic strategy decision, you will give the true count number needed to deviate on that particular play. For example, 16 versus 10 becomes stand on any positive count and hit on any negative number.

YOUR BEST BET

Alex surprised me with his focus and commitment. He quickly learned basic strategy, displaying an intense seriousness that had failed to surface during his entire four years at college. After practicing at home for a while, we decided to make the short drive to one of the local blackjack games. Alex made a few errors, but overall played very smoothly for the first time out of the blocks. He finished on a rush and won just over a hundred bucks.

However, Alex was still an underdog, despite his newly acquired blackjack knowledge. Playing perfect basic strategy is roughly equivalent to winning 99 out of 200 bets. This is close to even odds but still puts players at a slight disadvantage against the house. Yet this is far better than other casino options. Many people look at roulette as roughly an even bet when they wager on red or black, but because of the two extra green numbers, the wheel is not a fifty-fifty proposition. The typical player trying to guess in which color the ball will land wins about 95 out of 200 bets.

To put it in concrete terms, let's say Alex played four hundred hands (roughly four hours) of blackjack with his $10,000. With an average bet of $25, his expected loss (playing correct basic strategy) would be about $50. If he wagered the same amount at the craps table, his loss jumps up to $140, or nearly three times as much. If he headed for the roulette wheel, that sucker game would cost him over $500 for the four hundred spins, making it ten times worse than blackjack.

FINE POINTS

It's easy to see why blackjack should be the game of choice for your gambling dollar. Still, most people go to the casino to win and not just reduce their losses, and there are some additional techniques that can further shave the small remaining edge (approximately 0.5 percent, depending on the number of decks and the rules) the casino holds over basic strategy players. The easiest way is to find clubs with better rules. Fewer decks always offer better odds than more decks, although you need to be very careful these days because many "gimmick" games have cropped up in casinos. They may look like regular blackjack but have unusual and quirky rules that dramatically increase the house edge (like paying only 6 to 5 when you are dealt a blackjack).

Make sure you know exactly what you are playing before sitting down. There are a couple of services available that offer updated information on current rules and blackjack conditions across the country. The one I prefer is "Current Blackjack News" and is compiled by blackjack author Stanford Wong (see "Resources"). With the proper knowledge, you can slice the house edge in half just by being picky about where you play. Instead of losing $50 per session, now you lose only $25. That may not sound like much, but it really adds up over time.

A typical recreational player might make four gambling trips per year. For estimating purposes, let's say he plays about 25 hours per trip or 100 hours per year. With the same bankroll (10K) and average bet ($25) he stands to lose about $1,250 a year at a club with no bells and whistles. However, a classy casino like the Bellagio would not only provide a more elegant gaming experience, but because of its better rules would return an extra $625 to his pocket. Over eight years, that amounts to $5,000.

Finding games that offer the best rules is the most concrete way to improve your bottom line, but there are some slightly more abstract methods. If you are fortunate enough to play at clubs that still deal single-deck blackjack, there are some additional ways to increase your edge without actually counting.

For example, if you are playing at a fairly full table (four to seven spots) that deals two rounds each time before they shuffle, you can count the number of tens played on the first round. There should be an average of one face card seen (this includes all 10s, jacks, queens, and kings) for each player at the table (not counting the dealer). So in a four-spot game, the average number of face cards that you should see on the first round is four (from all four players and the dealer). This number then increases to five, six, or seven for each additional player.

Any time you see fewer face cards on the first round than this average number, you have a small edge and can increase your bet modestly for the next round. For example, if you only counted four face cards on the first round in a six-spot game, that is two *less* than the norm, which creates an excess of larger cards for the next hand, thus increasing your odds. You could also *reduce* your bet on the next hand when you have seen *more* tens than normal (eight in a six-spot game, for example). This is a simple technique, yet potentially strong enough to make you a slight favorite overall.

Surprisingly, many clubs still offer single-deck blackjack games. You might have to travel a little farther, but you can find them throughout Nevada as well as on a few riverboats in the Mississippi region.

The same principle can be applied to shoe games, but the gain is drastically reduced. Suppose Alex never played the first hand after a shuffle in the six-deck games, but instead watched to see if there was an excess of small cards. He then jumped in only when several players had split or doubled down and very few face cards were on the felt. The information from this one round could theoretically bring him close to dead even, but it is not very practical because six decks greatly dilutes the value of each small card.

COMPS

Most gamblers don't travel all the way to the desert to break even—they want to come out ahead. But is that possible without counting cards? It can be if we add one more element to the equation—comps.

"Comp" is one of the most glorious words in the gambling lexicon. It's jargon for the various complimentary items that the casinos give their more loyal players, including free rooms, meals, and shows. But as any veteran knows, nothing in a casino is ever truly "free." If you understand the comp system, there are some great values to be had. But for every player who knows how to work the system, there are a dozen people willing to burn through hundreds of dollars in their pursuit of a monogrammed T-shirt or a free hat.

It is indeed bizarre how much pleasure some people can get out of free items, but it is difficult to put a price on comps. Frugal individuals may not consider a comp to a fancy gourmet restaurant worthwhile because the tip for their free meal could cost them more than the entire price of a regular dinner. But to others such perks are like the MasterCard commercial—the comp is priceless. Scoring front row seats for David Copperfield might create memories they'd treasure the rest of their lives. For them, the value of the comp far exceeds their actual losses (which are easily forgotten).

As a high roller, I've received numerous free tickets to concerts and sporting events and have downed more than my share of sirloin steaks and succulent lobster. Several friends have accompanied me to casinos over the years, and I've snagged them free suites and fancy meals. So there is definitely an advantage to working the system, and getting comps for your friends can greatly help your popularity. But you don't have to be a high roller to drink from this well. Even someone with a modest $10,000 bankroll like Alex can benefit.

Remember our earlier illustration of how his projected loss for four hours of play totaled only $25 to $50? It wouldn't take very many comps to more than offset that meager loss. If he put up $10,000 in front money (or had a comparable credit line), he could easily procure a couple of hundred dollars of freebies per trip. In essence, he could take a few mini vacations per year with almost all expenses paid—if he played his cards right.

Max Rubin's book, *Comp City,* has several creative tips on how to maximize your casino rating and get a generous slice of this pie. He suggests that you look for full tables and play as slow as possible. The comp formulas most casinos use are based on hands per hour, and if you play fewer hands than the norm you are putting a lot less money at risk for the same gain in comp dollars.

Also, you bet biggest when the pit boss or *host* is watching, especially when you first sit down and ask to get rated. This tends to make them overestimate your average bet. Add in a few strategic bathroom breaks, and it is *possible* for a basic-strategy player to receive far more in comps than he should expect to lose in dollars.

It's difficult to recommend any one specific casino since conditions at the tables can change so quickly. However, a great example of a place where you can incorporate several of the tactics I previously discussed—and greatly increase your odds as well—is the Nugget in Sparks, Nevada, just outside Reno. This casino has traditionally always had excellent single-deck games with good rules. It is also extremely generous with its comps and has a superb collection of restaurants. The food and service always rate high in local surveys, and it is a very well-run, friendly club.

It's also possible to reel in a free cruise. Norwegian Cruise Line has an outstanding comp program and offers one of the best and most relaxed casinos on the seven seas. So you don't have to be a millionaire to qualify for the great benefits at many casinos around the world, especially at some of the smaller resorts.

ALL-YOU-CAN-EAT

Alex Strickland eagerly received this message of free food and expressed a willingness to milk the comp system like a Rocky Mountain goat. Alex bears a striking similarity to Friar Tuck of the Merry Men and has never met a buffet he didn't like. He is the type who doesn't even bother to slice the pizza, and the possibility of getting free pork chops practically made him salivate.

Yet Alex was like most of us—he still wanted more. There is certainly no disgrace in playing just basic strategy and merely breaking even. By doing so you are far ahead of most everyone else in the casino. But it was the possibility of winning money, not tempting meals, that really got Alex's attention. It's only natural that he expressed a desire to progress beyond basic strategy—he wanted to be a card counter.

But first, I had to clear up a couple of common misconceptions. Alex had a high IQ but struggled with high school geometry. He assumed only someone with a mutant brain would be able to memorize every card as the dealer removed them from play. I explained how card counting only approximated the distribution of high cards to low cards and assured him that almost anyone with the proper motivation could master it.

Alex was also concerned about the legality of card counting—he understandably didn't want to end up as the most popular inmate in Cell Block F. The idea that card counting must somehow be illegal is a fairly common myth, and is kept alive by some in the gaming community who want the public to believe card counters are common thieves or cheats.

This is far from the truth. As I explained earlier, card counting is simply using your brain in the casino. The very reason blackjack is the most popular table game is because people know it can be beaten by smart individuals.

CHAPTER SIX

The Advanced Player

The previous two chapters laid the foundation to help you reverse roles with casinos so that you're no longer a lamb being led to the slaughter. If you've mastered basic strategy and can mix in a few of the other tips, you're no longer a sucker, but a skilled player capable of breaking even against the house. Now it's time to advance a little higher and become the favorite every time you enter the doors of a casino.

COMPARISON OF COUNT SYSTEMS

Dr. Edward Thorp's initial Ten-Count strategy lumped all the non-face cards together and assigned them the same value. Besides sacrificing some accuracy, it was a bear of a system to actually use in the casino. Certainly some freaks of nature could master the Ten-Count system while in a yoga headstand chanting the mantra of the day, but it proved much too difficult for anyone else.

An early student of the game named Harvey Dubner simplified

Thorp's groundbreaking work into a much easier format. Instead of keeping track of complicated ratios, he devised a counting system that was very simple to grasp. He assigned a value of plus 1 to all the low cards (2–6) and a value of minus 1 to all the high cards (7–A). This count was christened the High-Low (hereafter referred to as *Hi-Lo*).

This elegant system provided a quantum leap forward from Thorp's Ten-Count system—it didn't take someone with a brain the size of Einstein's to keep track of all the numbers. All of a sudden the lucrative gates to the world of blackjack swung wide open, even for those of average intelligence.

For the majority of card counters, Dubner's innovative Hi-Lo system became all they ever needed because it correctly identified nearly every profitable betting situation. Since almost all the edge (at least in shoe games) gained from card counting is derived from raising your bets at the right times, the Hi-Lo seemed like the ideal system. However, some diehards wanted to squeeze the maximum gain from the tables and intuitively saw that more advanced counts could be created and higher edges obtained. This was because not all cards have the same importance when they are taken out of the deck. Hi-Lo lumped all the small cards together (2–6), but there is a considerable difference between them. Some have much greater impact when they are removed from play. The following table (reprinted from *Knock-Out Blackjack*, by Olaf Vaneura and Ken Fuchs) shows the approximate gain or loss each card has when it is removed from single-deck blackjack.

Card	Effect of Removal
2	0.40%
3	0.43%
4	0.52%
5	0.67%
6	0.45%
7	0.30%
8	0.01%
9	−0.15%
10	−0.51%
A	−0.59%

As you can see, some cards have a much greater effect on the odds. The strongest counting system would need to incorporate these subtle differences into their numbers because removing a 5 has more than twice the impact as pulling a 7 out of the deck.

This disparity inspired math geeks to grab their slide rules and search for counting systems that more accurately reflected the different strengths of the smaller cards. Hi-Lo is classified as a level 1 count since none of its values exceed plus or minus 1. More advanced systems are called multilevel counts because the cards have individual values higher than one.

The Zen Count (level 2), the Uston APC (level 3) and the Revere APC (level 4) have been some of the more popular *multilevel* systems. In the following chart, you will see several examples of various counts from level 1 to level 4. The two columns following each count show the betting correlation (BC) and playing efficiency (PE) for each system.

Count system	2	3	4	5	6	7	8	9	10	J	Q	K	A	BC	PE
KO	1	1	1	1	1	1	0	0	-1	-1	-1	-1	-1	97%	55%
Hi-Lo	1	1	1	1	1	0	0	0	-1	-1	-1	-1	-1	97%	51%
Hi-Opt I	0	1	1	1	1	0	0	0	-1	-1	-1	-1	0	96%	61%
Hi-Opt II	1	1	2	2	1	1	0	0	-2	-2	-2	-2	0	99%	67%
Zen Count	1	1	2	2	2	1	0	0	-2	-2	-2	-2	-1	96%	63%
Omega II	1	1	2	2	2	1	0	-1	-2	-2	-2	-2	0	99%	67%
Uston APC	1	2	2	3	2	2	1	-1	-3	-3	-3	-3	0	99%	69%
Revere APC	2	2	3	4	2	1	0	-2	-3	-3	-3	-3	0	99%	65%

One thing that astute observers will notice is the law of diminishing returns at work, especially for betting. Although advanced counts are definitely more precise, the extra gain gleaned from stepping up to level 2 is rather small. Even more surprising is how little additional profit is increased by learning level 3 and above. This is because the simplest systems capture most of the potential power of counting, which flattens out considerably beyond level 1.

Another thing you might recognize is that several systems count the ace as zero. Obviously, the ace is very important because it is the most significant card to consider when counters are raising their bets. Yet because an ace never busts any hand, it is hardly a factor for playing decisions (deviating from basic strategy according to deck composition). Therefore, the strongest systems are called *multiparameter* since they keep two counts—one for most of the cards and a separate one for aces. This allows them to retain the strength of high betting efficiencies while improving the accuracy of decisions.

UNBALANCED COUNTS

Most counting systems are called *balanced counts*. That means positive numbers are equal to negative numbers. If you counted down a deck using the Hi-Lo system, you would start with zero and end up with zero.

However, one of the counts doesn't add up (so to speak). The KO count is the best known of what are called *unbalanced counts*. It has one extra small card to count (the 7), so you'd end up with plus 4 at the end of the deck rather than zero.

This imbalance is deliberately created to eliminate the need to make true count conversions in blackjack. The KO methodology is explained in detail in the excellent book *Knock-Out Blackjack*, by Olaf Vancura and Ken Fuchs. Their premise is a very sound one— the authors feel it is mentally too taxing for most players to convert back and forth between running counts and true counts. (These terms will be explained more fully later in this chapter.)

There is a lot to be said for unbalanced counts, and sometimes less is more. The only downside is that ultimately you always pay a price (in card counting) when you sacrifice some accuracy at the altar of simplicity. The question is how much money are you giving up for something that is easier to learn and play?

Let's answer that question by going back to Alex Strickland and his $10,000 bankroll (which I will use as the benchmark for all win rates in this book unless otherwise noted). Assuming he took a gambling trip every three months and only had time to learn the

Microwave strategy, his loss would be about $2,500 for the year. If he mastered basic strategy and played average-shoe games, the loss is whittled down to $1,250. If he had access to better clubs with superior rules like the Bellagio, then the loss is only $625 for the year.

However, losing less is still losing, and learning to count cards is the best way to reverse this negative cycle and make you a winner. If Alex plays the KO count and spreads from $5 to $100 in normal six-deck-shoe games, he no longer is an underdog, but instead has an expected win of approximately $2,000 for the year. This amount increases slightly with the Hi-Lo count, but the difference between Hi-Lo and the KO count is negligible for most part-time blackjack players.

The conclusion? Any steps you take up this ladder are obviously beneficial. If you only learn basic strategy, you will still be far ahead of most blackjack players. So whatever you're capable of mastering is better than nothing, but the stronger your count system and skills, the more you will benefit, especially in handheld games (single or double deck).

When I taught Alex Strickland how to count, I started him right off in the big leagues with Hi-Opt II because that was what I used. This is a two-level, multiparameter count that requires a strong commitment to learn. Today, if an aspiring card counter approached me, I probably would recommend a different route. The reason is twofold. Unless a player is going to make blackjack his passion, the extra work for higher systems is often unwarranted. Also, many casinos now offer only shoe games, and recent research has shown that the simpler counts like KO and Hi-Lo are nearly as effective as the advanced counts for six- and eight-deck blackjack.

The best counting system for you depends on several factors, including the kind of blackjack games you play, how much you bet, and how many hours a year you expect to work. I would consider all these circumstances before recommending any one count.

However, most players starting out are going to fit into the recreational category and should learn Hi-Lo. I will explain the nuts and bolts of the world's most popular count shortly, but first let me cover one last item. Remember how Alex Strickland always liked shortcuts? When I first showed him all the charts and numbers needed to master Hi-Opt II, his eyes started rolling like reels in a slot machine. Finally, out of exasperation, he suggested an alternative plan. (Since then I've received the same request from many other people.) Rather than learning to count, he proposed following me around from table to table and simply betting higher on his spot whenever I increased my wagers. Presto! All gain. No pain.

I don't let friends do this because two or more players raising their bets at the same table, after seeing a flurry of small cards, always looks bad. However, other players (whom I don't know) often take advantage of my counting expertise (which I don't welcome) by jumping in at my table during positive situations.

If you're unwilling to teach yourself to count cards, theoretically you could also find a card counter and mimic his bets. The trick, of course, is identifying a *good* card counter. Practically speaking, if you can determine that, you can probably count on your own. However, some card counters have a certain look that sets them apart from the crowd. It's clear to the trained eye that they are not visiting the casino for fun—they came to make money and are sometimes rather easy to spot.

HI-LO

There is no "one-size-fits-all" counting system. If you intend to become a serious high-stakes player, or if you are willing to travel all over the land to find profitable handheld games, I suggest you just skim the following pages and learn the more advanced count in the next chapter instead. However, if you plan on primarily attacking the far more common shoe games and don't expect to quit your day job, then Hi-Lo is probably just the ticket.

This is not only the most popular count for intermediate players, it's also the weapon of choice for most blackjack teams for the simple reason that it avoids the stiff learning curve of multilevel, multiparameter counts. It works especially well for groups that constantly shuffle new players in and out of the team.

Hi-Lo is easy to learn. If you can add 1 and 1 and come up with 2, then you're a strong candidate to master Hi-Lo. First, let's review the respective values for each card.

Count Value of Cards

2, 3, 4, 5, 6	count +1
7, 8, 9	count 0
10, J, Q, K, A	count −1

You can see there are three groups. The twenty small cards (2–6) are counted as plus 1 when they are removed from the deck. The twelve middle cards (7–9) are considered the neutral cards and have no value. The twenty big cards (10–ace) are counted as minus 1.

It's helpful to think of these high and low cards as engaged in a continual tug of war, with the twenty big cards constantly trying to overpower the twenty small cards. Here is a case in which you'd want to root for the underdog, since the removal of an excess of small cards increases your edge. Conversely, if the big cards win the tug-of-war, the odds shift back to the house, and there is no betting advantage for the players.

This is best illustrated with the roulette wheel, which contains 38 numbers. Suppose we make a slight modification and create a wheel with 40 numbers—half of which are black and the other half red. In such a game, neither the players nor the house have any edge on straight bets on either color—it is dead even. *However, suppose after each number was hit, that number was removed from the wheel.* Now you have a whole different proposition. The odds will fluctuate rapidly back and forth between red and black. Take this example: during the first 10 spins, red comes up 8 times and black only 2 times. If you have a propensity for betting red because of some nostalgic Valentine's date back in high school, your chance for winning that romantically tinged wager plunges from 50 percent (20 out of 40) down to 40 percent (12 out of 30). However, black moves up to become a 60 percent favorite with 18 spots left in the remaining 30 numbers.

Our customized roulette wheel shows (in a highly simplified way) the reason card counting works. As cards are removed from play, they forever change the remaining deck composition. When the majority of cards removed are tens and aces (−1), the odds will favor the dealer. But whenever an excess of small cards (+1) are removed, the odds slowly climb past the 50 percent mark and will give astute players a chance to beat the house.

PRACTICE, PRACTICE, PRACTICE

The best way to learn Hi-Lo is to take a standard deck and flip through the cards one at a time until the value of each denomination becomes automatic. Fortunately, this is not too difficult after a little bit of practice. Remember, you don't have to differentiate for any of the four suits—the 5 of spades counts exactly the same as the 5 of diamonds.

Once you feel comfortable with that task, you can start keeping a *running count* (hereafter called *RC*) of all cards in the deck. This is done by starting off with a count of zero. As you flip through the deck, add or subtract the respective values of each card to your overall tally, or RC. After polishing off all fifty-two cards, you should be back at zero.

Let's take the example in which the first few cards in the deck were 6, 2, 8, J, 7, 5. Your brain would process this information into an RC of +1, +2, +2, +1, +1, +2. Each card is added to the RC in the order you see it. A small card adds 1 to the overall number, while a big card subtracts 1 from the total. If you have an aversion to negative numbers, here is a graph to show how this works.

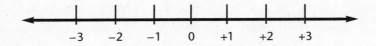

Another trick pros use is to never call negative numbers "negative 1" or "minus 1." It is much quicker to refer to them as "mi 1." Mi is short for minus. This may sound like a silly modification, but it really speeds up your counting. Another thing experts never do is refer to positive numbers as "positive 5." They would simply be 5.

This also streamlines and simplifies the counting process, although I will use the plus signs in this book to avoid any confusion while you're still learning the material.

Next, go through the deck two cards at a time. This may sound more difficult but is actually much easier. The reason is that many card combinations will cancel each other out in Hi-Lo. Here are several examples of cancellation at work.

All of the two-card combos shown above can essentially be ignored when counting since their total value is zero. Once you become acquainted with this fact, you often don't need to add or subtract each card, which is why many consider Hi-Lo such a breeze to learn.

For now, don't worry about your speed—the only thing important at this juncture is accuracy, which can be tested by removing one unseen card from the deck before you begin your count. When you're done, turn over the hidden card and see if it matches your count. For instance, if you ended up with a RC of minus 1, the last card (the one you had set aside) has to be a small card in order to bring the overall count back to zero. If it was any other card, then you made an error (or two) somewhere along the way.

Once you get to the point at which you can predict the last card correctly most of the time, it's safe to move on to your next assignment—speed. This drill is done exactly the same way—you flip over two cards at a time through a fifty-two-card deck, except now you're pushing yourself like a racehorse down the homestretch at Belmont, trying to coax out every ounce of speed.

Don't even bother timing your first efforts—it might be too discouraging. But before long, you should start feeling more in rhythm with the flow of the cards. At that point you're ready to dust off the old stopwatch from your track days and start recording your times. The ballpark goal most people shoot for is twenty-five seconds.

This may seem intimidating at first because most players are initially lucky to land in the fifty-to-sixty-second range. Part of the learning curve is just getting used to smoothly flipping the cards at a rapid clip. Once you get comfortable, start keeping a tally of your results. Your journal should show your time for each deck and whether the count was correct at the end.

The important thing is to not give up. It gets much easier after a little experience. If you want to be superefficient, you can practice counting down decks while watching TV or while pretending to listen to your spouse. It is actually good to have some distractions since that helps simulate the hustle and bustle of casino conditions. (Just don't tell your significant other that I classified him or her as a distraction.)

Recently, I decided to see how difficult it might be to count down a deck with Hi-Lo (since I don't normally use or practice that system). I surprised myself by correctly counting down three decks in a row, clocking in at 21, 18, and 18 seconds.

I don't mention this to dazzle you with my brilliance. My aptitude in math pales compared to some of the true geniuses of blackjack, like my buddy Mickey Weinberg, who graduated from Cornell. I cite this example to show how simple this elegant little count really is. Once you master the basics and understand the principles, Hi-Lo is quite easy to play.

PRACTICE CHART

Lawrence Revere recommended that players carry a small practice sheet with them to learn counting. Below is the one that I made and use. Feel free to modify it or copy it onto a file card. It can also be tucked into your wallet or shirt pocket. Then, whenever you're facing long lines at the bank or boring commutes, whip out this sheet to practice your speed and two-card recognition. This is something you can do in those public places where pulling out a deck of cards is going to either draw a lot of stares or get you fired.

8-T	A-6	7-T	3-6	2-7	2-6	A-2	5-7
4-9	T-T	A-6	5-T	3-5	8-9	7-T	A-9
A-3	8-T	T-T	2-9	A-4	5-6	5-T	4-8
T-T	2-3	6-9	3-T	3-9	T-T	A-9	6-T
7-9	T-T	5-9	3-T	A-T	4-T	A-5	4-6
6-T	5-6	7-T	3-7	2-2	2-7	A-9	T-T
2-T	8-T	7-7	T-T	2-8	8-T	3-7	T-T
6-5	T-T	9-T	4-5	6-7	4-9	5-8	2-5
3-5	6-8	A-4	8-T	A-8	T-T	9-T	3-T
8-9	8-T	4-T	5-7	3-5	T-T	3-8	4-7
3-5	3-T	A-6	6-8	4-T	7-T	6-9	T-T
3-4	4-T	A-7	T-T	2-7	3-6	T-T	2-6
A-T	2-4	2-7	A-2	2-T	2-7	A-5	T-T
4-T	4-5	5-T	T-T	8-T	2-3	3-T	T-T
5-T	A-6	3-T	3-4	4-6	2-8	7-8	3-T
7-T	5-T	8-9	2-5	9-T	6-7	A-T	2-3
T-T	A-5	8-T	4-9	5-9	6-T	T-9	3-T
4-7	9-T	4-T	4-8	9-T	6-T	T-T	7-8
A-8	5-T	2-5	T-T	A-4	A-T	2-9	A-2

RUNNING COUNT

Nearly all the advantage a card counter gains over the house in a shoe game (six- or eight-deck) comes from betting. Play decisions matter very little comparatively. It is possible to glean most of this gain without reading much farther. If you are able to correctly maintain a RC and play perfect basic strategy in the casino, you're ready to become the favorite, rather than the house.

Let's again use Alex Strickland's $10,000 bankroll as a benchmark for your wagers. If you have more or less than this amount, just adjust the numbers accordingly. What every skilled blackjack player is looking for is a high plus count. That indicates there is an excess of big cards (10–ace) left in the remainder of the shoe, which will favor the players rather than the house. A crude betting strategy to take advantage of these positive counts would be to hike up your bet during the high counts and stick with your minimum bet the rest of the time. The minimum bet would be $5 to $10, depending on how aggressive you want to be with your spread. Stick with this bet any time the RC is +4 or less (this includes all negative numbers).

From +5 to +9, bet $25. If the RC climbs into double digits, then bet $50 from +10 to +14. Jump to $75 for a RC of +15 to +19, and when the RC reaches into the stratosphere and breaks +20, take a deep breath and push out that $100 chip.

This is a tough method to tap into the edge that is constantly fluctuating back and forth between the house and the players at the blackjack tables. There is only one way to gain a verifiable advantage in any betting strategy—to wager more when the count is high enough to tilt the odds in your favor. Doing this will make overall winners out of disciplined players.

You could fine-tune it a bit more by moving your big bets up one notch over the second half of the shoe. For instance, now bet $100 on +15 or above and $75 on +10 to +14.

RC	First Half of Shoe	Second Half of Shoe
+4 or less	$5	$5
+5 to +9	$25	$50
+10 to +14	$50	$75
+15 to +19	$75	$100
+20 or more	$100	$100

NEGATIVE NUMBERS

If you still struggle with keeping the count when it falls into negative numbers, you might try starting off with a count of +10 rather than zero. If you go up or down from there, you will rarely dip into negative digits, and if you do, that might be a good time to leave the table anyway. Obviously, if you used this trick, you'd need to adjust your betting and play decisions to correspond with the different starting point ($50 at +20 rather than +10).

I never had any problems adding or subtracting negative integers, although I know some players who do. Personally, the only time negative numbers bother me is when they show up on the trip's win/loss sheet.

TRUE COUNT

The only reason I expect to have more winning days than losing ones is because I raise my bets during positive counts. The previous chart shows when to raise your bets according to the RC, but the maximum dollar-per-hour return would be to theoretically jump to your highest bet ($100 in our example) *any* time you have an edge over the house. This would also be the simplest betting scheme. However, such a strategy packs unnecessary risk, and players employing such aggressive tactics would be in danger of tapping out their $10,000 bankroll rather than winning.

A smarter approach is to modify your bets so they are in proportion to the actual edge you have on any given hand. A rule of thumb is that the higher the count goes into the positive numbers, the larger your edge. This is why the chart shows incremental increases in your bets based on how high the RC rises.

However, most counters never base their bets just on the RC because the value of the count changes depending on how many cards remain to be played. For example, if you took a 4 out of a pack of fifty-two cards, the odds would shift by about 0.5 percent in favor of the players. Yet you would need to remove six 4s out of a six-deck shoe to cause the same shift in the house advantage.

Here is a great way to illustrate that principle. If you added a teaspoon of sugar to an eight-ounce glass of lemonade, most people would find it just right—not too sweet and not too bitter. But if you were to add only one teaspoon of sugar to the entire pitcher of lemonade, the sweetener would be greatly diluted. It would take six teaspoons (if there were six glasses of lemonade in the pitcher) to accomplish a similar effect. The same concept applies to the true count, as the effect of each individual card value is diluted depending on how many decks are used. The bigger the pitcher or shoe, the less effect each teaspoon of sugar or small card will have.

Therefore, the only way to know the proper proportion and correct odds is with a *true count* (hereafter called *TC*). This conversion process scares off many players, but it can be learned with a little practice.

Here is the formula that shows the equation:

$$\text{True Count} = (\text{Running Count})/(\text{Unplayed Decks})$$

Getting back to the example of our 4s, a RC of +6 with six decks remaining to be played yields the same TC of +1 as a RC of +1 with one deck remaining (6 ÷ 6 = 1). This is because the effect of removing a small card from one deck (1 out of 52 cards) is significantly greater on the remaining composition than removing the same card from six decks (1 out of 312 cards).

This TC provides a much more accurate gauge for the proportions of high cards to low cards over the remainder of the shoe than an RC. And that is the information you need to know—whether there are sufficiently more tens and Aces than normal so your bets can be raised higher. To calculate a TC, it does not matter how many decks you started with, just how many are left to play. Each number in the TC is called a true point and is worth about 0.5 percent with the Hi-Lo count. In other words, every time the TC rises one point, your edge goes up 0.5 percent.

In most games, a TC of +1 brings you back to about even or slightly ahead of the house, and every positive number over that increases your advantage. For example, a TC of +3 yields about a 1 percent edge and a TC of +5 close to 2 percent. Here is how the thought process to determine that number works: The TC of +5 is multiplied times 0.5 percent (value of each true point). This gives a total of 2.5 percent. Then you subtract the starting house advantage (which is usually around −0.4 percent against the players). That leaves a total of approximately 2 percent for your edge. You can readily see how this more precise information allows you to bet correctly. However, you must be able to convert the RC to the TC to take advantage of this data.

TRUE-COUNT ADJUSTMENTS

There are several training techniques to learn TC adjustments for shoes. I learned with the Ken Uston method by buying over two dozen used decks from a casino and rubber banding every possible half-deck combination in a six-deck shoe (½, 1, 1½, 2, 2½, etc.). With practice, I became adept at eyeballing the different packs so that I could readily recognize how many half-decks sat in the discard rack. The RC is then divided by the number of half-decks I estimated remained (for example, an RC of +9 with 4½ decks remaining yields a TC of +2).

Today, I would recommend only adjusting by whole decks rather than half-decks. There is not a lot of gain from the additional precision, and it is much easier to estimate the cards in the discard rack to the closest deck. The previous example would then look like this: the RC of +9 divided by 4 yields a TC of +2 (actually 2.25, but the TC is generally rounded down to the nearest whole number).

However, I still suggest you buy a few decks and perhaps even a discard rack for practice. It's important to be able to check yourself at home to see how close your estimates are. Here is a great way to learn estimates for the six-deck shoe. Obtain five used decks from your local casino (it is best to purchase these at the gift shop rather than trying to grab them at the table). You want to use casino cards because the thickness of regular store-bought decks is often markedly different. Once you get home, take out a permanent marker and number each card sequentially from 1 to 260. (At this point you need to be careful to always keep them in this order.)

Now put all five decks in the discard rack. Either you or your mate (if he or she isn't still steamed over the distraction analogy) then pick up a portion of cards from the top of the pile and set them aside on the table. Now guess roughly how many cards remain in the discard rack, then flip over the top card and see how close you came to your estimate. The reason for using a partner is that you'd gain an unfair advantage by picking up the cards. Eventually, you'd be able to guess how many are left by the weight of the cards in your hand. This is an unrealistic practice since you can't pick up cards in the casino (without getting arrested).

Now let's see how this drill works. If you took about three decks off the top of the five-deck stack, it would look like two decks remain in the discard rack. The exact card number for two decks (in the discard rack) is 104 (number written by the Magic Marker). Anything reasonably close to that is accurate enough for TC conversions. However, if you guessed two decks were in the rack and the card number read 140, you were well off—it was much closer to three decks (156 cards) than to two decks (104 cards). Continue to practice until you're consistently within 5 to 10 cards of the actual number. This technique can be used whether you decide to round to the nearest deck or half-deck.

TRUE-COUNT CONVERSION

You can also mix in TC conversion practice by adding in another separate deck (it is smart to purchase a different color to avoid confusion and comingling). Take a card from the new deck and flip it over. This represents an imaginary RC number for practice. Say you turned over the 8 of clubs. If you've estimated there are two decks in the discard rack, then there are four decks remaining (hereafter called DR). So 8 (the RC) needs to be divided by 4, which gives a TC of 2. You can do this with several different cards, one after another, to practice this conversion before moving on to a different number of decks in the discard rack. You can also use red cards (hearts and diamonds) to imitate minus numbers and black (spades and clubs) for positive.

Let's look at a couple more examples.

$$\text{RC of } +4 \div 2 \text{ DR} = \text{TC} +2 \qquad (4 \div 2 = 2)$$
$$\text{RC of } +15 \div 5 \text{ DR} = \text{TC} +3 \qquad (15 \div 5 = 3)$$
$$\text{RC of } -12 \div 3 \text{ DR} = \text{TC} -4 \qquad (-12 \div 3 = -4)$$

Dividing by whole numbers (rather than half-decks) should be fairly easy with this drill. The exactness of decimal points for a TC is unnecessary, and it's generally best to round down to the nearest whole number.

$$\text{RC of } +6 \div 4 \text{ DR} = \text{TC } +1.5, \text{ or } +1$$
$$\text{RC of } -8 \div 3 \text{ DR} = \text{TC } -2.7, \text{ or } -2$$
$$\text{RC of } +12 \div 5 \text{ DR} = \text{TC } +2.4, \text{ or } +2$$

Some people have an aversion to division and prefer to multiply. This can be done by flip-flopping the equation. For example, the last sample problem above would be $12 \times \frac{1}{5} = 2$ instead. This can be simplified into the following conversion factors (CF).

Decks Remaining	CF
8	.1
7	.1
6	.2
5	.2
4	.25
3	.33
2	.50
1	1.0

Now, with an RC of +15 and a DR of 3, you'd multiply 15 by .33 (or $\frac{1}{3}$) to get a TC of 5. This is easier than it sounds. If you ignored the decimal point for a moment, most of the time in shoe games you multiply by 1, 2, or 3, which is very easy. For example, $15 \times 2 = 30$, and if you put the decimal point back in, it is 3.0, or a TC of 3.

When two decks remain, it's easier to think of one-half the RC rather than multiplying by .50. Also, it's best to add a little more precision and convert to half- or quarter-decks from that point on. This is when many close decisions come into play and much more of your money is risked. Here are the conversion factors for what is generally the last deck dealt out of a shoe.

Decks Remaining	CF
2	.50
1.75	.6
1.50	.67
1.25	.8
1	1.0

I prefer to use conversion factors because I think multiplication is easier and quicker than division, but I encourage you to use whichever technique feels more natural. The reason I list .25, .33, and .67 rather than .2, .3, or .7 is because it is often quicker to use ¼, ⅓, and ⅔ to multiply the RC at those places in the shoe.

PLAY DECISIONS

Determining the TC will help in two ways. The main advantage is in being able to bet the correct amounts at the right times. One important thing to remember is that a negative RC *always* equals a negative TC. So if you are calculating a TC only to determine your bet, you can save yourself the effort on any negative number because you will never change your bet (with the Hi-Lo system) until the RC rises over into the positive side.

The other reason you need a TC (rather than just a RC) is so you can vary your play decisions from basic strategy according to the count. It may sound stupid, after I took so much time explaining the importance of basic strategy, to tell you now that there are occasions when you throw it out the window. But there are very good reasons for these exceptions. When an excess of face cards are left in the shoe, it is sometimes wiser to stand on your stiffs and let the dealer bust. Also, you'd want to double down and split more frequently in positive counts and less often in negative decks.

The correct time to deviate from basic strategy is determined by a matrix number. However, you still play basic strategy on the vast majority of your hands. Some of these modifications according to the count can greatly increase your edge. Don Schlesinger, the gifted author of *Blackjack Attack*, determined the most important hands for changing your play from basic strategy. He dubbed these critical plays "the *Illustrious 18*." Here are the matrix numbers (as calculated by Dr. Eliot Jacobson for six-deck shoes) to use during those critical situations.

The Illustrious 18

Insurance	+3
16 vs 9	+5
16 vs 10	+1
15 vs 10	+5
13 vs 2	0
13 vs 3	−2
12 vs 2	+4
12 vs 3	+2
12 vs 4	0
12 vs 5	−1
12 vs 6	−1
11 vs ace	+2
10 vs 10	+4
10 vs ace	+4
9 vs 2	+1
9 vs 7	+4
10, 10 vs 5	+5
10, 10 vs 6	+5

What this chart means is that sometimes playing strategy (as well as betting) can be affected by the count. For example, now there are times when it is correct to stand with your 15 versus a face card (TC of +5 or higher) even though that is contrary to basic strategy. Taking advantage of this additional information (derived from the count) to alter some of your plays will increase your edge over the house.

You always want to round the TC down for playing decisions, and you only deviate from basic strategy if the TC equals or exceeds that number. Another tip is that in shoe games the TC is almost always less than the RC. A conversion is never required unless the RC is at least higher than the matrix number you need. For example, in 16 versus 9, you'd stand (rather than the usual play of hit) if the TC equaled or exceeded +5. However, if the RC is anything less than +5, you don't even need to do the math. Any fraction of +5 will be less than +5.

Sometimes, you may have a decision that is a toss-up—a hand that is borderline for the number. The best way to resolve such close calls is to go with basic strategy and err on the side of safety.

TACKLING THE TABLES

This chapter contains all the basics for you to become an overall winner at the casinos. However, at times this task may seem too difficult or overwhelming, and you may want to give up, but the reward for the work you put in now will be great over your lifetime. Disciplined players who adhere to the proper strategies will win far more often than those who play blackjack by the seat of their pants.

The important principle is to only use what you are able to master. A little knowledge sometimes can be a dangerous thing, and every time good information is dispersed to the gaming public it usually creates more losing players than winners. That is because few put in the work at home before entering the doors of the "palaces of chance."

The next step, once your speed and accuracy is adequate, is to take your game out of the kitchen and into the battlefield. However, it is very important not to rush this process. Practice should be done at home, not at the casinos. The cost of your education in the real world can be very high.

Assuming you're ready to tackle the tables, I suggest you start off betting small. Don't make my initial mistake and go in unprepared and overconfident. It is better to start slow and work your way up to higher chip levels. There are many things to keep track of when you first start card counting, and if you are also sweating over the amount of money at risk, you have a recipe for disaster.

If you've already learned a valid counting system (like the KO), there is no need to change if you are comfortable with that. However, more chips wait for you at each additional rung of the ladder. The higher you are willing to climb, the larger the gain. In the next chapter, I'll reveal some insider tips to help you maximize your return at lucrative handheld games. And those chosen few who are diligent and serious about their blackjack game can join the ranks of the true upper class in blackjack—the pros.

CHAPTER SEVEN

The Professional Player

Greater heights can certainly be reached if you're willing to take the next step up and learn how to play blackjack like the pros. The Hi-Lo system is more than adequate for most players and situations. However, there are scenarios in which it is wiser to use a more advanced count.

There are times when the extra gain of a highly complex count justifies the extra work. It hinges on three variables—bankroll, number of hours played, and quality of games selected.

Anyone who expects to bet big at the tables should seriously consider learning a more complicated system. A level 2 count will win close to 10 percent more per hour in shoe games than the Hi-Lo. For our benchmark $10,000 bankroll and one hundred hours per year, that's not much money—just a couple hundred bucks—so it may not seem like it's worth the effort. But if you increase either the average bet or hours played, that little bit extra can become a huge gain.

Take, for example the sensational MIT blackjack team, which was profiled in the best-selling book *Bringing Down the House*. They often bet $10,000 a hand, which would be the entire bankroll of many recreational players. Yet Kevin Lewis stated they played Hi-Lo because they "did not feel that the added value of more advanced systems outweighed the potential risk of casino error." Now there are several good reasons why many big teams stick to a simple count (for example, high personnel turnover). But if someone played on his own with a top bet of $10,000, he would give up approximately $50,000 to $75,000 a year by his reluctance to learn a more difficult system.

The other factor to take into consideration is the quality of the blackjack games you play. Card counters should always seek out the best conditions and rules. The next chapter will give some of my criteria for choosing the cream of the crop, but a general rule of thumb is this: the better the game, the more important your counting system, since advantageous rules or deeper penetration yields greater gain with an advanced counting system. This is most notable in handheld blackjack games. The difference can be huge in single-deck blackjack when playing with an advanced count as opposed to Hi-Lo.

For this reason, I recommend that anyone who plans on playing big money, serious hours, or a lot of handheld blackjack study a stronger count. The system I suggest you learn, if you want to become a pro, is one of the Hi-Opt (short for "Highly Optimum") counting systems, developed by Lance Humble. Their increased playing efficiency will translate into bigger profits. But there is an additional learning curve, and these systems will only increase your bottom line if you are able to use them in the casino without overtaxing your brain.

Most computer simulations show that the Hi-Opt II count is the top-rated system (although there is little actual difference between the best multilevel counts). Hi-Opt II is what I use, and I would never consider tackling the best games using only Hi-Lo. For example, at some of the great single-deck games I played, Hi-Opt II easily won me an additional $100 an hour over Hi-Lo.

Most of the juicy, single-deck blackjack games are now becoming a thing of the past—almost as dead as the dinosaurs. But many authors have prematurely predicted the demise of great conditions before. Ken Uston wrote twenty-five years ago that the gravy train had ended, yet over the last two decades, I've found one good game after another. Other high-stakes players gave up on handheld blackjack and only played shoes, but I won over a million dollars playing *just* single- and double-deck blackjack.

Consequently, most of this chapter will show you how to exploit those blackjack games. The future of handheld blackjack at times does look bleak, and if you live anywhere in the Boston-to-Baltimore corridor, it may seem like modern blackjack is only played with six or eight decks. But surprisingly there are still 88 casinos in the United States that deal single-deck blackjack, and another 266 casinos that offer double-deck games (according to "Current Blackjack News"). So if you are willing to travel a little, you may find that playing against one or two decks is still the easiest way to win and yields the best potential return per hour.

ADVANCED SYSTEMS

There are two well-known counts in the Hi-Opt system. The first is called Hi-Opt I and the second is designated Hi-Opt II. Here are the respective card values for each system.

	2	3	4	5	6	7	8	9	10	J	Q	K	A
Hi-Opt I	0	+1	+1	+1	+1	0	0	0	−1	−1	−1	−1	0
Hi-Opt II	+1	+1	+2	+2	+1	+1	0	0	−2	−2	−2	−2	0

Sharp eyes will notice the similarity of Hi-Opt I and Hi-Lo. The only differences are the 2 and the ace. The deuce is left out of Hi-Opt I because it is the least important of the small cards in the Hi-Lo system. The ace is not actually dropped, but is counted separately. This is the secret weapon of multiparameter advanced counts, because it allows experts to play their hands much more accurately. These are called *ace-neutralized* counts as opposed to *ace-reckoned* counts such as the Hi-Lo.

However, the benefit from keeping track of aces separately comes with a heavy price. Many find it too difficult to keep an RC and then adjust it depending on the number of aces played. I'm not going to sugarcoat it—multiparameter counts are indeed tougher. But let me explain the process, and you can determine whether it is worth the extra labor.

Either Hi-Opt count can be learned in the same fashion as Hi-Lo. Obviously, the individual values for some cards are different, but the practice drills will work in an identical manner. Going through the deck one card at a time, then two cards at a time, would again be the first step. However, it is helpful training to use a pack of cards with four extra aces (a loaded deck) to help prepare you for side-counting aces in a double deck game.

The second step is learning how to keep track of those all-important aces, since your count no longer compensates for them. Many players simply keep two counts going in their head, such as +5 and 2, meaning an RC of +5 with two aces gone. I think a better version of that is to use letters (at least with single and double decks). The previous example would instead be 5 B, meaning an RC of +5 and two aces (B being the second letter in the alphabet). This trick works pretty well except for those who missed *Sesame Street* the week it covered the alphabet.

However, I feel the best approach is to not fry your brain trying to manage two counts simultaneously in your mind. I believe it is much easier when you use some *external* system like fingers or chips to keep track of the aces. I employed the Uston method from *Million Dollar Blackjack* and counted them on my feet. Here is a table to show how that works.

1 ace	Toes on ground and heel raised
2 aces	Instep down
3 aces	Heel down, toes raised
4 aces	Outstep down
5 aces	Heel down, toes up and pointing to the left
6 aces	Heel down, toes up and pointing to the right
7 aces	Toes down, heel up and pointing to the left
8 aces	Toes down, heel up and pointing to the right

This technique will cover all the aces you'll ever see in a hand-held game. If you were to play shoes (which have twenty-four or thirty-two aces), you can simply start over again or use another modification, which I will explain later in this chapter.

The footwork required to perform this side count can be a little tricky to learn. On your first trip, you might end up accidentally brushing toes with the burly longshoreman sitting next to you, but before long, side-counting aces should become second nature. Once you have learned a method that works well for you, you need to know how to process the information. This is actually the hard part.

ACE ADJUSTMENTS

Normally, one ace should be seen for every thirteen cards. If there is any disparity from the usual number, the RC needs to be adjusted. This is generally only done for betting situations, and then only when the adjustment might make a difference on the amount you will wager.

This may sound a little complicated, so let me give you a few examples to show how it works. If you were playing in a double-deck game and approximately half a deck (twenty-six cards) had been played, you should have seen two aces. However, if only one ace had appeared, you have a situation in which the remaining cards are slightly ace rich (by one ace). You then need to adjust the RC up or down by the excess or shortage of aces. In this case you would add either +1 (for Hi-Opt I) or +2 (for Hi-Opt II) to the RC before making your TC conversion.

The chart that follows gives a few more examples of this process using Hi-Opt I. The first two columns show DR (decks remaining) and RC (running count). The column for aces shows how many aces were *actually* played, with the number in parentheses representing the number of aces that *should* have been seen at that point. The column ADJ (adjustment) shows how much of an adjustment (depending on the disparity of aces) needs to be made on the RC. The column ARC (adjusted running count) is the end result of this calculation and is multiplied times the CF (conversion factor) to give the final TC (true count).

DR	RC	Aces	ADJ	ARC	CF	TC
2.0	+2	0 (0)	0	+2	.5	+1
1.75	+5	2 (1)	−1	+4	.6	+2
1.50	−4	1 (2)	+1	−3	.7	−2
1.25	+7	5 (3)	−2	+5	.8	+4
1.0	+1	2 (4)	+2	+3	1.0	+3
.75	−1	1 (5)	+4	+3	1.3	+4
.50	+6	7 (6)	−1	+5	2	+10
.25	−2	3 (7)	+4	+2	3	+6

Still confused? Let's review by walking through this process. In the second example, roughly thirteen cards have been played in a double-deck game and approximately ninety-one (1¾ decks) remain. You should have seen one ace, but instead, two have already come out. This difference of one ace needs to be subtracted (ADJ) from the RC (+5) to get an ARC (adjusted running count) of +4. In this example, the excess ace reduced the count slightly.

The ARC is then multiplied by the CF to give the correct TC for betting (+4 × .6 = TC +2). After this is done, you revert back to the original RC. This step can be difficult and is where many mistakes occur, so you must be careful at this point.

These numbers are for Hi-Opt I, in which you adjust 1 for every ace. If you used the Hi-Opt II system, then you'd need to adjust plus or minus 2 for each ace.

The same principles from the double-deck chart could be used to adjust for aces in a single-deck game, except the number of normal aces would be different. Playing against only one deck is actually easier because the TC in single deck is always greater than the RC, and this greatly simplifies much of the conversion process. This means that it is only necessary to make TC calculations on *close* decisions. Often, the number needed to stand or to increase your bet will be evident without having to go through the several steps of adjusting the RC. Playing single deck at full tables where they deal two rounds is especially a snap because you only need to make one TC decision per deck for betting (between each round).

PROPER PROCEDURE

Learning the proper order for counting cards at the blackjack table can be confusing at first, especially in shoe games in which a dozen cards can appear within a few seconds. I will explain the technique I use, although the important thing is not so much the methodology, but its consistency. Never count cards in a random manner because you will inevitably miss a few or count some twice.

In a faceup game, I never begin my count with the first card given to each player. Instead, I start my count with the dealer's *upcard*, then count each player's *hand*, two cards at a time. The reason I wait until each player receives his second card is that many combinations cancel each other out and it's much easier to count in pairs. After that, I count each hit or double-down card *as it is seen*, beginning with the player at *first base* and ending with the dealer. The term "first base" refers to the individual sitting in the first betting spot immediately to the left of the dealer. Whoever plays last at the table is normally tagged with the moniker "third base."

In most handheld games, players still hold their cards like in the movies. Many people enjoy the old-fashioned tactile sensation this offers, but there is a downside for card counters—they don't see all the cards until the end of the round when the dealer flips them over to resolve the hand. This can be the source of errors, as sometimes you may catch a glimpse of another player's cards during one hand, while on the next hand you don't. Once again, consistency is the key here.

I usually try to sit in the middle seat, which gives me the best view of other players' hands, since seeing a few extra cards can make a big difference in single deck. My procedure in facedown games is to always count the dealer's *upcard* first. Then I count *my hand* and any *other hand* that I can see *every* time. After that I count all the other cards as they are *exposed*—hits, busts, double downs.

However, there are occasions where I do change my methodology, because sometimes gleaning a little extra information can change the play and save a big hand. The most common time to do this is on the second round at a full table. If you have a close decision to resolve, try to view as many cards as possible. Since you know the cards will be shuffled after this hand anyway, you don't need to worry about redundancy (counting the same cards twice), because you can drop the count once your hand is finished.

Let me give you a couple of additional examples of proper times to break procedure. The first is for an insurance count. I'm sure you remember that I said that insurance is a sucker bet. However, for card counters, it is the single most significant play to alter depending on the count. And in a one-deck game, there is actually a much stronger technique to take advantage of this edge.

As stated previously, the first card I always count is the dealer's upcard. If that card happens to be an ace on the *first* round of a single-deck game, I do an insurance count instead of using my normal count (Hi-Opt II). This is done by beginning with −4 and counting every non-ten as +1 and every ten (including face cards) as −1. If your insurance count reaches zero, the proportion of non-face cards to face cards will be exactly 2 to 1 (32 to 16, for instance, instead of 36 to 16, which is the starting point in a 52-card deck) and insurance would be a break-even bet. Any positive number indicates that you have an edge and should take insurance. Immediately after making the insurance decision, you should revert to your normal count and use that for the rest of the deck.

ESTIMATING

On particularly close decisions, I obviously try to see as many cards as possible, and a few tricks help you increase your knowledge. One way is to show your hand to another player whose cards are hidden from your view. Doing this may encourage him to commiserate with you and show his hand in return. Remember, blackjack is radically different than poker because all players battle against the dealer and not each other.

If this tactic doesn't extract the necessary information, you can resort to estimating. I don't recommend this for most hands, but in toss-up situations a calculated guess can be helpful. This is done by observing how someone normally plays his cards. A borderline insurance bet offers a good example. If the yahoo at first base, who ordinarily hits everything, immediately tucks his two cards under his chips, I *assume* he has a strong hand, possibly even two face cards. Therefore, it is reasonable to shift my decision based on this information. This also works with hit/stand decisions. For example, I might hit 13 versus a 2 if a couple of other players quickly stood on their hands, since I assume they're pat.

Another fine point in single deck is the distribution of specific cards. When you are sitting with 6-9, staring blankly at the dealer's powerful-looking king, garnering a little more information can be valuable. Seeing another 6 might change the correct play to stand. Generally, anytime an above-average number of the exact card you need is missing (a 7 for your 14 or a 5 for your 16 against the dealer's 10, for instance), the chance for success by hitting diminishes. Just don't go overboard with this technique, because it applies only to close decisions.

CARD EATING

Another tactic that works particularly well is a technique called card eating. Some blackjack authors recommend spreading to two hands on high plus counts. The theory, obviously, is to get as much money into play as possible during advantageous situations.

However, experience has led me to disagree with this advice for two reasons. The first is that the bullish move of jumping to multiple hands can often be a sure sign you're a card counter. Many pit bosses have been conditioned over the years to view players who frequently raise their bets with suspicion. Shoving out a boatload of chips into two spots can be a dead giveaway that you're an expert.

The other reason is related to the fact that I normally prefer to play alone or with as few other players as possible. In that setting, spreading to multiple hands will greatly reduce the number of rounds you will receive overall. In other words, spreading horizontally may not put that much more money into action. I learned early on (from Ken Uston) that the best strategy is to spread *vertically*, not *horizontally*. So when I raise my bet, I stick to one spot, increasing the stack higher, rather than going sideways.

Ironically, the only time I go horizontal (other than sleeping) is when the count falls into the negative numbers. This is called card eating. For example, in a double-deck game my normal minimum bet is $100. However, if the count dropped down the well and seemed unlikely to return to the land of the positive, I would spread to two hands of $50 each. This eats up cards and reaches the shuffle point quicker.

This tactic can increase a 1 to 3 spread to the equivalent of 1 to 4 or more, depending on the number of players. For example, if I was playing heads-up against the dealer with just under one deck left before the cut card, I'd normally get nine rounds before the shuffle. For me, in a negative count, that would entail $900 of betting (9 × $100). However, if I spread to two hands of $50 each, there would usually only be six more rounds dealt, and I've reduced my wagers to $600 (6 × 2 × $50). The result is that I bet $300 less during a negative count when the dealer held a big edge, which effectively increases my spread in a less-conspicuous manner.

I haven't really explained betting spreads yet and will save that discussion until the chapter on money management, but the general rule of thumb is this: the higher the betting spread, the higher your edge. However, it is unwise to employ too much precision in betting. So instead of always betting $100 on the bottom end, I sometimes push out odd amounts, like $120 or $107.50. Same story on the top end. Mixing together several colors can confuse the pit. A bet of $785 (rather than $800) makes it much more difficult for pit bosses to calculate your spread and often draws their attention to correct payoffs rather than to whether you're counting.

PREFERENTIAL SHUFFLING

Since single- and double-deck blackjack are so easy to beat, you probably wonder why anyone would ever play shoes. There are three reasons for this. First, not as many handheld games are left out there, since most casinos have gone exclusively to shoes.

Second, while it is much simpler for you to count down and beat the single-deck game, it's also much easier for the pit boss or surveillance people to recognize that you are counting. Many high-stakes pros avoid one or two-deck games solely for this reason. There is just too much scrutiny.

The third drawback is probably the most insidious, and is called *preferential shuffling*. What this term means is that sometimes (in a handheld game) the dealer will shuffle the cards earlier than normal. Say, for example, you were playing single deck at a full table and nearly every time you had a high count the dealer smugly grabbed the discards and shuffled up. This is a losing game.

One of the main advantages of shoes is that they have a cut card, and for all practical purposes, you can freely increase your bets without fear that the positive situation will be shuffled away. In single-deck and most double-deck games, there is no cut card and the dealer retains the prerogative to shuffle at will. Some paranoid clubs routinely instruct their dealers to do this whenever a player triples his previous bet.

Therefore, it's critical that card counters play only those games that deal deeply enough to provide an edge. What constitutes adequate penetration can vary depending on the game, the rules, and the amount of *bet spread* you use. I will expound on those criteria further in chapter 8, but the important thing is to find both deep and consistent games. If penetration is usually 70 percent, but drops to 50 percent on the high plus counts, you are facing an uphill battle even with great rules. The problem is that players aren't always aware that the level of penetration is fluctuating. It is very obvious when playing single deck at a full table, because it would mean that only one round is dealt before the shuffle, yet it's much harder to tell the difference when playing heads-up, especially in a double-deck game.

For this reason, I always count the number of rounds whenever I play any handheld blackjack game. By doing this, I'm able to tell if the dealer is consistently reaching the same shuffle point. Below is a chart listing the CF (conversion factors) I use for each round of a single-deck game. Some numbers are slightly rounded since a small difference between the play and bet decisions occurs each round. The first number is the CF. I then multiply the CF times the RC (running count) to get the correct TC (true count). The second number (after the slash) is to show how many aces should have been seen at that point in the deck.

Rounds	PLAYERS						
	1	2	3	4	5	6	7
1	1 / .5	1.2 / .5	1.2 / 1	1.3 / 1	1.4 / 1	1.5 / 1.5	1.7 / 1.5
2	1.2 / 1	1.4 / 1	1.6 / 1.5	2 / 2	2.5 / 2.5	3 / 3	3 / 3
3	1.4 / 1	2 / 2	2.5 / 2.5	3 / 3			
4	1.6 / 1.5	3 / 2.5	4 / 3				
5	2 / 2	4 / 3					
6	3 / 2.5						
7	4 / 3						

Let's walk through one example to show how this CF chart works. Suppose you are playing a single-deck game with two other players (three players total). After the first round, the RC is +3 with no aces played. With Hi-Opt II, the RC is then adjusted by plus or minus 2 to compensate for any disparity of aces from the normal amount. Since there should have been one ace seen at this point, you add +2 to the RC (+3), the ARC is now +5. The CF to use after round one in a three-player game is 1.2. This is multiplied times the ARC of +5 to give a TC of +6. You make a max bet.

After the second round, the RC is now −1, but there still haven't been any aces removed from the deck. Since 1.5 aces should have been played, the RC needs to have +3 added to it (to compensate for the ace-rich remaining deck); the ARC is now +2. This is multiplied times the CF of 1.6 for a TC of +3. You make a medium- to large-size bet.

The third round is the last one dealt at this club, so you no longer make any conversions for betting. However, you may still have a play in which you need to make a TC calculation for your play decision. In this case, the CF of 2.5 would be multiplied by your RC. You will notice there is also a slot for the fourth round in a three-spot game, but in this particular example (and in virtually all casino games) the dealer only dealt out three rounds before shuffling.

One of the best ways to learn these numbers is to deal hands to yourself at home. The easiest category to start on is the four-player game, since the conversion factors are very straightforward for that combination. Also, remember to adjust differently (plus or minus 1) for each ace if you play Hi-Opt I instead of Hi-Opt II.

I also keep track of the number of rounds in double deck, and have a corresponding CF chart for each of those, but estimating to the nearest quarter-deck will be sufficient for most people. However, here are the numbers for those seeking greater precision.

Rounds	PLAYERS						
	1	2	3	4	5	6	7
1	.5 / .5	.5 / .5	.6 / 1	.6 / 1	.6 / 1	.6 / 1.5	.6 / 1.5
2	.6 / 1	.6 / 1	.6 / 1.5	.7 / 2	.8 / 2.5	.8 / 3	.8 / 3
3	.6 / 1	.6 / 2	.7 / 2.5	.8 / 3	.9 / 3.5	1 / 4	1.3 / 5
4	.6 / 1.5	.7 / 2.5	.8 / 3	1 / 4	1.3 / 5	2 / 6	2 / 6
5	.7 / 2	.8 / 3	1 / 4	1.4 / 5	2 / 6		
6	.7 / 2.5	1 / 4	1.3 / 5	2 / 6			
7	.8 / 3	1.1 / 4.5	2 / 6				
8	.8 / 3.5	1.3 / 5					
9	.9 / 4	1.7 / 5.5					
10	1 / 4	2 / 6					
11	1.1 / 4.5						
12	1.3 / 5						
13	1.5 / 5						
14	1.7 / 5.5						
15	2 / 6						

If you've already learned to side-count aces with your foot, there is some good news here. You can use the other foot to keep track of the rounds. I use the exact same order, and if I need to go beyond eight rounds (double deck), I simply start over.

The bare minimum number of rounds that constitute a fair single-deck game are shown in the following table.

Players	Rounds
1	5
2	4
3	3
4	3
6	2
7	2

Some of these combinations are better than others, but all fall within the rule of 6. That rule refers to the sum derived when the number of spots and the number of rounds are added together. For example, 2 players and 4 rounds totals 6, while 4 players and 3 rounds totals 7 (which is obviously stronger than 6), but the best games are rarely seen anymore. You will notice that there are typically no good 5-spot single-deck blackjack games.

As I stated previously, I always prefer playing alone against the dealer and have often found single-deck games that dealt out six to eight rounds consistently. This is a very strong game, and playing heads-up yields the most hands per hour.

Higher-limit tables keep away most tourists, but additional tactics help you avoid crowded tables. One trick is to use props. For example, when I first sit down, I will often put my coat over the vacated chair to my left and then place a drink in front of the spot to my right. This discourages random players from just jumping in, because they first need to ask me to move all my stuff.

SHOE SOLUTIONS

I've gone into detail over the nuances of single- and double-deck blackjack because those were the games that provided the bulk of my income. However, many players will only have shoes available. If that is the case, you're probably wondering if the complicated Hi-Opt systems are still worthwhile to learn. By now, you can see how much work is involved.

There is a reasonably good compromise to this dilemma. The solution is to play a multiparameter ace-neutralized system for hand-held games and an ace-reckoned count for shoes.

I'm sure your immediate reaction is that this hardly sounds like a solution. Learning two separate counts may be child's play for a mathematical whiz kid like Mickey Weinberg, but how about the rest of us? Actually, it's much easier than it sounds. Here is how it works. If you want to play Hi-Opt I at a single-deck game, then you alter your count slightly and play Hi-Lo in shoes. Only two cards are different in each count, and you could even get by using the same matrix numbers (although it is better to use separate ones). Here are the Hi-Opt I single-deck matrix numbers for the Illustrious 18 (as calculated by Dr. Eliot Jacobson).

Insurance	**+1**
16 vs 9	**+5**
16 vs 10	**+1**
15 vs 10	**+5**
13 vs 2	**0**
13 vs 3	**−2**
12 vs 2	**+4**
12 vs 3	**+2**
12 vs 4	**0**
12 vs 5	**−1**
12 vs 6	**−3**
11 vs ace	**−1**
10 vs 10	**+4**
10 vs ace	**+3**
9 vs 2	**+1**
9 vs 7	**+4**
10, 10 vs 5	**+5**
10, 10 vs 6	**+5**

The same strategy will also work with Hi-Opt II. The Zen Count is extremely strong against shoes and is only slightly different than Hi-Opt II. All you need to change is the 6 and the ace. I've included a Hi-Opt II matrix in Appendix 2 for those of you who choose to tackle a more advanced system.

Both Hi-Opt counts will work fine against shoes, so there is no drawback financially if you want to stick with those. However, the difficulty lies in adjusting for aces. When you only keep track of four or eight Aces, it isn't too strenuous, but when there are twenty-four or thirty-two, it is a whole new ball game.

COMFORT ZONE

If you are a serious player, you may eventually view the Hi-Lo count as you would white bread—it will certainly work for making a sandwich, but there are far better alternatives. That is why I recommend the Hi-Opt systems, which I consider the Cadillacs of the card-counting world. If you are lucky enough to play a juicy single-deck game on a regular basis, then stepping up to a higher system is usually a smart move.

Ultimately, though, the most important thing is not finding the strongest count system, but how well you execute it. Otherwise, it may end up executing you. As the old proverb states, "The road to hell is paved with good intentions." For that reason, the best system is whichever one you can fully master.

CHAPTER EIGHT
Finding the Best Games

Where you chose to play can make a huge difference to your retirement plans. Although blackjack is offered in nearly every casino around the globe, not all games are the same. Casual observers usually aren't aware of changes in the rules or in the number of decks from club to club, but these minor variations can add up to major profits or losses. Playing at a casino simply because you like its decor or enjoy the pirate theme can potentially be devastating to your blackjack career.

A true pro seeks out only the very best games if he wants to become a winner rather than just another sucker donating the contents of his wallet. Determining where you can win the most money takes a certain level of expertise, as there are a number of factors that separate one casino from another. These variables make it difficult to decide where to play, and a number of players feel like they are lost in a jungle without a guide. So let me show you some of the criteria I used in blazing my path through the maze.

Obviously, the easiest place to play is whatever club happens to be closest to your front door. But if you live in some remote region, your options might be severely limited. Perhaps there is only one joint offering blackjack within a hundred miles. So you are left with a choice—either play in an inferior game or hit the road.

However, as a recreational player, you may still feel it is way too much work traversing the planet trying to find the world's best game. You fear that the escapist excitement your hobby currently provides will evaporate if you have to treat it like a job. That's fine, and you have every right to continue playing at the local club if fun rather than profit is your primary goal. It's just important to see how much per hour you are giving up for that pleasure.

Here is a table listing the positive or negative consequences of some common rule changes.

Positive Effects	
Double down after splits	+.13%
Resplit aces	+.06%
Late surrender	+.06%
Early surrender	+.63%

Negative Effects	
2 decks	−.32%
6 decks	−.51%
8 decks	−.53%
Dealer hits on soft 17	−.20%
No resplitting	−.03%
No soft doubling	−.11%
Double on 10 or 11 only	−.25%

At first glance, it might not seem worthwhile to take the time and expense to fly halfway across the country just to gain an extra few tenths of a percent advantage. But let's take a look at a typical scenario and see how much you gain or lose. All of the following examples are based on a $50 average bet and one long weekend of play (fifteen hundred hands).

All of the changes are measured against a benchmark single-deck game with Las Vegas Strip rules, which was an essentially break-even proposition for basic strategy players (it actually offered a slight advantage of .02 percent to players). Unfortunately, this game is pretty much extinct now, but it remains a good yardstick to measure all other blackjack variations. The number in the top far right of each table shows how much you would win or lose by playing basic strategy against that particular combination (rules and number of decks).

Barona (San Diego)	**(W $7)**
Single deck	+.02%
Hit on soft 17	−.20%
Double down after splits	+.13%
Late surrender	+.06%
Casino edge	+.01%

Golden Nugget (Laughlin)	**(L $135)**
Single deck	+.02%
Hit on soft 17	−.20%
Casino edge	−.18%

Circus Circus (Reno)	**(L $322)**
Single deck	+.02%
Hit on soft 17	−.20%
Double down on 10 or 11 only	−.25%
Casino edge	−.43%

Mirage (Las Vegas)	**(L $143)**
Two decks	−.32%
Double down after splits	+.13
Casino edge	−.19%

Excalibur (Las Vegas)	**(L $390)**
Two decks	−.32%
Hit on soft 17	−.20%
Casino edge	−.52%

Blue Chip (Gary, Indiana)	(L $307)
Six decks	−.54%
Double down after split	+.13%
Casino edge	−.41%

Grand Victoria (Elgin, Illinois)	(L $458)
Six decks	−.54%
Hit on soft 17	−.20%
Double down after split	+.13%
Casino edge	−.61%

As you can see, the difference adds up very quickly, especially if you take several weekend trips a year. However, none of the previous tables factor card counting into the equation. For a basic-strategy player, the best game would simply be the one with the lowest house advantage. But rules are only one of the criteria for expert players.

GAME SELECTION

Being able to evaluate all the different variables is one of the most important skills for anyone wishing to make their living at the black-jack tables. It's not easy to do and often is what separates the men from the boys. I'll give you a few general guidelines and then share some examples to show how I decided where to play.

The first parameter is very simple. The fewer decks being used, the better. In other words, one deck is easier to beat than two, and two decks is much stronger than six. Eight decks should be avoided as much as a visit to your mother-in-law.

The second guideline is to always seek out the best rules. Options such as surrender, double any two cards, or double down after a split always favor the players. Any restrictions or negative changes to the "normal" standard rules hurt the player and help the house, such as hitting on soft 17 or not being able to double down on any two cards.

The third principle is penetration, or how deeply the cards are dealt before shuffling. In my mind, this is the most important of the three main criteria. Stanford Wong was one of the earliest authors to point out how critical this factor was to card counting. Good rules usually don't make up for mediocre penetration. For example, if a casino offers a six-deck game with all the bells and whistles (surrender, double down on anything, resplit aces) but only deals out half the shoe (three decks) before shuffling, it would be a waste of time for any serious player.

On the flip side, even a game with lousy rules can become a magnet for card counters if they deal deeply enough. Reno is a great example of this. Many clubs commonly allow doubling down on only 10 or 11 and then make it even worse by hitting on soft 17. Both of these restrictions hurt the players, yet the combination of single-deck blackjack with deep penetration can potentially become a very strong game, despite the bad rules.

So with those three principles (number of decks, rules, and penetration) in mind, let me explain how I decide where to play. I typically go wherever I can achieve the highest return per hour of blackjack play. The best rules normally are found wherever a glut of casinos provides plenty of competition. This forces owners to offer more favorable options in order to grab their share of the gaming market, because many gamblers are surprisingly astute about what they want in a blackjack game and will vote with their feet if a casino has bad rules.

Historically, Las Vegas and Atlantic City have been good picks for basic-strategy players who are looking for the clubs with the thinnest house edge. They normally stand on soft 17 and allow players to double on any two cards.

Other clubs around the world also imitate these big boys, but there are many variations. In less-frequented Nevada border towns like Laughlin or Jean, they usually hit on soft 17. Mississippi is split into two sectors much the same way as Nevada, with the Gulf Coast typically using Strip rules like Las Vegas and the northern part of the state hitting on soft 17 like Reno. While it is true that many small-town casinos are a waste of time, occasionally a gem arises out of the desert sand. Wendover (on the Utah border) is a challenge to get to, but has rewarded its adventuresome explorers with one of the strongest single-deck games on the planet over the last two decades.

Common sense would assume that pros only visit the clubs with the very best rules, as the difference can be half a percent or more. That axiom would be accurate for basic-strategy players. Yet as stated earlier, there are other factors besides good rules for card counters. The trick comes in learning how to juggle all three variables (penetration, number of decks, and rules) to size up the best opportunity for your blackjack buck. With experience comes better judgment and discernment on this issue. I feel one of the biggest reasons novice card counters fail to win any serious money is because they play inferior games. You absolutely have to be ruthless in this category if you want to succeed.

BETTING SPREADS

I stated earlier that the simplest betting strategy would be to jump immediately from your minimum bet to the maximum bet on any advantageous count. However, this is unwise for several reasons. One is that such a betting technique attracts undue attention from the pit, and the other is that it would severely strain the limits of your bankroll. In the next chapter, on money management, I will cover optimal betting, but the basic premise is to keep your bets in proportion to your advantage. Otherwise you face the very real possibility of tapping out and heading home broke.

The secret to beating the house at blackjack generally hinges on one fact: you have to bet more when there is a high count—and less when it is negative. How much of an edge you obtain is often a reflection of how wide the *spread* is between your small bets and your big bets.

You don't need much to beat most single-deck games. A 1 to 2 or 1 to 3 spread is sufficient if the rules are good or if the penetration is very deep. However, if you do want to be a strong favorite over the house, then a spread of 1 to 4 will provide a powerful edge in most situations. For our benchmark bankroll of $10,000, that would be roughly going from $20 to $80. With the Hi-Lo count, you would bet $20 on any TC of +1 or less, $40 for a TC of +2, $60 for a TC of +3, and $80 for any TC of +4 or higher. Since there are more max-bet opportunities in the handheld games, it sometimes is wiser to reduce the risk by having more than a hundred top bets for single or double deck. (If your personal cash stake is different than $10,000, then just extrapolate the numbers for your betting range.)

SINGLE-DECK BETS		
	Hi Lo / Hi-Opt I	Zen / Hi-Opt II
+1 or less	$20	$20
+2	$40	$40
+3	$60	$40
+4	$80	$40
+5	$80	$60
+6	$80	$60
+7	$80	$80
+8 or higher	$80	$80

One advantage of those numbers ($20–$80) is that they contain a bit of built-in camouflage. Each bet consists of exactly four chips, and every bet is always capped by a red chip. This could confuse the eye in the sky into thinking you are always wagering the same amount. Casinos will carefully watch anyone who tends to change his bets frequently. Most gamblers tend to stick with the same amount on each hand, and the few players who spread their bets up and down are often suspected of being card counters.

The consequence of this unwanted attention might be preferential shuffling whenever you push out your maximum bet, or you could be asked to leave if the casino perceives you to be a true long-term threat. Fortunately, one advantage of good single-deck games is that you don't have to spread your bets very dramatically to become a winning player.

However, shoe games provide a much more arduous mountain to climb, and my betting advice on how to beat multiple-deck games will be met with extreme skepticism by some in the gaming community. That is because I suggest you use a very large *spread*. A lot of players prefer keeping their betting spreads small so the heat doesn't descend on them at the tables.

I certainly understand their logic, but I've always held a slightly different playing philosophy. My bet sizes are rather conservative in relation to my bankroll, but I've always been very *aggressive* in trying to gain a large edge whenever I play blackjack. I accomplish this by being extremely selective about the games I play and employing large betting spreads.

Here is my personal take on this issue. I'd rather win $100,000 in one year—even if it means I might get kicked out a lot—than eke out $20,000 year after year with a very small edge and a lot of negative fluctuations. Blackjack is difficult to beat in the first place, and I think it is best to do everything possible (within reason) to make sure you are a winner. Far too many counters worry about casino barrings and never really get an edge over the house. So if you can't take the heat, you'd better get out of the kitchen and look for a different vocation. Some players get so rattled they come apart like a cheap watch whenever a pit boss comes near. But if you've got the moxie to stand up to casino scrutiny, then here is the betting style I recommend.

DOUBLE-DECK BETS		
	Hi Lo / Hi-Opt I	**Zen / Hi-Opt II**
0 or less	$10	$10
+1	$20	$10
+2	$40	$20
+3	$60	$30
+4	$80	$40
+5	$80	$50
+6	$80	$60
+7	$80	$70
+8 or higher	$80	$80

For double-deck games, I typically used a 1 to 8 spread. With the $10,000 bankroll, that might mean $10 to $80. So now you would wager $10 on any negative count, then follow the same 20-40-60-80 sequence as in single deck.

Shoe games are harder to beat, but they do contain several interesting quirks that can be exploited. If your only available option is to sit through all six or eight decks, then a gigantic bet spread is often necessary to make it worthwhile. (This is because the house will have an advantage on approximately 80 percent of the hands in a shoe game.) I used a 1 to 20 spread, which is $5 to $100 for the $10,000 bankroll. Here you would bet $5 on negative counts, $10 on 0, $20 on +1, $40 on +2, $60 on +3, $80 on +4, and $100 on +5 or more.

SIX-DECK BETS		
	Hi Lo / Hi-Opt I	Zen / Hi-Opt II
0 or less	$5	$5
+1	$20	$5
+2	$40	$20
+3	$60	$30
+4	$80	$40
+5	$100	$50
+6	$100	$60
+7	$100	$70
+8	$100	$80
+9	$100	$90
+10 or higher	$100	$100

Betting off the top presents a bit of a predicament. Since you normally are at a disadvantage on your first bet after the shuffle, the obvious choice would be to wager as little as possible on your first hand. However, starting off with the same small bet every time is often a dead giveaway that you are a card counter. Mixing it up off the top is much wiser, although it is tough to do if you finished the last shoe with a monster bet. In those cases it is usually better to leave the table rather than drop way down.

REFINEMENTS

There are some additional tricks that can be employed in multiple-deck games. The practice of *back-counting* shoes (standing behind the table and counting the cards as they are dealt from a freshly shuffled shoe) and only jumping in and playing when you have an advantage is called *wonging* (in honor of its innovative creator, Stanford Wong). In its purest form, you only place bets on positive counts and simply walk away or refuse to bet when the house has the edge. Variations of this abound, the most common is to combine a healthy bet spread with the propensity to leave on negative counts. This could be just an occasional bathroom break at the right time or an MO that makes you walk away from the table every time it turns negative and search for a fresh shuffle elsewhere.

It's also possible to wong in on other counters. A number of players used to do that to me, and I'm hesitant to recommend it because it is highly aggravating to the recipient. But if you are in a club for a while, you might notice another person always raising his bets at your table at exactly the right times. If you feel he is pretty accurate, then you can use him as a back counter for future shoes. For example, say later in the day you are wandering around looking for a spot to play. You happen to notice your buddy with the thick glasses is firing black chips at the dealer. Since you remember that his normal bet is $25 or less, you can reasonably assume there is a high positive count at his table. If you were real confident in his abilities, you could even deduce what the approximate true count might be to aid your play decisions once you jump in.

Another technique I use in the bigger clubs is to always wong in for my first play on shoe games. In larger casinos like Foxwoods, it is fairly easy to do this because you normally aren't going to be watched until you make your first bet of the day. So I wander around the tables looking for a good high count before exposing myself (figuratively speaking) to the pit. After you've jumped into a table once, it is pretty difficult to repeat this stratagem without being noticed. However, in places like Vegas or Atlantic City where there are huge casinos lining each side of the street, it's very easy to float around from one place to the other without getting a lot of attention.

KEY CHARACTERISTICS OF CARD COUNTERS

Another important quality a professional blackjack player needs is drive. To stay under the radar of casino surveillance, I constantly moved around. My bread and butter came from aggressively pursuing the very best games anywhere in the world. While most pros habitually returned to Las Vegas, I visited small towns far off the beaten path.

For example, once I braved icy roads to play in Michigan's remote Upper peninsula when one casino there set up a potentially lucrative Over/Under 13 side bet. In the last decade, I took advantage of the gambling explosion across America's heartland and played on numerous riverboats and Indian reservations. Mississippi combined high limits with the world's best single-deck blackjack. A casino in Minnesota made me an offer I couldn't refuse, and so I spent a week playing a sensational double-deck game with special rules. Once, I drove all night to take advantage of a 2-to-1 promotion on blackjacks.

If you want to make a living at blackjack, you have to have a strong desire to play only optimal games—wherever they may be found. To win on a consistent basis requires hard work and a willingness to find the very best blackjack conditions. Card counters need a great deal of perseverance and persistence to overcome the many obstacles facing them.

Currently, tribal casinos offer some of the best blackjack games, and their number is simply exploding, especially in the state of California. However, some players are hesitant to play in any unregulated site. I have one high-stakes friend who absolutely refuses to play on any Indian reservation since they lack the oversight of a gaming commission. He fears there would be no recourse if he were mistreated.

While I understand this concern, I've always had a very positive experience in casinos owned by Native Americans. I've won a ton of money in them and actually enjoy the atmosphere more in their clubs than in the glitzy Nevada casinos. While some large tribal casinos, such as the two in Connecticut, certainly rival or exceed the big dogs on the strip, the smaller ones are the most enjoyable to me. They often have a rural American feel to them and are much warmer and friendlier than the megaresorts of Las Vegas or the sterile environment of Atlantic City.

CHAPTER NINE

Money Management

Overbetting tends to be the biggest downfall for aspiring professional gamblers and can cause someone to go broke even when he holds an advantage. This is the one area where more would-be card counters fail than any other. The casino has an almost unlimited bankroll, while most players are seriously underfinanced for the amount they bet. This imbalance greatly favors the house when the pendulum of fluctuation brutally sways back and forth. Casinos can absorb virtually any negative swing, but many players are wiped out with one bad run of cards and never return to the tables.

If you doubt this concept, just try betting one-half of your bankroll on every high positive count and see how long you last. My guess is the game will be over well before the fat lady sings.

Why do otherwise smart gamblers occasionally overbet? The main reason is that most of us live in a very nearsighted manner. We look mainly at the dot (the present point in time) rather than the longer line of our existence. This creates a tendency to put much greater emphasis on the short term, causing us to get fixated by daily results rather than the long run. As a result, many players develop an innate need to show a profit for the day before they can head off to bed.

If you want to be successful in the casinos, this myopic form of gambling is a dangerous habit you must absolutely purge out of your system. The only thing that matters in blackjack is whether you win overall. War provides a reasonably good analogy for this concept. Smart generals don't risk their entire resources on each skirmish. They are willing to accept some losses and even retreat to fight another day if the situation calls for it. And your goal as a card counter is to win the war, not each individual battle.

Expert blackjack players hold only a slim edge over the house, and even the very best pros still have many trips when they're absolutely crushed by the casinos. It's fairly common to end up in the hole on about two out of every five days you play. So if you are unwilling to walk away a loser on those days, then you are either going to be putting in a lot of marathon sessions or you're going to get desperate. And desperate people do foolish things. I've seen players who are normally very disciplined go on tilt and risk a disproportionate amount of their bankroll in a stupid attempt to finish the day ahead. If you are inclined to have this mind-set, here is a startling secret—*the casino will still be open tomorrow*.

It is *critical* to have strict guidelines for betting and to *always* adhere to prearranged maximum wagers. If you ever bet more than you should out of a desire to get even, it is very unlikely you will be successful in blackjack. Part of the fallacy for overly aggressive betting comes from the logical belief that a good card counter is supposed to win. While that is certainly true, you can't win every hand or even every session. Accepting losses is an important ingredient to becoming a world-class blackjack player.

CAN I QUIT MY DAY JOB?

The main question on the minds of most potential card counters is not related to handling the losses—it's "How much money can I make?" It is the potential for riches that draws many into casinos in the first place. Whenever I speak to others about my vocation, they invariably make comments about what an easy job I have. Or how nice it must be to just hop over to a casino anytime the allure of materialism bites and I need to make a major purchase.

While the life of a professional gambler does have its own mystique and glamour, the financial rewards in blackjack are often far less than some might expect. The reason for this primarily boils down to the fact that it is very difficult to play anywhere near as many hours as you might work in a normal job—not because of fatigue or brain drain, but because the casinos simply won't tolerate it. For example, if Caesars allowed me to sit peacefully at its tables from nine to five every day, and I could happily get in forty hours every week, I'd easily clear a million bucks a year and still be able to take a couple of weeks of vacation.

Now, large casinos can easily absorb a loss like that, but they got to be big by plugging all the leaks. And it would be bad business for them to allow hordes of card counters to descend on their tables like locusts looking for easy pickings. Hence, there has evolved a cat-and-mouse battle between skilled players and the house. The casinos tolerate a certain amount of damage to their castle walls, but the boiling oil is sure to come out if you try and scale too high.

This creates certain limitations on how much money individual card counters can scurry off with. Practically speaking, it is hard for solo players to get in long days at the tables. A full-time pro might only *work* three hundred hours over a twelve-month period. So instead of raking in a million a year and spending his vacations on a yacht in the Mediterranean, his expected return each year drops down to a much more pedestrian number. Therefore, many card counters are destined to spend their summers on the Allagash River in a canoe shooing away pesky mosquitoes rather than on a boat in the French Riviera fending off amorous Scandinavian blondes.

STANDARD DEVIATIONS

A ballpark estimate of how much you can hope to make card counting is to take your top bet and multiply it by 25 to 30 percent. This is roughly what you will average per hour of play. That translates to about thirty bucks an hour with our benchmark $10,000 bankroll, which means a serious effort might only net $10,000 a year. Even worse, the recreational player (one hundred hours a year) might only bring home a meager $3,000. Hardly enough to quit the day job.

Yet thirty bucks an hour is still attractive enough to entice many people, especially when a few comped meals and shows are thrown in. If you desire a greater return for your labors, there is a simple solution to push you into a higher wage bracket—just start with a bigger bankroll and bet more. If you had $40,000 to work with, your potential hourly return should be over a hundred bucks an hour. And unless you're an attorney or a BMW mechanic, that's starting to sound like pretty good money.

However, the problem is that unlike other jobs, you don't get paid by the hour. Your actual return will vary dramatically from your *expected value* (EV). These wild fluctuations are what drive many people out of the business and fall under the mathematical term "standard deviations" (SD).

Here is an example to explain SD. If you were to flip a coin 100 times, the average results should be 50 heads and 50 tails. However, as everyone knows, there will be a certain amount of fluctuation in any short-term trial. Sometimes heads will clock in at 51 out of 100, and maybe the next test it will finish at 43 out of 100. However, there is an exact formula for predicting how often the results of these coin flips will land within certain parameters.

One SD would range from 45 tails to 55 tails (a difference of 5 either way from the average). This would occur 68.3 percent of the time (roughly two-thirds). Two standard deviations would range from 40 tails to 60 tails (a difference of 10 from the average). This covers 95 percent of all tests. A wild swing of three standard deviations would give us between 35 tails and 65 tails (a difference of 15 from the average). This range covers nearly every situation and occurs 99.7 percent of the time.

The same principles apply to blackjack. If your EV for ten hours of play might be $300, then that number would only be an average. In the short run, there will be a wide range of results up or down from that number (the mean). Approximately two-thirds of the time (one SD) your tally for the ten hours of play would fall somewhere between a loss of $700 to a win of $1,300 (actual numbers depend on type of game and bet size). Two standard deviations would vary from a loss of $1,700 to a nice win of $2,300 and would happen nineteen out of twenty times. Three standard deviations fluctuate all the way from a stiff loss of $2,700 to a hefty win of $3,300. All these are possible ranges during that short ten hours of play.

Baseball provides an excellent parallel to the swings a professional gambler will experience. The New York Yankees traditionally are the best team in baseball. If the Yankees were to play the worst team in the league (say the Detroit Tigers), the boys from New York would be favored every time they took the field. But being the favorite doesn't mean they will win every game. Some days their mighty juggernaut would still taste defeat against vastly inferior teams.

Now suppose we fortified their outfield by bringing back Ruth, DiMaggio, and Mantle from the dead. Even with that powerful lineup, the men in pinstripes would still endure some losing days. However, if the games weren't stopped at nine innings, but were *unlimited*, the Yankees would undoubtedly prevail. There would be some sequences of innings where they would be outscored, but over time their superior strength would virtually guarantee victory.

The life of a card counter is somewhat similar. If you've prepared correctly and stay focused inside the casinos, you are now the favorite rather than the house. Even so, many days will test your sanity with devastating drains on your bankroll. Even the best players still lose about one out of every three short trips. This statistic surprises many who assume that once they acquire the magic secret code of card counting, they can treat casinos like an ATM machine. However, reality is far different than fantasy, and the only way to prepare for these negative swings is to make sure you have adequate resources at your disposal.

YIELD PER HOUR OF DIFFERENT GAMES

Earlier, I gave a rough formula for estimating how much you could expect to win per hour at blackjack depending on the size of your bankroll. Throughout this book I will mostly focus on the big picture. Consequently, some of the numbers will be more approximations than precise, hairsplitting fractions. I feel it is extremely important to give players more of a general feel for how the game works. Far too many blackjack books get lost in the minutiae of details and leave readers hopelessly lost on where to begin. However, if the following explanations on risk, optimal betting, and proper bankroll requirements are too light on the math for some readers, then I suggest you purchase Don Schlesinger's excellent book *Blackjack Attack*. He has charts and graphs to cover nearly every nuance of the questions asked by the more technically inclined.

With that caveat out of the way, let me go into a little further detail on the all-important subject of what your return on investment should be in various types of blackjack games. The following statistics were derived from simulating millions of hands (using the Casino Vérité software program) to determine how much per hour a card counter can expect to win with a $10,000 bankroll.

	Hi-Lo	Hi-Opt II
1-deck (Reno), 1-4 Spread		
50% penetration	$16	$21
67% penetration	$31	$44
2-decks (Mirage), 1-8 Spread		
50% penetration	$21	$24
67% penetration	$30	$35

A quick perusal of these numbers should make a couple of things very evident. One is that the gain increases dramatically with a more advanced system—especially in single-deck games. However, the most important factor in getting a good game is penetration, although you can partly make up for bad penetration with a larger spread. That is why my personal philosophy always revolved around being very selective over which tables I would play and being very aggressive about jacking up my bets. Far too many card counters lose or eke out a meager existence because they are afraid to jump their bets. This tentativeness comes from a fear of not wanting to draw any attention from those stern-looking pit bosses. But I think it is far better to win and get kicked out than to lose and feel welcome. Too many players settle for inferior games with bad cuts because they don't get heat at those clubs. Again my advice is to play the strongest game possible and let the chips fall where they may.

Many authors would disagree with me on that point and would consider such a recommendation roughly akin to Charles Manson carving that swastika on his head before his meeting with the parole board. They feel it is much wiser to reduce your spread (say 1 to 4 at double deck instead of 1 to 8) in order to maximize your longevity. I do agree that you need to strike a balance. I'm not advocating that you always greedily grab for the biggest edge possible every time you sit down. But let me repeat an earlier point—blackjack is extremely difficult to beat. Most players who undertake this endeavor will fail. And every inch of advantage that you sacrifice on the altar of longevity reduces your chances of winning and greatly increases your negative fluctuations.

At the risk of sounding heretical, I recommend you err on the side of aggression rather than passivity. If you truly become a winning player, then you will have to face the possibility of getting kicked out for being too good. I view that as an occupational hazard. If I'm going to get eighty-sixed (not allowed to play anymore in their casino), I'd rather it occur after a big win than a small one that took days to grind out.

Also, there are occasionally great games that crop up around the world. Some players try to milk these and make them last as long as possible. Again, I see some wisdom and sensibility in that approach. However, what invariably happens at those clubs is that a high-stakes pro (or team) will hear about the gravy train and play at that casino like a pig until the game is removed or changed. So my advice is to be fairly aggressive when you stumble across those once-in-a-lifetime situations. I did that at one single-deck game at the Jubilee Casino in Mississippi that was so good I could have flat bet and still had an edge. Yet I knew anything that easy to beat wouldn't last long, so I spread from $200 to $1,000 until it ended. Maybe it would have lasted slightly longer if I hadn't won so much. But longer play multiplied by a lower EV doesn't always translate into higher numbers.

HANDS PER HOUR

Another component of return in dollars per hour that rarely gets addressed is speed. Many experts search under every rock trying to squeeze every last tiny fraction of a percent advantage out of their system. But the simplest and surest way to increase your bottom line is to play with fewer players.

The reason for this is that most simulations are based on playing one hundred hands per hour. This is actually on the high side but is a reasonable compromise. However, if you were to play heads-up (alone against the dealer), you will most likely play closer to two hundred hands per hour, which effectively doubles your EV per hour.

On the flip side, if you mostly get stuck at full tables, the number plummets to sixty or seventy hands per hour, depending on how crowded it is or how drunk the patrons are. Therefore, I rarely sit down at a table with more than two other players. This is by far the easiest way to increase your take-home pay in blackjack.

Now let's look at some simulations for shoe games.

6 decks (Las Vegas Strip), 1-20 Spread

	Hi-Lo
67% (2 decks cut off)	$14
75% (1.5 decks cut off)	$17
83% (1 deck cut off)	$21

Here again we see how better penetration can affect your potential return. At first glance, it may not seem like there is much difference monetarily between clubs that deal down to one deck and those casinos that cut off at two decks. However, that small $7 per hour increase represents a sizable 50 percent improvement in your win. Over time, that can translate into a lot of money. And if your chip levels are higher (say with a $100,000 bankroll), the difference is $70 an hour, which really adds up fast.

As mentioned earlier, the spreads in shoe games tend to flatten out more than in single deck and minor changes don't have such a major impact. Therefore, you need a much bigger spread between your small and big bets to obtain any worthwhile edge—if you play all shoes from shuffle to shuffle. Most experts don't attempt to beat shoe games in this manner. The edge is often too small and the game too tedious to beat for any significant amounts. But if you combine a reasonable spread with a fair amount of wonging, the gain increases rapidly.

Remember to be selective about which shoes you play or back count. Not all dealers offer the same penetration—even within the same casino. So look for the best cuts possible before you invest time in that shoe. Also some tables have gone to CSMs (continuous-shuffle machines). These can sometimes look like normal games, but they are not and should be avoided by card counters.

RISK OF RUIN

While most players are understandably drawn to the question of "How much can I make?" the real question remains "How likely am I to lose?" The formula to answer this is known as the *risk of ruin*

(*ROR*). The fear (of somehow losing everything) hangs like the sword of Damocles over the head of every experienced gambler and in some ways provides a healthy dose of reality to keep them from growing overconfident.

Even though card counting is gambling, it doesn't have to be a high-risk venture. If you are properly funded and bet correctly, your chance of losing the entire bankroll should be 5 percent or less. This is a fairly acceptable risk for most people, especially since the return can be far greater than most traditional investment vehicles.

However, there can be a big difference in the level of risk, depending on whether you have a bankroll that can be readily replenished or one that if lost will leave you homeless. If your gambling is a recreational sideline, then it is likely you have a steady stream of income from your regular job, which could replace your playing stake if you ever tapped out. If that is the case, then you could be slightly more macho in your betting, assuming you are truly willing to live with the risk.

A more traditional bankroll is one that if lost will end your gambling career for good. This must be handled entirely differently, almost like you are walking on eggshells. That's because once they crack, the game is over. I viewed my bankroll that way and bet fairly conservatively in relation to it. Those choices always involve trade-offs, because the more aggressively you bet, the quicker you will double your bank. Conversely, if you are risk averse, your dollar per hour return will incrementally shrink.

I tried to find a medium ground of acceptable risk in which my bankroll normally doubled about every three hundred hours. Mathematically, the odds favored success in this venture nineteen times out of twenty (which leaves one chance out of twenty to lose it all). The exact figure for this depends on whether you spend your winnings after each trip or keep them in the bankroll, and on whether you change your optimal bets as the bankroll dwindles.

The best way to treat winnings is to not touch them—at least until a certain point. If every time you hit a lucky streak you then turn around and spend that money, the risk of your bankroll evaporating during the next bad run increases dramatically. In other words, don't use fluctuations to pay your rent. And especially don't use big wins to go on big buying sprees. After you've safely built up a buffer, modestly dipping into the profits can be done without jeopardizing the entire venture.

OPTIMAL BETTING

The smartest way to bet is to always wager in direct proportion to your advantage for that hand. I touched on this subject in chapter 8 (in the tables that show how to size up your bets in relationship to the true count), and now I will explain in greater detail.

Most advantage players pattern their betting strategies from a common model known as the *Kelly betting system*. J. L. Kelly, in a paper he wrote for a technical journal in 1956, theorized that the wisest way to balance risk and reward in gambling was to bet the exact percentage of your advantage. For example, if you had an advantage of 2 percent on the next hand, you could safely wager 2 percent of your bankroll, or $200.

This optimal style of betting minimized the chances of ruin and maximized the potential for winning. Ideally, this "Kelly Criterion" would change as the bankroll shot up or down. However, in practice it is very difficult and somewhat dangerous to do perfect Kelly betting since you usually have to bet more than zero when there is no advantage, and not all bets are practically divisible into fractions. Occasionally, other factors like table maximums and minimums work against perfect Kelly, as do some types of camouflage betting many card counters are forced to employ.

Furthermore, betting exactly Kelly can be extremely volatile and will put most players at greater risk than they would like. Card counting is an emotionally demanding profession in which over 98 percent of the time you will find yourself below your all-time high. Mathematicians call this "a random walk with an upward drift." My solution was to turn down the dial on the risk meter slightly and to bet what is commonly known as one-half Kelly. That means I never bet more than half of the edge on any given hand. So with a 2 percent advantage on a $10,000 bankroll, I'd recommend a bet of $100 instead of $200. In handheld games, the risk averse might want to drop the top bet down a little lower because single- and double-deck blackjack offer many more betting opportunities than shoes.

MAX BET

Additionally, I always capped my maximum bet regardless of the advantage. I think it is mandatory to have a set betting spread in mind before you ever sit down at the table. Consequently, I never bet more than 1 percent of my entire bankroll on any hand, no matter how high the edge. And I only pushed that amount out when the count showed at least a 2 percent edge in my favor. This method of betting will greatly reduce your fluctuations and limit your risk to an acceptable level (at least in my eyes).

Another key component of optimal betting is to modify your betting levels in proportion to the shifting tides of the overall bankroll. If you started with $10,000 and a maximum bet of $100, then a bad weekend at the tables (losing $4,000) would lower your top bet to $60. Theoretically, this should always be done as the winds of fortune fluctuate your bankroll up or down. Practically speaking, however, it is only wise to do it occasionally. I would recommend it only after major swings of at least 20 percent, if not more. Please don't confuse this betting change with streaks or cards being due because that is not the reason you are altering your bets. It is only based on the ROR, and how best to balance the chance for gain with the desire to remain solvent.

Let me cite another example from early in my card-counting career to explain this concept further. After I had slowly built my bankroll up to an acceptable level playing blackjack in taverns, I decided to take an extended road trip to Nevada. I hoped that I would be able to double my bankroll of $6,200 with a month of full-time play. At that point in my card-counting education, I had learned enough about optimal betting to recognize that I should never push out more than 1 percent of my entire bankroll on any one hand. Having one hundred top bets yielded an acceptable level of risk, and I began the trip by playing mostly single-deck games in Reno at $15 to $60. The games were beatable, but the cards were horrible. I couldn't win a double down to save me. In the first week, I dropped $3,800 of my bankroll—a brutal bath of over sixty top bets. The setback was unnerving, but I didn't get overly rattled. I had strong confidence in my counting system and abilities after months of consistently winning at the small clubs in Oregon.

Fortunately, I had taken my entire bankroll with me (since I didn't know everything about trip bankrolls at that time). Over the next three weeks, I slowly got the money back. At the end of the month, I found a tremendous single-deck game at the Nevada Palace in Las Vegas where they dealt virtually all the cards every time. So I stayed an extra week and beat them like a drum. This strong finish enabled me to still double my bank for the trip despite the horrible start in Reno, and I drove home a very happy man.

It wasn't until a few months later that I came across a blackjack book that explained optimal betting in detail. Then I realized how lucky I really was. When my bankroll had been depleted from $6,200 to $2,400, I should have been reducing my maximum bet after the big losses (from $60 to $50 to $40 to $30) since I no longer had one hundred top bets. Fluctuation can be very fickle, and if I had one more bad swing I might have been totally wiped out.

Ironically, some players actually start betting more when they're losing because they think the cards are bound to turn around soon. However, your bankroll doesn't remember previous results, and the past never affects the future in that sense. In other words, your bankroll doesn't know when it is supposed to swing back the other way to correct itself, so only bet according to what you currently have in the bankroll, not where you think it should be.

BANKROLL

"Bankroll" is a term that is frequently misunderstood. Some players equate it with the money they take with them on the flight to Vegas. Others think of their entire net worth as their bankroll. Or to the truly intrepid, it is solely the cash stashed under your mattress that only sees the light of day during gambling trips.

All of those examples are related to bankroll, but none precisely define it. The classical description of bankroll is a liquid amount of money that is 100 percent available for gambling. It is important that these are funds you can afford to lose and that you are willing to put at risk. Make no mistake about that—even though you have the edge, there is still a very real risk in this undertaking.

If you want to attack the casinos and make some serious bucks, you have to have adequate funds with which to work. The old adage of "It takes money to make money" is definitely true in card counting. Because of the inherent swings in gambling, anyone without the proper bankroll could be wiped out by the first serious negative fluctuation.

I started off with a ridiculously inadequate amount to ply my trade and was extremely lucky to begin on a positive climb. In most cases, even the world's most skilled blackjack players can tap out unless they have a bankroll large enough to weather the volatile ups and downs of card counting.

At the time, I simply didn't know any better. I had little concept of what the proper parameters were for a bankroll and bet sizing. Fortunately, you don't have to start off as naively or as undercapitalized as I did. This chapter will give you the ballpark guidelines on how much money is needed to reduce the risk to an acceptable level.

RAISING THE FUNDS

The first step is to put together the bankroll. Hopefully, you can think of several sources (other than robbing convenience stores) to obtain this money, but the most obvious is extra cash or disposable funds not currently invested. If this still leaves you short, there are many other wells that can be tapped, each with their own pros and cons.

Many of us have assets that we wouldn't hesitate to dip into if we found a super investment opportunity. However, the problem often comes from trying to explain to friends or family members that blackjack is really an investment. Try casually mentioning to your wife that you're thinking about taking out a second mortgage on the home so you can put together an adequate bankroll and you're likely to be sleeping on the couch for the next month.

So while tapping into a home equity line of credit might be the most logical solution, it is one that should be undertaken only if you are *absolutely* positive you do have an edge—and only if you are *certain* you can convince the skeptical doubters in your family that you haven't gone off the deep end.

There are several other possible options to raise money. If you already own stocks or mutual funds (outside of retirement plans), it is fairly easy to borrow against them without actually having to sell them off. Most brokerage funds allow you to access up to half the value of your account with a debit card. One advantage of doing this is that the interest charged on your "loan" is tax deductible.

Another method is to use your credit cards, although I would be very hesitant to recommend that step to anyone. The fees are normally very high (although in some cases the cash advance charges are waived) and the risk is much greater. The reason for this is because you are now playing with money you don't really have, and if you do lose (a very real possibility) you will be left with huge bills that need to be paid rather than a slightly smaller stock portfolio.

A better option for borrowing is surprisingly available from your new opponent. Casinos will extend credit to almost anyone and are much more liberal about "loans" than your typical bank, although many clubs have tightened up their standards after years of getting stiffed by losing gamblers. To obtain credit, a casino expects you to have a balance in your checkbook that exceeds the amount of credit you are requesting. For example, if you wanted a credit line of

$5,000 at the MGM, the casino would first need to verify that you have at least that much sitting in your bank account on a regular basis.

This technique is similar to the nothing-down strategies some aggressive investors used to make their fortunes in real estate. If you get a line of credit, in essence you are putting up none of your own money. If you start out as a winner, then everything is great, and you have highly leveraged yourself into a bankroll courtesy of the casino credit lines.

For anyone just starting out in their card-counting career, I would never recommend either tapping into your home equity or funding your bankroll with credit cards. The risk is simply too high. If you borrow against your stocks and lose, you might have to sell some shares of Microsoft. But if you took out a second mortgage and lost, then you might lose your dream house and end up in a cheap apartment. The credit card scenario is similar in that you will end up owing money you don't have, and the high interest rates might make it difficult to ever pay the balances off. Needless to say, declaring bankruptcy because you blew all your money gambling is not going to increase your social status in the community.

Likewise, borrowing money from relatives is unwise because it might end up alienating your family. Of course, you might be able to convince them you are a good bet and try to get them to bankroll you. I've had numerous friends who wanted to invest in my black-jack play, but only after I established a track record of winning consistently. Many big teams are financed by outside investors drawn to the potentially high returns available in blackjack. However, I don't recommend taking any funds from close friends or relatives. It is bad enough losing your own money, but it can be even worse when other people are involved in your bankroll. Believe me, it is no fun to return home broke and tell your uncle Roger that you dumped all his savings over the weekend.

TRIP BANKROLL

The easiest way to explain the difference between your overall bankroll and your trip bankroll is to take our benchmark $10,000 as an illustration. As stated previously, you don't need to keep all ten grand in small bills under the sofa or drag it with you on each trip. Strutting around the world with a thick wad of C-notes creates many potential hazards. There is the obvious risk you could get robbed, which happened to me once. Or it might tempt you to bet more than you should on trips when things are not going well in an ill-fated attempt to get even. Or you could get the money confiscated at airports or by state troopers who suspect that you are either a drug dealer or a terrorist transporting cash for some illicit purpose. This has happened to many innocent, God-fearing citizens of our country. For that reason I always carry a notarized letter from my attorney and from my CPA stating I am a high-stakes gambler who needs to carry a lot of cash on my travels to and from the casinos.

The important point is that you never take the entire bankroll with you. Part of the $10,000 could be parked in some brokerage account to leverage your earning potential. This is only workable if you have absolutely no qualms about liquidating those holdings at a moment's notice. Otherwise, if you are at all hesitant about dipping in after a big loss, it is not really part of your bankroll.

For short trips, taking $3,000 with you is usually adequate and would weather most swings. For longer trips, half of your bankroll might be wiser. This $5,000 ideally should be in cash. There are many accounts that will allow you to tap into your holdings with a debit card, but that doesn't always work in all situations, especially on weekends when you are out of town.

If you bet correctly, it is rare that you will lose more than 20 percent of your bankroll in one day. But it can happen. Let me give you a couple of examples. I maintained a bankroll of $100,000 and usually took up to forty grand with me in cash. I viewed this as my trip bankroll. Once I arrived in paradise, I'd safely tuck away $20,000 into a safety deposit box and take the other half out into the field with me. This served as my session bankroll.

For me, that constituted twenty top bets, usually a sufficient amount to withstand the brutal daily swings. However, there are times when the cards will go cold and that large stash in your fanny pack will evaporate faster than a sailor's paycheck during shore leave. These disasters don't happen very frequently, but I've had my share of days when I crawled back to the hotel room with little or nothing left of the $20,000. I've also had a couple of trips where I got pummeled and dumped my entire trip bankroll—once for $40,000 and another time for $50,000.

Fortunately, those nightmarish declines into the abyss are rare, and I've never lost more than half of my bankroll since that first naive trip to Reno (where I lost $3,800 out of $6,200). Furthermore, I've never had any long extended periods when I ended up in the hole. However, I have spoken with a number of good card counters who have had losing years (something I've been able to avoid). There are a couple of reasons why I have been more successful than the majority of expert blackjack players, and they are not always related to how well I can count. The main reason is that I am very selective, and I absolutely refuse to play inferior games. Also, I am fairly conservative in the relationship of my bets to my bankroll—and I recommend you do the same. But to make money in blackjack, you have to be willing to take some risks. So it is imperative that you never play with money you can't afford to lose. If you do, those inevitable bad days will be nerve-racking, and you'll probably spend all your winnings visiting a shrink.

STOP LIMITS

The gut-wrenching nature of being a professional blackjack player is far too harrowing for a lot of people. The never-ending volatility of their new profession drives many into early retirement from the game. Even those few who have skin tough enough to endure the financial and emotional gyrations are often scarred for life by those horrific days when their entire bankroll almost vanished down the toilet.

The result is that some counters adopt a technique more commonly employed by average players rather than by skilled experts. Their reaction to the cruel swings of fluctuation is to set stop limits. Logically speaking, it seems to make sense to place hedges around your bankroll to keep it from dipping too low. But most of the time, these boundaries are based on some mistaken belief that you can somehow magically know when to leave the table.

Let me succinctly answer that common misguided notion—there is absolutely no way to know when to quit. It is impossible to predict the future, because the cards have no memory of any recent streaks. Your bankroll hasn't got a clue whether you are up or down for the day, and it isn't "due" for any correction regardless of whether your cards have been running hot or cold.

If the game you are currently playing is still profitable and you're not too tired, then you should keep playing. But if you're exhausted or the conditions for winning have deteriorated, then it might be a good time to pack it in and see if the buffet is still open.

The human tendency is to quit earlier on the days (or trips) when you're ahead. Doing so will provide some short-term benefits; for example, you won't have to go to bed with deep regrets over the financial bath encountered during the last hour of play. However, stopping earlier than planned will have only one long-term consequence—you will play fewer hours and conversely win less money during your blackjack career.

There is absolutely no advantage to quitting prematurely—unless you are retiring for life. Otherwise the overall tally of wins versus losses will simply continue whenever you play your next hand—whether it is the next day or on a future trip. It may make you feel good to walk away a winner, but in most cases you are only postponing results.

However, I am not saying stop limits are always bad. There is just no logical place for them in the mind-set of a pro. For normal players, they are often extremely helpful and can keep someone from going on tilt and blowing their entire wad in one weekend.

True professionals have to be immune from such impulses or else they rarely become successful, but that doesn't mean we never second-guess ourselves. I've certainly had many times when I *wished* I'd stopped for the day when I was way ahead. My brain will be forever etched with the painful recollections of those days when the dam seemed to burst right at the end of a session and a solid win got washed away by the torrents of fluctuation. However, that is only selective memory at work. Unquestionably, there were as many times where I won big during the last hour; it's just that those moments are easily forgotten because, after all, *you're supposed to win* and positive results are expected.

I knew a card counter named Dennis who was a fairly good player, but his skill level suffered because he allowed a few silly superstitions to creep into his mind. One of his habits in particular provides an excellent illustration of another fallacy associated with stop limits.

Dennis kept meticulous records of every blackjack session he ever played. This is a smart thing to do and is a trademark characteristic of nearly every successful gambler. However, Dennis used the results of his log in an erroneous manner. Whenever he had exceptionally good luck and his overall tally greatly exceeded his expectancy, he feared a correction might soon be coming. So he'd back way off from his normal stakes ($50 to 100) and start betting only nickels ($5 chips) until his luck evened out.

The absurdity of such a scheme should be readily evident even to those with little mathematical background. The cards (in blackjack) do have memory because the past does affect the future (within each shoe). But previous results (any past wins or losses) will have absolutely no bearing on the future. Your bankroll doesn't know whether it is up or down. It does not *correct* itself because it is supposed to swing the other way. In the long run, most aberrations will average themselves out and you will end up close to the mean, but it never happens because you are due.

Let's go back again to the illustration of 100 coin flips. If during the first 90 flips 50 came up heads and 40 came up tails, it might make sense to think that the next 10 flips would be tails, since a normal distribution would be 50 tails out of a 100 flips. However, as most everyone should readily recognize, each new flip is independent of any past results. The odds of flipping tails on any of the next 10 flips remain exactly the same as it began and is unchanged by the current disparity between heads and tails.

My conclusion? The most effective way to make money is to play as strong a game as you can find and then play as long as you can without getting heat or feeling too fatigued. I think it was Confucius who said, "In the long run, the card counter who plays the most hours returns to the village with the most chips."

KEEPING A LOG

The one really smart thing Dennis did was to keep accurate records. I can't overemphasize how important this is. It accomplishes at least three purposes. First and most important on this list is the confidence factor. There is absolutely no substitute for the reassurance a card counter gets by poring over his logbook after a particularly brutal day at the tables. Only those who keep good records will be able to know for sure that they are indeed winning overall and that the previous downturn constituted nothing more than just a temporary blip.

The second advantage of a journal is that you can use it to keep track of sensitive information about each casino. I have been kicked out of so many places, I would have trouble remembering them all if it weren't for my log. It is critical to record any particularly relevant data from every casino session. Here are a few mandatory items you should keep track of: name of casino, date, win/loss, time played, any pseudonyms or disguises you might have used, which shift you played, and whether you received any unusual heat (and from whom). It is easy to forget some names and faces after you've played hundreds of casinos. Unfortunately, your foes often don't forget you (especially in this high-tech computer age with the advent of facial-recognition software), and it is best to be prepared before you return to the lion's den. Most computer database programs are useful in keeping your results and important information organized; I've included a sample log in Appendix 1.

The third reason to keep a log is because the law requires it—but only if you have winnings that need to be reported to the IRS. However, the way the tax code is written on gambling is somewhat ambiguous. You are required to file for any winnings you have, and then you are supposed to itemize any offsetting losses. Unfortunately, the tax code doesn't clearly define what time frame is acceptable for record keeping (whether by the hand, by the hour, by the session, by the casino, by the trip, by the month, etc.). As I understand it, technically anyone who experiences any type of win is expected to report it and then offset that gain with any losses incurred.

Obviously, the law was originally intended for large lottery wins or big slot jackpots. At table games, there is no *W2-G* handed out when you win over $1,200. Consequently, blackjack players are expected to write down where they played, when they played, who else was at the table, the table number, and, of course, the win/loss result. Practically speaking, the paperwork required to comply can be a nightmare. For pros who move around a lot, it is not always possible to record the results of each session, let alone each table. Then it becomes a question of *where you draw the line*. Is it for each casino, each day, each trip, or each month?

However, despite inherent difficulties, it is imperative that you figure out a system for keeping track of your wins and losses. Evading pit bosses is sometimes necessary to succeed at blackjack, but evading taxes is illegal and will get you into a lot of trouble. It may feel like it is free money when you are raking in chips at the tables, but all gambling winnings are taxable (at least for U.S. citizens).

CURRENCY LAWS

Another annoyance for many high-stakes counters is the requirement of casinos to file a *CTR* (*Currency Transaction Report*) whenever a player buys in or cashes out for more than $10,000 in a twenty-four-hour period (as determined by the casinos). Since pros typically try to keep a low profile and avoid getting too well known, this law becomes an albatross because you have to show a valid ID·

when the form is filled out. Consequently, many high rollers do anything possible to avoid this process. They might hoard chips from the more commonly visited casinos and simply refuse to ever cash out more than $10,000 at any one time. While there are several good reasons why you might not cash out when your session is done (the line at the cage is too long or a pit boss is chasing you out the door), there are some obscure laws that make avoiding CTRs a crime. Deliberately trying to dodge a CTR can be considered structuring and might be construed as a criminal offense. The difficulty of interpreting this statute is that intent is the big issue.

My advice here is to err on the conservative side. I am no big fan of some of the more convoluted legislation that our government enacts, but I do feel the wisest course is to abide by the law even if there are negative consequences. I was audited for a total of five years during one ten-year period because CTRs flagged me as a high-stakes gambler, but I still think it is better to be honest and upright than to take a chance at committing fraud.

There are many creative ways to circumvent the system, but the risk versus the reward is often too high. Aside from the obvious legal and ethical considerations to obey the law of the land, I feel it is unwise to slip off into the "cash is king" underground. I wouldn't have such a large investment portfolio today if I had chosen to thumb my nose at Uncle Sam and not pay my taxes. My only real estate holdings would most likely be in Liechtenstein or some other obscure location. The most successful people I know in the gambling world all own million-dollar homes. Mickey Weinberg lives in a posh gated subdivision on the outskirts of Las Vegas and is neighbors with Vanna White, Gladys Knight, and several other wealthy stars. Allan Brown has a beautiful palatial home in the foothills east of Sacramento. A couple of other ex-blackjack players I know have retired to the upscale community of La Jolla. The reason they are able to sleep comfortably at night in such luxury is because they were willing to bite the bullet and report their winnings. If you don't, all that money does you little good because it is difficult to invest, and ultimately you are only shooting yourself in the foot by fighting the system. Otherwise, you might end up owning the best mobile home in the trailer park rather than the mansion on the hill.

CHAPTER TEN
Camouflage

Card counters need a certain amount of camouflage to escape the ever-present crosshairs of casino surveillance. Otherwise, some of the actions and attitudes we unwittingly adopt make us stand out as readily as a brown rabbit against a snowdrift. However, having to add subterfuge inevitably increases the complexity of the task facing budding card counters. Now, instead of simply learning to beat the game, a skilled blackjack player must also learn how to get away with winning. If you're too strong a player a casino might kick you out; but if you're too weak, you could end up losing. The trick is learning how to juggle those two balls.

TELLTALE SIGNS

I can often spot a fellow card counter very quickly, sometimes before he even sits down. There is a certain look a pro exudes that distinguishes him from tourists, especially in the way he cases the tables. A winning player is much more selective about where he will sit. He searches for dealers who offer the best cut and for pit bosses that look the least threatening. It is similar to the way a predator sizes up the herd—probing for the weakest point to attack.

However, finding the best game must be done in a manner that allows you to blend into a crowd. Far too many card counters practically wear a big red C on their chest as they break into a run trying to get to a table with a monster plus count. It is far better to *act* enthralled by the surroundings—drink in the ambience of big slot winners and the pageantry of paradise. I often *pretend* I'm watching the football or basketball game on one of the overhead TV screens rather than the cards at the table (which I'm back counting). Then I might slip into a chair after a particularly bad turn in the sporting event, but during a big positive upswing in the count at the blackjack table.

It is important to find the right conditions—it just has to be done in a natural manner. The difference between a stingy dealer who cuts only two decks from a shoe and one who generously deals down to one deck is enormous for a card counter. Therefore, it is helpful to subscribe to services like Stanford Wong's "Current Blackjack News" to arm yourself with this knowledge before you enter each casino. This way you don't have to spend as much time scouting, since you will already know where to find the best rules and penetration.

PARTY TIME!

Another trick is to join a table with some big hitters. Usually, I prefer playing alone, but being surrounded by high rollers is a great way to become invisible to the pit. If you can get into the party mood and yuck it up with real gamblers, then you may look like just another one of their buddies. This is especially effective when a big event like a boxing match or the Super Bowl weekend has drawn a large crowd to town. A little acting never hurts. If you pretend you are betting way over your head just to fit in with the group, the eye in the sky may think the law of conformity is at work, and you're simply betting more because of peer pressure.

It's always important to blend in with the other patrons in the casino. Most of them are never as serious or as studious-looking as card counters. Take a cue from them by loosening up and acting like you're on vacation—not putting in overtime at the office. Try to find moments when you can talk without losing the count. This is easier in single-deck games because you can drop the count on the last round. While playing shoes, I never start my count until the second card comes out; this is a good time to make a quick comment or joke, or to look away from the table. Many will find it easier to be chatty when they are winning, and tend to clam up while losing, so be careful not to fall into this trap. I think if you practice talking and counting at the same time at home, you will find it surprisingly effortless in the casino.

There are also times when it might be best just to drop the count. If a pit boss is closely scrutinizing you, it can be beneficial to pay no attention to the cards for a while and just flat bet. You are obviously giving up a little during that time, but it can provide a lot of longevity later.

On the other hand, that technique can backfire. Once I practically had pit bosses crawling all over my table at the Treasure Island Casino in Vegas. So I decided not to raise my bets any higher for the rest of the shoe while they evaluated my play. Unfortunately, the count went ballistic and I started winning every hand. Despite that, I still kept my bets at $200. It ended up being one of the greatest shoes I ever played. If I had fired away at my normal level of $1,000 top bets, I would have won about $12,000 instead of $2,500. That is the downside of camouflage.

CHIPS AHOY!

How you handle the chips can also be a factor in how you are perceived. It is only natural after years of play that you will become quite proficient and adroit at stacking, weaving, and manipulating chips. I used to have a cute way of flipping my small bets out into the square like tiddledywinks. It looked cool, but was a stupid thing to do. Any sharp pit boss would immediately recognize that I was an experienced player and a potential threat.

A clever way to tackle this problem is to play with the wrong hand. This is a very simple technique that will pay big dividends in projecting the correct image. It is almost impossible not to look clumsy in handling cards or chips when you pick them up with the wrong hand.

Keeping your chips in neat stacks can also be detrimental. Card counters by temperament seem to be drawn to precision. We are wired to bet the exact amount called for by the count, and many of us have an innate desire to know how much we are up or down at any given moment. It is far better to act a little messy and disorganized. Then each bet looks a little more random, rather than the end result of some long mathematical calculation. Also, this makes it easier to salt or squirrel away chips. If you occasionally slip a big chip or two into your pocket at opportune moments, it may deceive pit bosses into thinking you are *losing* rather than *winning*. Just remember to cash out at a later time when the same pit boss isn't watching or it will defeat the purpose.

Another red flag occurs when card counters drop down to a minimum bet after a shuffle. If you just finished the previous shoe with a $100 bet, it looks bad to start the next one off with $5. A better strategy is to compromise somewhere between your high and low bets or to simply walk away from the table. Take a short break to check out the craps action or go to the restroom. When you come back, it should be okay to find a new table and start over with your bottom bet. In handheld games, the edge against you is very small off the top, and it won't cost much to occasionally start off with your bigger bets in those situations.

TOOLS

One technique to help you keep a low profile is to not get rated. However, this may also look suspicious to casino personnel because most players understandably want to receive comps. It is helpful to have some responses ready to deflect the inevitable badgering for your name and address. Here are a few examples:

"No thanks. I'm already getting spammed to death from my last rating card."

"I get so many mailings now from casinos, my mailman thinks I need to join Gamblers Anonymous."

"After what happened to William Bennett, I'd rather keep my big losses to myself."

PROPS

A couple of other tricks I use fall under the heading of props. Props can be very effective in conveying the right image to the pit boss when you first sit down. One is the way you dress. If you have thick glasses and a slide rule sticking out of your pocket, you're going to stand out like Hugh Hefner at a religious revival. So ditch the engineer or CPA apparel and dress like a tourist. Personally, I have never been a suit-and-tie person, but there are other ways you can look the part of a bona fide gambler. If you're betting larger amounts, it's usually important to have some telltale sign of your decadent wealth. I used a fake Rolex. Others wear gaudy jewelry or narcissistic items that practically shout, "I'm rich and you're not."

You can also look nonthreatening to your opponents in other ways. Sitting down with a keno or sports parlay card can speak volumes. It tells them you are just another all-around gambler who seeks out many types of action.

Also, give the impression right up front that you won't be there long. Glance at your watch nervously and act like you're already late for your dog's funeral; then it won't surprise them when you quickly bolt from one table to another on negative counts. It is also good to stand rather than sit. You'll look like you're in a hurry to find that last great run before catching your flight. Here are some possible lines to convey that image:

"Just a few hands before kickoff."

"One last shoe to try and get even."

"I'm hoping for one last miracle."

It's smart to accentuate your losses and minimize your wins when talking with club personnel. If you do win, try to act like you finally got lucky for once. However, don't try to lay this on too thick because the pit boss might see right through it and soon show you the door.

URBAN MYTHS

Whenever I do radio interviews on card counting and mention how many times casinos have kicked me out, I frequently get asked the same question: how can casinos legally bar anyone just for using his or her brain? The general public is understandably appalled by this obvious injustice.

The basis for this policy is derived from the restaurant business, which has traditionally reserved the right to refuse service to anyone. However, this parallel quickly breaks down at the blackjack tables, because card counters are not thrown out for being drunk, belligerent, or rowdy, which are the usual reasons for the restaurant rule. Yet it is still vigilantly applied in the gambling industry. With the exception of Atlantic City, virtually every casino around the world operates with this barring option in its arsenal. (The New Jersey Supreme Court ruled that casinos within that state could not bar anyone simply because of his or her skill.)

On a personal level, I would like to play blackjack without this fear hanging over my head. However, from an economic perspective, I understand that casinos are making a business decision when they bar card counters. Consequently, the blackjack profession is not for the faint of heart.

I have been shown the door about two hundred times during my career. I consider getting barred an occupational hazard, and if you are a winning card counter, it will happen to you. However, in certain situations, casinos may still view you as a threat, even when you are not winning. Many times I have been kicked out while losing. Once I was down nearly ten grand at the Riviera Casino in Las

Vegas. Yet the shift manager still booted me, creating a spectacle by forcibly dragging me against my will across the gaming floor to the back room, my feet thumping in cadence against the carpet while stunned casino patrons witnessed the scene and speculated on what heinous crime I must have committed to deserve such a fate.

THE HEAT IS ON

You will often be given some warning signs when the heat is about to come down. The phone might ring, pit bosses might start whispering about you, or a suit may suddenly materialize behind your table and glare menacingly in your direction. Normally, the best response is just to leave when they are about to boot you. However, if you think they are just checking you out to make a determination of your skill level, it might be best to surprise them with your nonchalance. Most counters shrink under the microscope and tend to act like a cornered rat in those situations.

Maybe I have a little more chutzpah than most, but I rarely get intimidated. It is almost like a staring contest in which the pit boss is trying to see who will blink first. Rather than looking guilty or act like you're about to walk the plank, a better strategy is to smile back at him or her, or even ask for a comp.

If you do get barred, it is best to leave right away without making a scene. Some casinos have an old-school attitude toward counting, and it is best not to push the envelope in those clubs. The confrontational nature of the business has jaded a few casino executives into a "shoot first, ask questions later" mentality.

EIGHTY-SIXED

Some of you may still not be convinced that casinos actually kick people out. Perhaps you think it is just an old wives' tale. Believe me—they can, will, and do throw out anyone they think will beat them in the long run. Most skillful players attract a lot of attention and are watched from their very first bet. And the larger your chip size, the more likely you are to be noticed. If you always bet small or use a fairly conservative approach, it decreases the chance you'll get kicked out. But it still happens.

In contrast to me, Alex Strickland rarely got barred during his blackjack days—mainly because he never used aggressive bet spreads or played bigger money. However, once he got booted from Binion's Horseshoe Casino on Christmas Day while playing only small stakes. (I don't know which is sadder—that a Scrooge-like casino eighty-sixed him on Christmas or that Alex had nothing better to do than to play blackjack on December 25.) So if you do decide to become a card counter, the potential threat of getting kicked out of a casino is a very real obstacle—even if you never become a high roller.

BARRED OR BACKED OFF?

While I often lump the terms together, there is a difference between being "barred" and being *backed off*. When a casino bars you, it is more serious and usually implies you have been read the trespass act and told never to return. But when a casino "backs you off," it is generally done in a much more polite manner and often involves a simple tap on the shoulder followed by the apologetic explanation that "You're just too good for our blackjack tables." Normally, in that scenario, you are allowed to stay in the casino and are welcome at any of the other games.

Of the many times I've been booted, most fall under the latter category. However, there have been seven times where I was taken to the back room and illegally detained against my will. Four times I got unceremoniously thrown out of my hotel room in the middle of the night. Twice I was threatened and once I was handcuffed—all because I used my brain to beat the casino's game. Those events all happened several years ago, and I'd like to think most casinos are more enlightened now about card counting. Hopefully, they have learned the difference between skillful play and cheating and will treat their patrons with more respect in the future.

The other point to clarify is what happens when you are kicked out. Many card counters incorrectly assume that once you are barred, you are effectively done for life. I have met a number of players over the years who said they used to count, but weren't allowed to play blackjack any longer.

Such a statement is almost always incorrect, and the entire issue of barring a player is frequently misunderstood. Part of the confusion stems from erroneous assumptions about the infamous *"black book."* The only people featured in that publication are Mafia types not allowed inside the doors of *any* Nevada casino. There is also a book that the *Griffin Agency* maintains that contains pictures and information on a number of "undesirables." These faces range from the truly criminal to harmless card counters. Despite this collection of data, there really are no card counters who can't play blackjack at least somewhere in the world. One reason for this is that surprisingly few casinos share information.

However, once you get extremely well known, it can become very difficult to ply your trade. For example, I had been politely shown the door at the Eldorado casino in Reno one summer after a big win. I avoided going back for at least a year. Once I returned, they barred me again after only five minutes of play. So you can see it is important to take steps to prevent events like this from happening.

TIP-OFFS

Howard Grossman is certainly one of the most colorful and controversial players in the blackjack industry. He has worn nearly every hat in the business—from blackjack dealer to successful card counter. His stellar playing career speaks for itself, and Howard is one of the sharpest individuals I've met in the business; yet some counters despise him. The reason for this animosity stems from Howard's unpopular decision to switch to the other side of the table. When he tired of counting, he offered his expertise to the casinos and was hired as a pit boss. From there he worked his way up the ladder to shift boss, then casino manager, before eventually becoming a highly paid casino consultant.

This switch branded him as "Benedict Arnold" to many in the card-counting community. Yet by crossing over to the dark side, he has gained some keen insights into what is the best camouflage for expert blackjack players. His main recommendation is to stay far away from the normal image a card counter conveys in a casino. He feels some of the telltale signs that give away pros are just in the way they walk around the casino. They often have an intelligent look, an air of confidence, and almost a different posture about them. His advice is to go against type and don't look like you have ice water in your veins. Here are a few of his suggestions for demeanor at the blackjack tables.

1. Show some emotion
2. Act excited
3. Get mad
4. Look stupid
5. Don't buy in for much
6. Pretend to be chasing your losses
7. Always look like the fool rather than the genius

THE DUMB ACT

How you act when you first sit down can be critical. As in many other areas of life, first impressions are extremely important in blackjack. If you can disarm your opponents with a few "fakes" at the start, you might be able to enjoy many hours of heat-free blackjack. They may conclude you are not going to be a threat to them and quit watching, convinced you're just another loser.

Mickey Weinberg was a master of the dumb act (evidently, it takes someone very smart to pull it off). He could pretend to be drunk, ask stupid questions, commit every faux pas possible in the game of blackjack, and generally come across as a complete idiot at the table. I never had the personality to try such a tactic; besides, laying on such a dramatic act often slowed the game down to a crawl—which I always hated. Mickey, however, is a meticulous person who has the patience of Job.

Some of the tricks he used to convey the image of a novice were little things that directly violated blackjack etiquette and generally caused everyone at the table to cringe or head for the door. For example, when he first sat down, he would hand his money to the dealer rather than lay it flat on the felt, then leave his wallet on the table. If it was a faceup game, he usually tried to pick up the cards after they were dealt. Often it might take several reprimands from the dealer to break him of this offensive habit. He also liked to start out by verbally shouting his decisions to the dealer, rather than using hand signals. When he split or doubled down, he'd reach out to manually count his chips (another major taboo) to see how much he needed to match his bet. It was always amusing to see him combine several of these nitwit plays. For example, he'd say, "I think I'll stand on that blackjack," and then attempt to tuck his two cards (which he wasn't supposed to touch) under his chips.

Don't be afraid to loosen up and have fun inside the casino. You may not want to try the dumb act, but a carefree and relaxed attitude can go a long way in this business. But if you act uptight and are always trying to prove how smart you are at the tables, it is unlikely you will take a lot of money out the door.

CHAPTER ELEVEN
Ploys

Arrogance is very seldom a positive quality. However, there are some professions in which being brazen is expected and even admired. Barry Bonds can get away with having a king-sized ego because he is the best baseball player on the planet. Tiger Woods can speak condescendingly of other golfers because his game is certainly on a different level than everyone else on the tour. But such cockiness from card counters is rarely tolerated at the blackjack tables. Pit bosses are very astute at picking up on arrogant vibes, and, while it really isn't their money, they will act a lot differently depending on how they are treated—since they don't take kindly to being played for fools. A card counter may believe he is light-years ahead of the pit boss in intelligence, but to be successful at the blackjack tables, he needs to check his ego at the door. If he insists on always trying to prove how smart he is, it is unlikely he will be allowed to win much money.

Yet some card counters swagger through the casinos with the brashness of a heavyweight boxing champ looking for his next knockout victim. It is very easy to get into the mentality of "us against them," but it is much better to show restraint in your clashes with the casinos. As the old saying goes, you attract more bees with honey than with vinegar. So even though I advocate being aggressive about obtaining a strong edge at blackjack, it doesn't mean you have to become confrontational and treat each session like a war. This inherent conflict between sharp players and the house should never escalate into a battlefield. I think it is quite reasonable that both sides should maintain a healthy and civil respect for one another. It might not exactly be a symbiotic relationship, but both parties should be able to coexist without hostility. I've never viewed casino personnel as the archenemy, and I don't think there is any reason to treat anyone on the other side of the felt in an adversarial manner.

PEACE TREATY

Bill Zender is widely considered one of the sharpest casino executives. He has been a card counter, a pit boss, a casino manager, a consultant, and even a part owner of a casino. Zender spent two years with the State Gaming Control Board in Nevada and also owned a dealing school in Las Vegas. He is the author of four books, including *Card Counting for the Casino Executive*, a text applauded by expert blackjack players.

His book echoes my premise that casinos and counters do not need to wage war. Zender believes most clubs are better off dealing deeply and spending less energy worrying about card counters. He tried this controversial experiment at the Aladdin Resort & Casino when he was its vice president. The rules were among the best in town, and he instructed the casino's dealers to cut off only twenty-six cards from their six-deck shoes.

The results of this "peace treaty" were astounding. The deeply dealt shoes reduced the amount of time spent shuffling and sped up the games. Consequently, the hold (casino profits) improved dramatically under his watch. There were some sharp players who took advantage of this great game (I hit them for $26,000 in five fun-packed hours), but overall they still made more money proportionately than any other casino on the Strip. Zender's philosophy was simple—casinos should take adequate time to carefully check out any possible card counter, rather than throw him out too quickly. He reasoned that many clubs barred players who really couldn't beat them in the long run.

FRIEND OR FOE?

An excellent parallel for the cat-and-mouse struggle that card counters wage against casinos is found in the world of sports. I had the good fortune to play basketball throughout high school and college and I rose to a fairly high level despite my physical limitations (I was only 5' 10" and possessed the vertical leap of a turtle). The main reason for my success was a killer instinct. Whenever I stepped onto the court, I always played to win. If the game was on the line, I did whatever it took to put the other team away. However, that doesn't mean I hated my opponent—I simply played as hard as possible within the rules, and that included outsmarting my opponents.

One key aspect of victory in sports comes from the art of deception. Because of my shorter stature I often had to use pump fakes to get off a shot when driving to the basket through the tall trees. Many games, such as football or chess, are like that. The masters are adept in creating feints or ruses that mislead the opponent into missing the actual point of attack. The same skill is necessary for those wishing to extract large amounts of money from casino vaults.

EYE IN THE SKY

Before you learn how to fake out the casinos, you have to know what they are looking for. Therefore, it is helpful to understand how things work on the other side of the ceiling. The following is a brief description from Bill Zender about the normally off-limits eye in the sky.

The surveillance room is filled with monitor screens, recording equipment, tape storage space, and console control equipment. The room is usually kept dark to aid in the viewing of the monitors. The number of cameras varies, but today it is normally a regulatory requirement to have every table game, every slot bank, the vault and count room viewed and recorded twenty-four hours a day.

The eye in the sky is typically staffed with ex-security personnel who are trained in game procedure, card counting, and some facets of theft and cheating. One complete wall of the room is entirely covered with monitors; with larger screens intermixed for better viewing quality. In front of the monitors are the console control stations. These stations allow the surveillance operators to control cameras and monitoring equipment. From each station they can direct the pan, tilt, and zoom (PTZ) cameras and switch pictures from one monitor to another.

While the surveillance operators will oversee the real-time activity on the casino floor, the main purpose of modern surveillance is to record the events as they happen on the floor. Almost every casino keeps a seven-day library of videotapes for future reference. In most instances the surveillance department will also keep a tape collection of specific incidents, as well as big player files, cash transaction occurrences, and a file of suspicious players.

RED FLAGS

So what exactly do they watch for up there in the eye when they're not playing solitaire on their monitors? The main criterion for evaluating a potential card counter is whether he spreads his bets and how he plays his hands. First of all, surveillance wants to see if you know basic strategy, and next, whether you correctly alter it during bigger bets.

These sharp eyes overhead also look for certain behavior patterns that might identify you as a winning blackjack player. Anyone wearing a baseball hat or sitting at third base will score very high on their list since those characteristics have traditionally been associated with card counters. The more ways you can fit in with the crowd and avoid this stereotype, the better. Otherwise, you might tip off surveillance that you are a pro rather than a tourist. If you are young and look like you're in the casino on business, rather than pleasure, your demeanor may send someone scurrying to the computer to input you into their facial-recognition software.

However, despite how intimidating this new Big Brother technology sounds, Bill Zender feels it is only as good as the people interpreting it. He believes there are many ways to *fool* this program and its operators. To begin with, a lot of the viewing angles from the overhead cameras are difficult to get an accurate picture. If you add in a few other variables, such as a player wearing glasses, it is very easy to screw up the program, since it requires precise measurements around your eyes. Zender once tested the facial-recognition software with a picture of a guy already in their database, and the program popped out four other probable matches, but not one of the correct person.

THE COST OF COVER

As your bankroll increases, so will the size of your bets. It is only natural that the level of attention you receive will also increase proportionately. At some juncture, you may feel that some types of subterfuge are necessary to continue in your new vocational pursuit. The overriding questions then become "How much do I need" and "What is the ultimate cost?"

The best camouflage is very simple and straightforward. All you have to do is lose overall. Then your blackjack play will be welcome at virtually any club. However, that obviously defeats the purpose of becoming a card counter. Therefore, some players have decided to make a few errors to reduce the amount of their advantage, but to still retain an overall edge. The theory is that these strategic blunders will buy you additional time by convincing the pit you are just another moron.

UNUSUAL PLAYS

The general consensus among blackjack authors is that certain plays (like not insuring blackjacks) distinguish the pros from the tourists. For this reason, the conclusion of most experts is never to split face cards and, additionally, to make some misleading plays to throw off the bloodhounds. I understand their logic, but I don't totally agree with them. Splitting tens certainly is an attention-getting play, but it is also a highly profitable one. To forgo that opportunity means a direct reduction in your expectancy. Personally, I cannot recall a time I was ever barred simply because I split face cards. There have been other obscure plays where I can actually pinpoint the moment the pit decided to show me the door. Once, at Lake Tahoe, I split a pair of 9s, caught an ace, and doubled down on the soft 20. Within minutes two security guards arrived at my table. The play, though correct, was far too unusual. In retrospect, it was not a wise choice.

The key to splitting face cards (or other unusual plays) is to set them up earlier with smaller bets. The expected loss is minimal on some bonehead plays, and they can establish you as a *balls-to-the-wall* gambler well before you get to your big bets. Author Fred Renzey lists several examples of cheap plays such as doubling down on a hard 12 for a lesser amount (as low as a dollar). I haven't tried out his ploys, but the basic premise of his argument makes good sense.

VOODOO LOGIC

Another variation of this theme is to pretend you are superstitious—when it is to your advantage to do so. Some examples of this are asking, "Would you mind waiting until the end of the shoe?" (in order to preserve the sacred order of cards) during high counts, or saying on negative shoes, "I think I'll sit out and let this hot dealer cool off." Also, don't be afraid to ask the pit boss for advice on toss-up hands (if it doesn't matter which way you play it). Appearing to need help is a good way to look like a weak player.

BLACKJACK COMMANDO

Some ploys are worthwhile only in certain situations. When I am in Vegas or Atlantic City, where there are several casinos side by side, I tend to play very short sessions at each club and adopt more of a hit-and-run style. The beauty of that Rambo approach is that I rarely reduce any of my edge, yet still receive little exposure at any one casino because I move around so much.

Since blackjack is difficult to beat, I hate to give up potential profit just to lessen potential heat. However, there are occasions when I think it is justified. One is when I pick a casino to use as my "home base." At that club, I might lower my bet spread slightly and employ a little extra cover in order to get comped. For instance, I might choose to stay at the MGM Grand in Vegas and play just enough there to score a free room and meals. Then I would refuse ratings at other clubs to preserve my anonymity, which would allow me to play more aggressively at those casinos.

Another time it is wise to reduce your edge to gain longevity is when playing a local casino where you'd like to return many times. Also, if you are at an isolated casino where you don't have the luxury of easily walking to a new club after getting kicked out, you may need to scale back the attack slightly.

PLAYING TO LOSE

Faking your opponent out in a sporting event is an excellent analogy to describe the deception often necessary to succeed at the blackjack tables. But what if you took it a step further? Would there ever be a time when you might want to deliberately blow a layup in a big game? As a basketball purist, I cringe at such a thought. However, there are some other sports where deliberately going into the tank is acceptable and even admired. Golf and pool are two examples in which it is not uncommon to see one player purposely misplay his shots to hustle opponents into higher stakes in later matches.

Some advocate the same approach for card counting. Blackjack author Ian Andersen is one of the best at explaining various ploys to accomplish this. His philosophy is to consistently make several basic strategy mistakes, such as always insuring a blackjack, standing on all 16s versus a 10, and not hitting A-7 against 9, 10, or ace. The beauty of his Ultimate Gambit, as he calls it, is that most of those decisions become either closer calls or correct plays at higher counts. Since that is when most of your money is at risk, the seemingly foolhardy strategy doesn't actually hurt as much as it might appear to the pit boss (who will usually peg you as just another loser).

Ian Andersen is also excellent at pointing out that we don't need to treat our casino opponents as the enemy. Instead, he looks at them more as customers and partners. I fully agree that these innovative and creative steps will greatly increase your longevity, especially if you intend to become a professional high-stakes player like Ian Andersen. The only drawback is the cost. If you play the game either primarily for the thrill of beating the house or because you want to score great comps, such a style is perfect.

However, if you are primarily in blackjack because you want to make money, then it is a much tougher call. At some point you have to question whether the reduced return still justifies the time and energy. Using the Ultimate Gambit in shoe games dealt to 75 percent will yield $164 an hour with a bankroll of $155,000 (which is the amount needed to keep the risk of ruin down to an acceptable level of 5 percent). So a pro employing such trickery would win about $50,000 for a normal year of play (a little over three hundred hours).

While $50,000 a year is not bad, it still might not be worth the risk and time. There are some passive investments (such as trust deeds and tax liens) that yield 12 to 18 percent per year, without having to work one week every month. So getting a 32 percent return (by playing blackjack) is not much of an improvement, considering the hundreds of hours that are required over a passive investment.

Additionally, there is much greater fluctuation whenever you have a reduced edge over the house. Andersen stated his worst run ever was when he lost on twelve straight trips. Since I've employed a more aggressive playing style, I've always tried to maintain an edge of about 1.25 percent over the house, or about twice the advantage of the Ultimate Gambit. Consequently, my odds of losing twelve trips in a row is extremely remote (approximately 500,000 to 1). Let me give an example to put these numbers in perspective. Let's say I suddenly switched religions and believed that reincarnation was possible. And suppose I had incredibly bad karma and my penance was to come back as a Hare Krishna–chanting card counter for my next twenty thousand lives. Even then, a streak of twelve straight losing trips would happen only once over my next twenty thousand lifetimes—assuming I played one short trip every month for twenty-five years during each subsequent rebirth.

I don't mean to disparage any author who advocates camouflage. I admire Ian Andersen's willingness to deliberately play big money at losing games like craps or baccarat in order to gain longevity. He obviously has a tremendous amount of discipline—many lesser mortals who try his tactics might end up going on tilt and losing their shirts. And I believe his clever ploy of misplaying hands would provide excellent cover and trick surveillance into viewing you as just another sucker. Even Bill Zender admitted that if Ian Andersen had employed the Ultimate Gambit at his club, he probably wouldn't have detected him as a card counter. So if it could fool someone as sharp as Bill Zender, it definitely would extend your longevity in most clubs.

However, the overriding question that remains is whether the cover is worth the cost. For most players with smaller bankrolls, the answer is usually no, but it is difficult to judge how much extra longevity you are gaining for what you are willingly giving up.

Suppose your EV (expected value) was to win $100,000 a year

and you deliberately made enough mistakes to reduce your edge to $50,000 for the year. If such camouflage only bought you twice as much playing time, it would not be worth it. In that case, you would be working twice as many hours to win the same amount of money. If this ploy allowed you to play four times as many hours, then it becomes a little more viable, although there is still a strong case to be made for one year of winning $100,000 being slightly better than four years of work for $200,000.

So again the question comes back to whether the additional cover you are gaining is worth what you are sacrificing. Many high-rolling blackjack pros feel some camouflage is absolutely necessary, since the more they bet, the more cover they need. However, for the majority of card counters with smaller bankrolls, my personal opinion is that the reduced win rates and increased fluctuation make a lot of the ploys very debatable. I am convinced that the two cheapest and most effective forms of cover are to simply move around a lot and to talk a lot. Moving makes it very difficult for casino personnel to gauge your strength, and being chatty makes you appear much more like a gambler than a card counter.

CHAPTER TWELVE
Team Play

Among the many legendary blackjack stories, nothing quite matches the mystique of team play. Yet it is a misconception that only those card counters who play for big-money teams can strike it rich in blackjack. While there are certainly some benefits to joining one of these huge syndicates, there are also negatives. In this chapter I will share a few horror stories about how incompetence, skimming, and stealing devastated some groups, while other card counters have found blackjack teams exciting, glamorous, and their ticket to big money.

However, our friends on the other side of the fence fail to share the public's romanticized image of card-counting teams. Most pit bosses are already ticked off that a bunch of Robin Hoods chip away at their bottom line, but when the Merry Men start banding together and send troops to the blackjack tables, casinos respond quickly and harshly. Many shift managers fear looking like fools— or worse, losing their jobs—because some team hit them hard.

Sometimes this threat has been overblown and the wins by large groups exaggerated. Yet without question, highly capitalized blackjack teams have accomplished some of the biggest scores. I know one group that hit the casinos for over $5 million, and the word on the street is that the MIT team won at least $10 million.

It is largely because of the well-publicized success of the MIT team that many players currently want to join a blackjack team rather than attempt to count on their own. There are certainly some advantages to being part of a bigger, well-financed group. But there are also some disadvantages, and in this chapter I will try to give a fair assessment of the pros and cons of team play versus taking on the neon Goliath by yourself.

HISTORY

If you read *Bringing Down the House*, by Ben Mezrich, you might think that team play is a fairly recent innovation. However, this is as erroneous as Al Gore inventing the Internet.

The strategy of team play goes way back, and was first popularized by a group Ken Uston joined in the 1970s. This California-based team won millions from the casinos in a blitzkrieg-style attack, and Ken Uston quickly became a well-known name throughout the country. The notoriety he created captivated the imagination of the gambling public, who loved hearing stories about smart players turning the tables on Las Vegas and actually beating the house. For many blackjack players, Uston's appearance on *60 Minutes* became a landmark event in TV history, roughly on a par with the Beatles' memorable performance on *The Ed Sullivan Show*. A number of people (including myself) either first heard about or became card counters because of Ken Uston.

Uston's considerable gifts and charisma certainly helped spread the buzz about blackjack, but it was the concept of highly organized groups of card counters (as profiled in Uston's book *The Big Player*) taking on the casinos that really grabbed everyone's attention. These earliest blackjack teams had developed an elaborate system of hand signals and techniques to exploit the shoe games that casinos thought were virtually bulletproof against card counters.

While Thorp's earlier book, *Beat the Dealer*, didn't produce the hordes of skilled card counters some predicted, the casinos still took steps to protect themselves. The main change was an end to the golden era of single-deck blackjack (in the 1960s), as shoes became the norm at most clubs. This made the games very difficult to beat because it took a large betting spread and a lot of patience to win against multiple decks.

However, it was this change that ironically created a new opportunity for innovative card counters. It took a few years, but eventually some skilled blackjack players figured out a way to fully capitalize on shoe games. They enlisted the aid of other card counters and stationed them at different tables around the casino. These *spotters* (counters who either stood behind the table and didn't bet at all or sat down and bet very little) would then signal the *Big Player* (or *BP*; the big bettor for the team, who hid behind the slot machines or flirted with the cocktail waitresses until called onto the stage) when a high count occurred at their table.

This mad stroke of genius packed a powerful two-pronged punch. First, it leveraged the efforts of the Big Player, since he could effectively reap benefits from several tables. And second, it eliminated making a long string of minimum bets while waiting for the count to climb. With this system, the BP rarely varied his bets, creating additional camouflage.

At long last the latent fears first raised in the hearts of casino owners were confirmed. Now, a viable method of attack seriously threatened their blackjack tables. When this approach was first employed, it totally fooled many casinos. The spotters were virtually invisible to the pit, and the BP looked like just another gambler randomly stopping at the blackjack tables to plunk down a stack of chips in the middle of a shoe. However, it didn't take the casinos long to figure out what was going on. Uston's team soon got heat at nearly every club in Vegas, as surveillance became more adept at unmasking their cover.

MO

There have been a number of variations on the theme of team play over the years as teams have tried to stay one step ahead of the casinos. Uston's group positioned its card counters at different blackjack tables, where they generally sat down and didn't move. They would make only minimum bets regardless of the count and (initially at least) never drew much attention from the pit.

When the shoe at their table reached a high count, they used a hand signal to call in the Big Player. The count would then be passed with additional signals similar to those used from ship to ship.

I prefer putting spotters behind the table and always use verbal signals to pass the count. This has three advantages. First, the back counters never have to play the hands or bet any money in the negative shoes, which provides an excellent entry-level position for new players to break into the game. Second, verbal signals can't be detected by the overhead cameras, but even the most covert hand signals could be deciphered with the modern aid of replaying them over and over again on videotapes. And standing behind the tables makes it much easier to move when the count is going south and the odds favor shifting to a new table to back-count.

DIVIDING THE DOUGH

Some teams are funded entirely by one person (often the BP), but it is also common for teams to solicit investors, and some bankrolls end up being a hybrid of outside money combined with cash contributed by the principal players. The traditional way to split the profits is 50 percent to the investors and the other 50 percent to the players, to be divided among them.

Again, there are numerous variations on this theme, and most teams require their members to play together until a bankroll is either doubled or a certain amount of hours have been reached. The reason for this is that the incentive to keep playing drops dramatically (for noninvesting players) when a team falls behind. It is not uncommon for some counters to bail out like rats deserting a sinking ship when they think there is little realistic chance of making any profit. One way to alleviate the potential problem of players quitting early is to simply pay spotters by the hour.

PROS AND CONS

The biggest reason to form a blackjack team lies in the increased yield. Don Schlesinger calculated that adding one spotter can increase your profits by 76 percent and two spotters can potentially push it up by 132 percent. Playing against mostly positive counts dramatically shoots up the return per hour, and when the team is big enough to have a couple of BPs, it can help even out the fluctuations.

Another perk of team play is that a lot of people are naturally drawn to the camaraderie that a group offers and find it much more fun than being the Lone Ranger. Now, with such a rosy picture of team play, you may wonder why anyone would opt to count the conventional way. However, there are also many drawbacks to team play.

What sometimes is the greatest strength can also become the Achilles' heel. Extra teammates greatly leverage your blackjack play and provide potentially higher returns, but those very same people can also be the worst part of joining a team. A group of card counters is rarely stronger than its weakest link. Just one inept player on the team can jeopardize the entire bankroll. And if you are unfortunate enough to hook up with an individual who has a few bad habits in his closet that he forgot to mention (drugs, booze, or loose women), then your money may disappear down the toilet faster than financial aid to Russia.

Another potential disadvantage is the loss of control inherent in joining a team. Professional gamblers often gravitate to their chosen vocation because they are independent types who enjoy a flexible lifestyle. If you have a strong aversion to punching the time clock, then a team might not be the best fit for you.

BLUEPRINT FOR A BLACKJACK TEAM

Rick Blaine, the author of *Blackjack Blueprint*, has been involved with some of the larger blackjack teams over the past two decades. His experiences prompted him to write a book outlining the critical guidelines and considerations for operating such a team. The main issue he stresses is the importance of writing out a plan beforehand. This might seem like common sense to most people in the business world, but it is truly amazing how many teams fly by the seat of their pants. Novice groups especially seem to learn the hard way, through trial and error.

Here are some items he suggests every team cover before they ever make their first bet.

Who is the manager?
What are the responsibilities of each player?
What are the methods of compensation?
How long to play?
What to do when a player quits the team early.
Whether tipping is allowed, and if so, how much?
Which expenses are the team's and which are the player's?
Who holds the money and keeps the books?
How are distribution of winnings to be handled?

Blaine has put together some very large, well-funded teams (with multimillion-dollar bankrolls), and he feels that leadership is the single most important ingredient in the success of any blackjack team. It is an axiom of any endeavor in life that the more people involved, the harder it can be for everyone to agree. The lack of central leadership can wreak havoc on the best-laid plans.

Therefore, it is best to spell out the critical issues in advance—especially those related to money. Experts say arguments over finances are perhaps the biggest causes of marital strife. The same is true on blackjack teams, except you can leave out the "perhaps." Distribution and handling of money is the number one problem. Blaine advises every group to make those matters crystal clear right up front—who will get what and when they will get it. Players quitting early, improper expenses, and disagreement over winning percentage have gutted many good blackjack teams and ruined friendships. So it is wisest to write it out first, rather than fight it out later.

Blaine recommends a minimum bankroll of $300,000 to $500,000 for any serious team effort. The main reason for this huge sum is that those chip levels make it much easier to get comps and airfare. This is a big factor if you are wisely rotating your play around to a lot of different regions. The costs of transporting, housing, and feeding a large group can be prohibitive if comps aren't factored into the equation.

I heartily agree on the need to be light on your feet. The longer you stay at any one club, the chances of the welcome mat remaining out for future trips diminishes rapidly. I also readily endorse his premise of setting up a blueprint for your blackjack team. A manual that covers training, operations, and procedure should be mandatory before hitting the tables.

A CORPORATE ATTITUDE

I have played on several blackjack teams during my career—some small, and some large. I hooked up with a couple of Uston's old cronies and also played with the illustrious Czech team for a while. (These Europeans were certainly one of the most colorful and intriguing blackjack teams of all time, and their exploits will likely be the subject of my next book.) How many of those groups do you think put their plan in writing like Rick Blaine wisely suggests? Zero. But if they had, it would have saved a lot of grief later on. I have seen some arguments escalate into near fistfights, simply because everything hadn't been spelled out in advance.

The best groups I played with always treated blackjack as a business and not like a spring break party for their frat house. If your team is run like a corporation, the probability of winning increases exponentially.

PICKING A BLACKJACK TEAM

Finding a blackjack team is not easy for beginning card counters. You can't exactly make a connection through the want ads like many other vocations. The two largest teams I played on both came about from contacts I made at the tables. Inevitably, you will bump into other card counters as you travel around the country plying your trade. As I stated in the chapter on camouflage, it is fairly easy to spot another counter, especially when he's playing at your table and both of you are jacking up bets in unison like a synchronized swim team.

There might also be times when you detect a team at work in the casino. Most novice players naturally want to meet other card counters, especially bigger bettors. It is exciting to talk with a fellow counter and finally find someone who can relate to your world, and there are some benefits in knowing other counters. The companionship a team provides or that comes from hanging out with fellow pros can be helpful, and it eases the loneliness of traveling when you have a few buddies to hang out with around the country.

However, there is the downside of guilt by association, and you might come under closer scrutiny by casinos, depending on whom you break bread with. Ian Andersen recommends *never* making friends with other card counters. His advice is prudent, and I definitely think it is wise to keep to a minimum your contact with other card counters anywhere on casino premises, even in its restaurants. I know my name moved much higher up the "most wanted" list after playing on a couple of big-money teams. So if you are only joining a team because you lack social interaction and friendship, you might consider buying a dog instead.

SHOULD YOU JOIN?

Ultimately, I'm not sure why I joined my first blackjack team. At the time I thought it was strictly a financial decision—it had a much bigger bankroll (mine was only $15,000 then). Consequently, I felt playing with a team would offer a far higher return than plodding along at my own lower betting levels.

Looking back now, I think that was only part of the motivation. I believe a bigger reason was the thrill and excitement of actually playing for a team. I envisioned myself becoming part of a highly skilled group of professionals, sort of like the crack Navy SEALS team—except in this endeavor, I didn't have to wear fins, and I expected the pay to be much better.

That glow quickly faded when the group struggled to win over the next few months. I didn't have any problems betting and winning with the bigger money, but there was one really bad player on the team. He continually put us in the hole, and I strongly suspected a few of his vices were the problem (a strong propensity for shapely women ranked highest on the list).

It is aggravating when one losing player drags down the entire team's performance. We finally got the bankroll back on the plus side just before reaching our target goal of five hundred hours, and I wisely chose not to reenlist with that group for any future play.

The next team that I joined was definitely all about the Benjamins. They were hardened professionals and had put together a very serious bankroll ($500,000). I joined that group with no more giddy visions about the allure of team play—I just felt this was my one chance to really hit it big.

Unfortunately, that team didn't work out very well, either, despite the star-studded lineup. I did make a little money for my time, but it ended up being a very tiny percentage of the amount I actually won for the team. The problem? Too many chiefs and too few Indians. Typically, blackjack players don't make good employees, and a team packed with oversize egos can be a recipe for disaster.

Despite the fact that I didn't make much from either of those groups, there were some residual benefits. The comps were absolutely incredible—I stayed in exquisite penthouse suites and enjoyed some fabulous perks. It also gave me some experience at the higher chip levels. Playing bigger money can be unnerving for many players at first, and it is a much easier transition when it is someone else's cash and not your entire life savings out there on the table. I still vividly recall one of my more memorable sessions for a black-jack team I played on with Mickey. I won $20,000 right off the bat, then proceeded to lose all my winnings and another $20,000 more within the first hour of play. If that had been my own money, it would have been very disconcerting, since twenty grand seemed like a great deal of cash at that time. Nowadays Mickey probably keeps that much hidden under each cushion on his couch.

FORMING YOUR OWN TEAM

Finding good players is a critical component of any blackjack team. However, it is not an easy task gauging the ability, honesty, and loy-alty of other people. For this reason, most counters are better off playing alone rather than joining up with a team. Yet you can mini-mize this potential problem by only hooking up with people you know and trust.

I have twice put together teams comprised solely of friends who I recruited and trained. The first consisted of Alex Strickland and two other friends from our college days. The advantage of those guys was that I didn't have to question their honesty or do back-ground checks or insist on regular polygraph tests (which some teams require). The group had moderate success but ultimately fiz-zled out. Apart from Alex, neither of the other two had the disci-pline and commitment to become successful blackjack players.

I pretty much gave up on team play at that point and decided to go it alone. However, several years later some circumstances tran-spired that led to the forming of the world's fastest card-counting team.

THE WORLD'S FASTEST BLACKJACK TEAM

The good games in blackjack tend to run in cycles. Conditions can be great for a while, then paranoia strikes deep and casinos every-where tighten their games. I found myself in that quandary a while back. After years of crushing single- and double-deck blackjack, I suddenly found very few handheld games left worth playing.

Consequently, I decided to shift my assault more to shoes. Since the edge was markedly smaller for multiple-deck games, I felt that using a couple of spotters for the bigger clubs would be the wisest way to increase my winnings. Alex Strickland signed on right away, but I still needed a couple more players for optimal efficiency.

At that time I was very involved in the track community, since living in Eugene, Oregon, allowed me to rub shoulders with many elite runners from all over the world. As fate would have it, some of the top athletes I met were also extremely interested in blackjack. I ended up teaching three of them (Karl Keska, Greg Whiteley, and Mike Bilyeu) how to count. Coming from a sport in which one is measured by the stopwatch, they readily understood the need for speed and precision in counting, and soon they accompanied me on trips to Nevada.

Were we the fastest? Perhaps not in the normal measurement of counting down a deck, but there is no question that we could kick any other team's butt on the track. Karl Keska went on to become one of England's top distance runners and turned in a standout performance at the 2000 Olympics in Sydney. Greg Whiteley held the American road-racing 5K record for a number of years and represented the United States on one of its world championship teams. Mike Bilyeu's stellar running career provided a stepping-stone for a small movie role and some modeling ads for Reebok.

Besides their foot speed, these three all brought another big asset to the tables. They were extremely focused and disciplined from their years of hard training on the running trails. This quality enabled them to become excellent card counters, and they became far more successful than the earlier group of friends I had put together.

The fitness of the group also had tangible benefits. I found out very early in my career that the best way to be successful in blackjack is to move around—a lot. However, this can be difficult and sometimes expensive (with cabs) when you are constantly bopping in and out of every club. So our solution was to jog between each casino. This obviously only worked in places like Las Vegas or Atlantic City, where the resorts are packed closely together.

The advantage of such a strategy lay in its simple efficiency. Rather than wasting precious time moving around and parking cars, we were able to go from club to club in minutes. The usual order of attack would leave me to finish up the last hot shoe at a club like Caesars Palace while the rest of the team took off to set up next door. By the time I wrapped up at Caesars and arrived at the Mirage, one of the spotters often already had a positive shoe to call me into, which tremendously reduced any downtime.

This technique worked extremely well, but I do need to throw out a couple of disclaimers. You shouldn't actually break into a run until you are outside the casino *and* you draw far less heat if you don't wear numbers on your tracksuits.

HAVING A PLAN

The Track Team was easily the most fun group I ever played with and one of the most successful. The extra counters helped me win far more than I could have on my own, and the spotters got to partake of the many comps and perks that casinos offered me. Our team didn't write out a detailed plan like Rick Blaine suggests (which we should have done), but we were very organized. We always had a plan of attack and determined at the start of each session exactly where we would play (specific pits within each casino) as well as how long. We had strict rules against talking to each other anywhere in the casino or being seen together in any public place as a group. And most important, we always had a contingency plan for what to do if things went wrong.

However, there were a few times that I forgot to cross all the Ts. The first track star I taught to count was Mike Bilyeu. For his inaugural trip to the big leagues, we drove together to Reno, where I set him up to back-count for me at the Hilton. I had played there on my own a month earlier and beat the casino for $16,000. At that time there were some great four-deck shoe games, so I figured having a spotter would double my pleasure.

Unfortunately my pleasure was very short-lived. Before I could even make my first bet, several security guards surrounded me and whisked me away to the back room. Mike looked totally bewildered as he watched them drag me off, and he obviously didn't know what to do. This certainly wasn't what he expected when he signed on to become a card counter. He finally went out to the car and waited.

After a long ordeal of playing 20 Questions with the surveillance people, they finally relented and marched me up to my hotel room. They gave me five minutes to pack up my belongings (including all of Mike's things), and then escorted me through the casino and out the doors.

With both security guards and the shift manager watching me, I couldn't very well head straight to the car, so I laboriously trudged across the long parking lot and off the property before finally hooking up with Mike at a gas station.

If I had been smarter, I would have arranged an alternative meeting site, just in case something had gone wrong. This would have prevented Mike from driving conspicuously around the parking lot while I pretended not to know him. Since that disaster, I always make Plan B crystal clear with teammates before the day's play.

SHORT-TERM TEAMS

Another technique that many card counters use is teaming up for specific situations. If you know another player whose skill level and honesty are impeccable, it can often be advantageous to work together. Mickey and I have combined talents and money several times, such as when we traveled to Asia. For long and expensive trips, this tactic will make it much more likely you will return a winner.

You can also invest in other blackjack players if you believe they are competent. I've done this with several people who were good counters, but who didn't have the bankroll necessary to make playing on their own very viable. However, players are sometimes tempted to use their own money for some games and the investor's for others. This obviously can lead to some ethical nightmares. And it can strain your friendship when you bankroll a close associate who loses your money. My worst loss ever was in in Puerto Rico. Mickey had a piece of the action for my blackjack play on that trip, and I don't think he will ever let me forget it.

MINITEAM

Some of the benefits of team play are available without actually having to form a full-fledged team with BPs and spotters. This can be done by pooling funds from several individual players. Say, for example, that you have four other card-counting buddies, each just barely eking out a living off the casinos while playing on a fairly tight $20,000 bankroll. If you were to throw your lot in together like five pirates on the high seas, you would suddenly have a treasure chest weighing in at $100,000. With that amount of firepower, you can do an awful lot of pillaging and plundering.

Now your top bet becomes $1,000 rather than $200 and each one of you could play separately, but bet to the higher bankroll. Since you are all playing at different tables, the results would be independent. In other words, everyone could play to the combined bank ($100,000), rather than their original one.

That was one of the reasons Mickey and I joined forces on a few trips (the other was to reduce fluctuation). However, if you try this tactic with more than two people, the logistics of transferring the money around can be difficult. If one person is losing big and needs more cash, it isn't always easy to get the funds quickly. One of the other players might be in a different location with his portion of the bankroll, and it can be an ordeal to keep enough capital readily available for everyone to play at the same time.

THE TRIANGULAR TEAM

A modified approach I'd also recommend is a small, fast-moving group of three players. An ideal situation is to enlist your wife or girlfriend as the BP and then find another person to help you back-count shoe games. Having her do the betting is great camouflage because casinos are still rather chauvinistic and many old-school pit bosses immediately dismiss women as potential threats.

And if she balks at having to learn card counting, there are ways to simplify this technique. It's possible for her to only make flat bets when she is called in. You and your buddy could do all the counting and have her learn a modified basic strategy for positive shoes. This will dilute your overall edge, but will still yield a winning game.

There is value in playing and working together with a loved one, both financially and emotionally. If you don't end up fighting over the money (or fighting over the girlfriend), then the entire experience can be very worthwhile and remove many of the negatives of traveling alone.

NETWORKING

Having teammates and card-counting friends also provides other perks. I've obtained a ton of information by maintaining contact with expert players. It can be very useful to compare notes with other people you respect—you might find the latest hot game or get a feel for casino tolerance on a particular shift.

Also, teammates can be your eyes and ears in valuable places. It is not uncommon for *floormen* to talk openly about a player after he is gone. If one of your spotters still happens to be hanging around, he might pick up some useful intelligence on how the pit really views the BP.

An amusing version of this "fly on the wall" scenario happened at the Sands Casino in Las Vegas. I set up to do a short play there with Alex and Greg, as the Sands was always a pretty tight club, and it was difficult to play long sessions.

I will sometimes back-count shoes myself, in addition to using spotters, and on this particular day I got a hot one right out of the gate. I laid down four $100 bills on the felt and calmly said, "Money plays." The pit started buzzing like a beehive, as it rarely got much big action. I won the first three hands and the count continued climbing, so I tucked the cash back into my pocket and started firing away with the small stack of black $100 chips in front of me. The cards all went my way, and I never had to reach back into my pocket again for more cash. By the end of the shoe I had won $9,600. Now the beehive was really buzzing.

There weren't any $500 chips at the table, so I had huge mounds of black chips spread in front of me. Typically, after a really big win, I would immediately leave and cash out later. However, because the chips were so heavy and the casino was soon to be closed, I decided to go to the cage right then. It took a few minutes, but I finally got paid and starting jamming the large stack of C-notes into my fanny pack when I noticed Alex Strickland was giving me the hot signal. He evidently had a monster count on his shoe and was miffed that I was cashing out rather than running over to his table. I had already won far more than the usual choke point for the Sands, so I waved him off and headed out the front door.

Normally, spotters never play any serious money at the table they are back-counting—no matter how high the edge. The reason is that it is a blatant way to blow their cover. However, since the old casino was scheduled to shut down and be imploded, Alex figured he had little to lose, so he jumped in and started playing the high count with his own money. By doing so, he was able to relay what happened within seconds of my departure.

A stocky woman with short-cropped red hair, evidently from surveillance, suddenly came running into the pit angrily waving a faxed picture of yours truly, shouting, "I knew it was him. That was Kevin Blackwood! And you just let him beat us out of ten grand!"

THE DOWNSIDE

Howard Grossman's card-counting career shared some strong similarities to mine. He started out with a minuscule amount of money and ran it up into a large sum playing on his own. He also dabbled in team play and was involved in several high-profile teams, but just like me, he had mixed emotions about the experience.

Grossman saw firsthand how sometimes the pitfalls of team play can overshadow the potential benefits when one group he put together starting disintegrating. He strongly suspected some of his teammates were skimming money from the bankroll or stealing for personal expenses. One player (let's call him the Larry the Lush) just could not win, while another player (Freddy the Fox) had results that continually fell short of what was expected. Howard finally resorted to anonymously watching the Fox at the tables. Not surprisingly, the Fox came to the next team meeting reporting a much lower result than the independent observer. Further investigation revealed that Larry the Lush was blowing money on vices, including sending team money to his girlfriend on a regular basis. Howard quickly disbanded that team before any more of his money went down the drain.

Similar problems also occur even on the largest and most successful teams. Howard felt that cocaine and big egos destroyed Ken Uston's teams. It got so bad that they couldn't even keep the books straight for the wins and losses. There was almost always some discrepancy—which is rather odd for a group that makes its living by being proficient at math.

Because of these potential risks, Howard and I both are somewhat ambivalent about team play. Hooking up with a good team can be fun, exhilarating, and extremely profitable. But getting stuck with a bad team can be devastating and disastrous. The difficulty lies in knowing ahead of time which of these two groups you are actually joining. You may think you are linking up with a team of world-class blackjack champions, but they may instead only be world-class chumps.

You can increase your odds for success by looking for people who have a good track record in blackjack and are highly organized. I think that any group that employs some type of blueprint (like Rick Blaine suggests) is much more likely to avoid many of the hazards that sink lesser teams.

Just don't get too carried away and become unreasonably rigid—

even though everything should be outlined, it is good to have a little flexibility. But keep in mind that no amount of planning will make up for unqualified or untrustworthy players. If you can't find strong card counters who are 100 percent honest, you are walking a dangerous tightrope. There is a tremendous amount of temptation present when someone is handed a stack of cash and sent off alone to a casino.

CHAPTER THIRTEEN

Tournament Blackjack

Should you consider playing in a blackjack tournament? There are several reasons why the answer to this question is a resounding yes, but the main appeal of a blackjack tournament is obvious—the payoff for a small initial investment can be astronomical. Tournaments currently are experiencing a strong resurgence around the country, and the Las Vegas Hilton offers $1 million for first place in its annual event. That's enough cold hard cash to get most hearts pumping faster than a jackhammer.

To win the big prize, you first have to survive one of the twelve monthly tournaments to even qualify for the finals. Although luck definitely plays a great role in blackjack tournaments, you don't need to tie a horseshoe around your neck before you sit down at the table. If you correctly learn a few strategy tips, you'll greatly improve your odds and have a much better chance of victory.

Normally, the casino game of blackjack differs from poker because skilled players take on the house rather than each other. Blackjack tournaments reverse this formula and pit everyone at the table against each other instead of against the dealer. This format produces exciting finishes that typically come down to the very last hand. And you don't have to be a pro or a math whiz to win the big bucks. That is the beauty and appeal of tournament blackjack. The knockout format is a great equalizer, and average players have nearly the same chance of winning as skilled professionals. A case in point is Ed Rhoades, who also proved that nice guys don't have to finish last. Sometimes they can win a million bucks.

LUCKY EDDIE

Ed Rhoades has won six tournaments to date, but he was just a recreational player with no knowledge of proper strategy before he played in his first tournament. He not only didn't have a plan of attack, he didn't even plan on playing. While visiting Atlantic City with a friend, he entered his first tourney totally on a whim. The event featured two tournaments (blackjack and craps) held concurrently at Harrah's Marina Casino and Harrah's Boardwalk Casino. The preliminary rounds took place in both casinos over several days with the finals at the Marina.

Once entered, Ed stunned the competition and won $15,000 for first place in the craps tournament. At that time (1984), International Gaming Promotions offered a special bonus (a luxury car) to anyone who could win two consecutive tournaments. The suits in charge understandably became nervous that Ed might also go on to win the blackjack tournament and claim the bonus, but the marketing director reassured them. He stated that Ed didn't even know basic strategy and had virtually no chance at winning the blackjack tournament.

But they had underestimated the mild-mannered Ed Rhoades. He maintained his focus and not only won the $50,000 first-place blackjack prize, but he also picked up a sizable bonus—a brand new Rolls-Royce worth $110,000. In addition to the money and fame, he acquired a new nickname—Lucky Eddie.

Lucky Eddie went on to win a few more tournaments, the most notable being a $50,000 first-place prize at the Frontier in Las

Vegas in 1985, but eventually he quit playing tournaments. He started playing again only a few years ago and won a couple more small ones. Then he decided to take a shot at the biggest payday in the history of blackjack and signed up for the Million Dollar Black-jack Tournament. He fought his way to the final table and bounced in and out of the lead right up to the end. Even though he only won two out of the last five hands, his wins and strategic bets came at the right time, and Lucky Eddie was crowned the first million-dollar champion at the Las Vegas Hilton in April 2003.

CAN YOU WIN?

The amazing story of Lucky Eddie shows that anyone can win at a tournament, even if you're a novice. However, while it is possible to triumph in your very first tournament, it is highly unlikely to hap-pen in larger events. I doubt Lucky Eddie could have beaten the large skilled field at the Hilton without the wisdom gained from his previous tournaments. A smart player will learn from his mistakes and greatly improve his chances of winning. This chapter will in-clude several general principles to take you from recreational player to tournament expert.

But what about someone who is already a card-counting pro? Are there any good reasons to consider playing in blackjack tourna-ments? There are several positive and negative points to consider before answering this question. In the past, most card counters, myself included, saw only the downside and failed to recognize the powerful edge tournaments potentially offered. I felt the increased exposure and high degree of luck made them a waste of time for a high-stakes pro. It took some creative blackjack players like Stan-ford Wong to look outside of the box and see the true benefits of tournaments. For the advantage didn't lie in the traditional mathe-matics of card counting, but in two other factors—overlay and com-petitive edge.

OVERLAY

"Overlay" is a common gambling term used to denote any situation in which there is a positive expectancy. This happens frequently in tournaments because normally all the entry fees (100 percent) are returned to the players as prize money and casinos often add extra dough to sweeten the pot. Here is an example provided by Kenneth Smith, whose Web site (www.blackjacktournaments.com) is the premier place to get information for upcoming tournaments, including the Las Vegas Hilton's Million Dollar Blackjack Tournament. In a recent blackjack tournament held in Tunica, Mississippi, Bally's Casino generously added another $25,000 to the prize pool. The entry fee was $500 per person, and this extra $25,000 created a total prize pool of $135,500. Since only 221 players entered, this created an EV (expected value) of $613 for each contestant, giving a hefty overlay of 22.6 percent for the $500 entry fee.

The rationale for this liberal marketing strategy is similar to the loss leader ads used by Home Depot, in which they promote cheap garden rakes (sold at slightly below cost) and hope that you buy a new riding lawn mower while you're in the store. Likewise, the casino knows it is good business to pack its floor with a few hundred blackjack players, especially since they will have a lot of free time between rounds. The bottom line is that most players end up losing far more overall than the potential small gain offered in the tournament.

Another windfall is that some tournaments will guarantee the prize money. For example, let's say a casino expected to get 200 players (at $500 a pop) for their tournament and offered $100,000 in prize money. But perhaps only 143 players actually showed up. If the prize money was guaranteed (always read the fine print), then the EV for each player jumps to $700 for their $500 investment, yielding a very positive equity (140 percent return). Furthermore, there are often nonmonetary benefits for tournament players as well, including free rooms, meals, hats, souvenirs, and shirts, all of which can add value to your bottom line.

COMPETITIVE EDGE

Another advantage comes in the edge a skilled player will have over his fellow competitors. Surprisingly, this has little to do with card counting. The most effective tournament strategies are primarily all about risk management. To win your table, at some point you need to risk a large chunk of your playing stake.

Stanford Wong devised some of the earliest strategies to gain an edge over your opponents at the blackjack table. His calculations showed that the mathematical odds of advancing in a tournament could be dramatically improved by learning some general guidelines. He put together a team to refine his theories and later wrote about his findings in *Casino Tournament Strategy*. Here are some of the more important principles taken from that groundbreaking book.

1. **Succeed or bust.** The best tournament strategy is to either advance to the next round or bust out trying. Develop a killer instinct and always go for the win.

2. **When behind, play for the swing.** When losing, look for hands in which you can create a big swing, either with the betting amounts or by play decisions, to seize the lead.

3. **When ahead, go with the flow.** If you have the lead, try to mimic your competition by correlating their bets and reduce the chances of big swings.

4. **When in doubt, push it out.** In the late rounds, medium-size bets often will do little good. Even if you win, you still won't grab the lead; but if you lose, you have too few chips left to stage a comeback. It is best to bet the max and hope to get back in contention with one hand rather than with a bunch of small bets. It's not always best to bet as much as you can, but it's almost never the worst.

5. **Always be alert for openings.** Just because it looks like your opponent has a lock, don't assume he will make the right play. Give him a chance to make a mistake and allow you back in the game.

6. **Two bets to win.** When you need more than your original bet to win the final hand, you must double or split any hand you get. Just don't double for more than is needed, and if you do split, you

should usually stand on any stiffs because your best chance of winning both bets is if the dealer busts.

7. **Hope for the worst.** If it looks unlikely that you will win on the last round, even with a max bet, try to retain the largest stack of unbet chips. That will make you the winner if the dealer beats everyone at the table. (The dealer will win more hands than she loses.) The following table (also from Stanford Wong's book) lists the probable outcomes of various tournament situations and helps explain why this strategy is often a good percentage play.

Probability of Win, Push, Lose

One Player

Win	44%
Push	8%
Lose	48%

Two Players

Both win	30%
Either or both win	58%
A wins and B pushes	2%
A wins and B loses	12%
Both push	1%
A pushes and B loses	5%
Both lose	31%

Three Players

All win	23%
Two win; other loses or pushes	19%
One wins; others lose or push	25%
None win; all lose or push	34%
All lose	22%
Two lose; other pushes or wins	27%
One loses; others push or win	25%
None lose; all win or push	27%

Mastering these strategy tips will give you an edge over most opponents. In this chapter, I will profile four very successful tournament pros to illustrate how to incorporate these principles into various tournament situations. But before we introduce those intriguing individuals, let's first examine how a tournament operates.

TOURNAMENT FORMAT

As stated earlier, the main difference of blackjack tournaments is that participants compete against each other, rather than the house. This creates a dynamic more similar to poker than to regular blackjack. The usual format consists of a series of elimination or knockout rounds. Typically, the tournament will start with a random draw and place five or six players in designated seats at each table. Whoever finishes with the highest total of chips advances from each table, although some tournaments promote the top two to the next round. All betting limits are fixed in advance. In some cases, you play with real money, but most times the chips used in tournaments are nonnegotiable, or "funny money." They have no real value, so you can never lose more than your original entry fee. Either way, every player always starts with the same amount of chips and can't buy in for more during the round or carry over winnings from the previous table. However, there are many tournaments where you can reenter into a later round, if you had no luck and crashed out prematurely at your first table.

The number of rounds in each tournament varies, depending on how many players entered. In smaller "minitournaments" there may only be two rounds total, but in larger tournaments it might take four or five rounds to reach the final table. Each round either consists of a fixed time frame or predetermined number of hands (usually twenty to fifty) and is the same for every table.

To walk away with any money from a tournament, you typically have to fight your way to the final table. The prizes are very top-heavy and only a few players win any cash, while most lose their entire entry fee. Even if you have a great run in the early rounds, all your "profit" will be worthless unless you win the table and advance. This creates some very wild and wacky finishes for the lucky few who make it to the final table.

POSITION

Another unique quirk that distinguishes tournaments from regular blackjack is the use of the button. Usually, the player at first base is always the first one to bet and play each hand. However, tournaments use a button to rotate the position of each hand. This is done in the interest of fairness and provides everyone with roughly an equal number of turns at each table position.

This may seem unimportant, but it becomes critical for play and betting decisions. For that reason, it is helpful to calculate where the button will be near the end, especially on the last hand. If you anticipate you will be on the button (having to bet and play first) on the last round, you need to be more aggressive in the middle rounds. However, if it looks like you will have the luxury of betting after everyone else on the last hand, you can be slightly more conservative and try to catch up with a max bet at the end, if necessary.

Positioning also means that any player to your immediate left will have a better chance to catch you late in the round, since he will bet and play after you do on five out of every six hands. He can also match your bets and margin you when he holds the lead. For this reason, the best time to make a move on the opponent to your left is when he is on the button, and you get to bet last.

THE DREAM TEAM

Allan Brown is widely considered one of the world's most successful gamblers. He is so trustworthy and honest that I'd be willing to play poker with him over the phone. Although he started out as a card counter, he later successfully expanded his winning talents into other aspects of gambling, including sports betting. His skill at analyzing profitable betting opportunities places him at the pinnacle of his profession.

Allan also was among the first card counters to recognize the possibilities of tournament play, and he formed one of the earliest tournament teams in blackjack. He decided it would be more fun (and profitable) to join forces with the better players rather than compete against them. His motivation for the team was partly social (he enjoyed the camaraderie) and partly economic—he reasoned that teaming up would rapidly increase the team members' learning curve and lead to more wins. Proper tournament strategy was still fairly unknown at that time, so skilled players kibitzing together each night about unusual hands and tactics greatly aided their cumulative knowledge.

But the single biggest advantage in forming a team was in the reduced fluctuation. Despite their superior skill, the best players rarely win blackjack tournaments, since the element of luck always remains a huge factor. This high variance devastates many players and can wipe out anyone with too small a bankroll. Allan had reached thirteen semifinal tables before he made it to a final. So by combining their efforts, the team members greatly increased the likelihood that one of them would make it to the big-money round.

The strong band of talent Allan assembled soon became a commanding force on the tournament circuit and dramatically changed the tournament format. Today, a large number of casinos use an invitation-only process to keep away skilled pros like Allan Brown.

THE BIG HAND

Allan Brown discovered early on that tournaments were all about betting. His team would often try to bury the competition early rather than leave it to chance or luck on the final hand. They developed a very aggressive style, which often meant they ended up first or last. This can be embarrassing, as it is only human nature to want to look good in front of other people. But the gains from going for the jugular are huge.

Allan's most memorable win came at the Frontier casino. He entered the last hand down $800 to the chip leader. Since the max bet was $500, he knew his only chance was to get a hand he could double down or split. Allan's hopes rose when the dealer dealt him two face cards. Normally, this is a strong winning hand, but here Allan had no choice if he wanted to win. Spurning the sure thing, which would have locked up second place for him, he calmly slipped out another $500 and split the face cards.

His first ten received an ace for a total of 21. Then, unbelievably, his second ten caught another ace. Both hands won and the place exploded. Allan walked away with the $50,000 first-place prize and provided the crowd with one of the most dazzling finishes in the history of blackjack tournaments.

BEYOND BLACKJACK

Allan believes that those who can think quickly on their feet during the heat of battle have a big advantage in tournament play. One of the members of Allan's team who personified this trait was a sharp poker player named Russ Hamilton (Russ would later win the $1 million first prize in the 1994 World Series of Poker). Although the initial plan was for the team to attack only blackjack (its area of expertise), Russ Hamilton believed other tournament games like craps offered an even bigger edge. He observed a group of Caltech alumni, tagged "the Engineers," dominate several craps tournaments, including winning $500,000 for first place at the Tropicana in Las Vegas. Russ noticed that the Engineers and Stanford Wong's team did extremely well at these dice tournaments, so Russ learned their strategy and taught the rest of his team. Soon Allan Brown's group branched out into winning craps, keno, and baccarat tournaments.

His team excelled at these games because few players understood the correct strategy for betting, especially near the end. The important thing in most tournaments is to go for the win (depending on how the prize money is split). But getting to the final table doesn't mean you should start dreaming about that new condo on Maui. Allan once had three guys from his team at the final table of a baccarat tournament. First place paid a cool million dollars. Yet despite their high hopes and obvious edge over the other players, not one of the three snagged the grand prize.

GO BIG OR GO HOME

Blair Rodman was a key member on two of the most famous tournament teams (Stanford Wong's, then Allan Brown's). More recently, he was the best-known pro to survive all the grueling qualifying rounds at the inaugural Million Dollar Blackjack Tournament and make it to the final table. When the seat assignments at that tournament were determined, one of the first things Blair did was to mentally calculate his probable betting position for the very last hand. After deducing he would be in a bad spot at the end, he decided to bet aggressively and try to capture an early lead. The Travel Channel had arranged to televise the entire event, so Blair expected the other players to wager conservatively, since it was unlikely anyone wanted to make an early exit on national TV. He theorized that a big lead might unsettle his opponents and cause them to bet too aggressively and make mistakes while trying to catch him. In the earlier qualifying rounds, Blair had already witnessed a number of people crack under pressure, including one player who had the win locked up but incorrectly surrendered on the last hand and lost.

An early high count gave Blair the opening he needed, and he seized the lead with his large bets. However, one catastrophic hand (splitting 7s three times and doubling down on one) unluckily dropped him all the way from first to last place when the dealer hit to 21. Knowing he would be close to the button on the last round, he decided to go all-in with six hands to play.

Most people never would have made such a bold play so early. But a seasoned pro like Blair understands the value of having the lead *before* the last hand. Unfortunately, it didn't work, and Blair became the first casualty at the final table. However, his willingness to go for the win is a mandatory characteristic for every serious tournament player. If you fear being the first one to exit from your table, that reticence will hinder your chances of winning the biggest prizes. Tournaments are generally set up to reward the brave, rather than those willing to play for second place.

CONTRARIAN

Kenneth Smith established himself as one of the best-known players on the tournament circuit during an amazing streak over a three-year period where he finished in first place in five out of nine tournaments held at the Isle of Capri Casino in Mississippi—a feat practically unparalleled in tournament circles. That astounding win ratio demonstrates how proper strategy can dramatically increase your chances for success at blackjack tournaments.

However, learning the optimal tournament strategy is often complex, and even the simplest-looking situations can have complicated solutions. Kenneth started off with a fairly basic tournament strategy. Since you rarely win by hoping to get better hands than everyone else at the table, Kenneth usually wagered the opposite of his competition. Most of the time that meant betting small and waiting for the high fliers at his table to flame out.

This straightforward technique worked well until other players in tournaments got smarter. Now Kenneth has to mix up his strategy depending on the circumstances and caliber of the competition. He currently uses a hybrid approach, based on whether his opponents are timid or bold. But his fundamental philosophy remains the same—contrarian betting is often the wisest strategy. For that reason, most of his bets are usually either really small or very large.

TOURNAMENT LINGO

Experienced tournament players have coined several phrases to describe the various scenarios that occur on the last hand. Here are a few of these terms and examples provided by Kenneth Smith.

Taking the high: This means you've made a large enough wager so that even if all players win their bets, you'll win the table and advance. This is easy to do when you're in the lead, but may also be an option when you bet after the leaders at your table.

Taking the low: This means you've left enough unbet chips in front of you so you'll be in the lead if the dealer beats the entire table. By making a small bet, you hope the dealer has a strong hand, and wipes out your opponents' larger bets.

Playing for the swing: This describes playing your hand to increase the likelihood that you will win your bet while your opponent loses his bet. An example would be hitting to a higher total than your opponent's hand, and hoping the dealer's total ends up somewhere between your two hands.

Free hit: A free hit is a situation in which busting your hand is no worse than standing with your current total. Therefore, you can safely take another card with no cost, even if the card causes you to bust.

Because of these principles, basic strategy sometimes gets tossed out during tournament blackjack. Just as betting properly in tournaments often has little relationship to the count, there are also times where the best play is to hit your hard 18 or to double down on a blackjack—plays anathema to any correct basic-strategy chart.

THE KEY TO A LOCK

Another term commonly used in tournament circles is "lock." This involves a situation in which a certain play or bet will guarantee victory. A basic example of a lock is when you have such a large chip lead that no one else can catch you on the last hand, even with a double down. In that case, you should just bet the minimum and not put your sure win in jeopardy.

There are also plays that will lock up your victory. These frequently occur when you have the luxury of making your decision after your main competition has already played. Here is one scenario to show how this works and how easily you might overlook a potential lock. The chip leader has $1,100 and is on the button. He bets

$400. You have $1,000 in front of you, so you bet the table max of $500. He goes first and busts his stiff, leaving him with $700. Meanwhile, you're sitting pretty with a pat 20. Most people would assume they have the win locked up. But if the dealer somehow strokes out a 21, your dreams of retiring in the Caribbean will disappear faster than an ice cream cone at the beach, because the unexpected loss would leave you with a total of $500, and you might not even hold on to second place.

However, if the tournament rules allow surrender, there is an easy way to guarantee victory and prevent the worst-case scenario from happening. If you surrendered your 20 (an unusual play to make), you would end up with $750 and lock up first place (assuming none of the other competitors were within striking distance). Remember, the object is simply to win. It doesn't matter by how much, so always look for ways to maximize your end play.

WEIRD PLAYS

The nature of tournaments creates a format in which they often come down to the very end, creating crazy finishes. Consequently, there is a big difference between trying to overtake the leader late in the rounds and trying to win it outright on the last hand. To accomplish victory, bizarre and brave plays are often needed when time is running out.

One of the most common techniques for these desperate situations is doubling down for less. This is a play that would never be correct at a normal blackjack table, but it can be a very valuable weapon near the end of a blackjack tournament. This is particularly effective if your turn to play comes after your main competition. Since he has already finished his hand, you will have a pretty good idea of where you will end up in the chip totals. For example, suppose you have a solid lead going into the last hand. Your closest pursuer tries to catch you with a max bet, but you wisely covered his bet with just enough money so that if both hands win, you would still prevail. However, he throws a monkey wrench into your well-laid plans when he splits his deuces and makes a couple of pretty good hands. This reverses the situation. If you both win now, he will overtake you. So you might need to double down in order to get enough extra money out on the felt to catch him. However, it is often smarter to double for less, to protect yourself on the low end, just in case all hands lose. So instead of doubling for the full amount (which might be your first impulse), calculate the exact amount you need to win and don't bet a dollar more.

STRATEGY SHORTCUT

One of the most frustrating aspects of tournament play occurs when you are trying to catch the leader, especially when you have to bet first. If the chip leader is sharp, he will either match your bet or wager an amount sufficient to lock in both the high and low. Therefore, it can be extremely confusing trying to determine the correct bet to make near the end of a tournament. Added into this difficult mix is the fact that most tournaments have time constraints forcing you to rush your decision. Also, the pressure of making a colossal blunder in front of other people can be intimidating and play havoc with your math skills.

Kenneth Smith devised a great shortcut to deal with these nerve-racking and mentally taxing situations. His Rule of 2, 4 & 5 is a powerful way to simplify the complicated calculation process necessary to overtake the leader near the end. You can create several extra ways to win if you wager at least the following multiples of your deficit (each example assumes you are $100 behind the chip leader).

- **Bet 2 times your deficit ($200)**: you win with a double down over a single bet win by the leader.
- **Bet 4 times your deficit ($400)**: you win with a blackjack over a single bet win by the leader.
- **Bet 5 times your deficit ($500)**: you win with a double down even over a blackjack by the leader.

If you are unsure which of these is the correct amount for any given situation, it is generally best to go with the largest bet (5 times your deficit). The 2, 4 & 5 rule is a great tool for handling those tough decisions and will greatly improve your chances of coming from behind to win the big money.

THE KING

Anthony Curtis is one of the most recognizable faces in the gaming community today. His frequent television appearances and insider expertise have made his name and newsletter (*Las Vegas Advisor*) familiar to nearly every savvy gambler. His energy and charisma make him instantly likable, and many women consider him the most eligible bachelor in Las Vegas now that Elvis is dead.

Curtis and I share similar backgrounds. We both got involved in card counting about the same time, were very serious about becoming world-class players, and learned difficult multilevel counting systems. We also both started playing with woefully inadequate bankrolls, but I was fortunate to hit a good run right out of the blocks, and I quickly moved up to the bigger chips. Curtis wasn't as lucky initially, but eventually his cash-flow problems disappeared when Stanford Wong invited him to join a new blackjack tournament team. Wong's deep financial pockets allowed Curtis to take a shot at bigger paydays, and he took full advantage of this opportunity, becoming one of the leading players on the tournament circuit.

WORLD MATCH-PLAY CHAMP

Anthony Curtis still vividly recalls waking up one morning in 1986 and thinking how golden his life was. Over the previous few days, he had played some of the greatest blackjack ever seen on the planet, as he skillfully maneuvered his way to the finals of the World Match Play Championship at the Las Vegas Hilton Casino.

The unusual rules made it one of the more unique tournaments ever held. Everyone played exactly the same community hand on every round. This put the criteria for winning on playing correctly, rather than hoping to get hot hands. An experienced counter like Anthony Curtis definitely excelled in this setting, because the Hilton liberally dealt every card in a single-deck blackjack game and offered every imaginable good rule, including resplit aces, double down on any two cards, and early surrender.

Curtis squeezed every possible ounce of advantage out of all these options, including the seemingly bizarre play of surrendering a hard 19 in order to lock up a win in the quarterfinals. There were other top-notch experts in the tournament, but none of them seemed to be able to put all the elements together as well as Anthony Curtis.

In the semifinals, he faced one of the top blackjack players in the world, Allan Brown. Curtis felt like all his senses were locked into a zone, and he put away his most feared opponent. He still considers it his greatest moment at the tables—even Stanford Wong stated that Curtis made some of the smartest plays he had ever seen.

Since the final and its $76,000 first-place prize was scheduled to take place the next day, Curtis thought he might be able to milk his good luck just a little further. He contacted a previously reluctant cocktail waitress from the Lady Luck Casino and asked if she would be interested in watching him play at the final table. For some odd reason, the prospect of Curtis winning a huge sum of cash changed her attitude. She warmly agreed to join him, and Curtis didn't disappoint his date. He dominated the final and became the 1986 World Match Play champion. The two new lovebirds went to the closest bar to celebrate the victory and bask in the afterglow. The entire $76,000 in prize money sat stacked in alluring bundles of cash inside a box on their table.

Just when the budding romance was starting to heat up, Stanford Wong entered the bar and casually walked up to them. Without even acknowledging the girl, he gave Curtis a pat on the back and dumped the contents of the box into a shopping bag. A sheepish

Anthony Curtis had to explain to his date how the huge win wasn't exactly all his—he had to share it with a team. When she realized his portion came out to less than $4,000, her passion mysteriously disappeared.

Despite the bad luck at love, it still was his most memorable day gambling. Curtis nailed down many other big tournament wins— $50,000 (twice), $60,000, and $125,000, but he still considers winning the World Match Play Championship his finest hour. That victory also firmly established Anthony Curtis as one of the all-time top tournament players. His triumph also illustrates another important principle—if you are more skilled than your opponents, you should seek out tournaments that reward expert play. In general, the better the rules and penetration, the more potential there is for your card-counting ability to influence the outcome.

WORLD SERIES OF BLACKJACK

In the past, I skipped tournaments for two reasons: As a high-stakes card counter, I didn't want the additional visibility, and I felt there were greater profits in regular blackjack. However, I feel I overlooked the strong advantage sharp players could gain over their opponents in tournaments.

I recently got invited to play in the prestigious World Series of Blackjack Tournament that is televised on the GSN network. This gave me a terrific chance to see if I could apply the principles from the various experts in this chapter. Since I had virtually no tournament experience, I was hardly the betting favorite in the eyes of the skilled tournament veterans. But I surprised everyone by beating a tough field in my first round and I eventually finished in fifth place overall.

Almost as important as the money I won was the exhilarating atmosphere of close competition. Like most tournaments, my destiny came down to the final card. Unfortunately I lost out to the legendary Stanford Wong on the very last hand. Had the dealer not busted, I would have moved on to the final four and had a shot at becoming the 2005 World Champion of Blackjack and collecting its $250,000 prize.

After getting over the disappointment of coming so close and still coming up short, I realized Allan Brown was right. There is a benefit in tournaments well beyond the monetary gain—they are just plain fun to play. And your pleasure can be greatly multiplied by mastering a few strategy tips. With a little practice, you might follow in the footsteps of Lucky Eddie Rhoades and return home from your next tournament with a million dollars in cold hard cash.

CHAPTER FOURTEEN

The Dark Side

The vivid term "Axis of Evil" didn't originate with President Bush. For years, many card counters used this phrase to describe the gambling industry and the appalling ways it dealt with skilled blackjack players. The worst casinos always seem to hire unenlightened pit bosses who lump card counters together in the same category as cheaters, thieves, or other common criminals. This attitude causes some expert blackjack players to retaliate and use dubious means to win. They feel the game is so heavily stacked against them that "anything goes in love and war."

This ongoing struggle between casinos and card counters creates many ethical dilemmas. Lots of pros have inevitably redrawn the thin line separating right from wrong. I wish this chapter contained only stories about other pros and their questionable practices—weaker-willed men than I who caved in and did the type of things that shocked their mothers. But that would be a work of fiction. The truth is that I also struggled with ethical decisions. The constant harassment jaded me, and I did some things that I later regretted. However, at the time it seemed like a fair way to respond to this system of injustice. When you've been handcuffed and thrown up against a wall or had your life threatened in the back room of a "family-friendly" Las Vegas Strip casino simply for counting cards, it becomes very easy to rationalize.

This chapter will examine what potential dangers lurk on the dark side that lies within all of us. It will also explore a few of the techniques (other than card counting) that will give you an edge at blackjack. Some of these are legal, some are questionable, and some may get you *RFB* at the state pen for three to five years.

BITING THE APPLE

The first gray area I explored was what is commonly referred to as *hole-card play*. This occurs in casinos where the dealer is a little sloppy and exposes her hole card. There are three main variations of this—*front-loading*, *first-basing*, and *spooking*. My introduction to this unusual world came through a chance encounter with one of the most interesting characters in the history of blackjack, Howard Grossman.

When I first met Howard, we were playing at the same table at the Pioneer Casino in Laughlin, Nevada. My initial impression was that Howard didn't even look old enough to be playing blackjack in a casino. He slouched down so low in his chair, I thought he must have still been a teenager. However, once I watched him play for a while, I realized he was actually much older—and was definitely up to something.

He didn't bet higher during the positive counts or even play his hands correctly, but he won like crazy—and something told me it wasn't luck. Howard looked far too sharp to be a crazy gambler, and before long I figured out what he was doing. The dealer had a very wide sweeping motion when she tucked her hole card. Since I sat right next to Howard, I soon noticed why he was slouching down so low. At certain angles the hole card was exposed to players sitting in the middle of the table. Howard then adjusted his playing strategy based on this valuable information.

When the dealer went on her break, Howard also left the table and walked outside. I followed him and introduced myself. At that time Howard worked full-time as the shift boss at Vegas World Casino and no longer played on any of the big-money card-counting teams. Pros are normally very tight lipped when they find a great situation, but since Howard only played blackjack on the side for some additional income, he readily opened up and explained his technique to me. It was called front-loading, or surreptitiously reading the dealer's hole card, and provided an incredibly strong advantage (several times better than card counting).

Howard had done a lot of front-loading over the years, beginning on Ken Uston's teams. At one time they hired a person to scout out casinos for the best hole-card opportunities. This valuable advance information enabled Howard to create a book listing the names and shifts of sloppy dealers at each club. They also took notes on whether the dealers were rubber-banded, or returned to the same table each time after their break.

Many years later Howard still remembers my original response to front-loading. I told him I thought it had to be wrong. I even called it a sin (no doubt the result of being raised in a strict Baptist church), and I flatly stated I had no interest in winning money that way. Howard didn't agree with my logic. He asked me how I would respond if the dealer inadvertently flipped over her hole card and I knew she was stiff. Would I still hit my 16?

Of course, the answer was no. You'd have to be a fool not to take advantage of such a mistake. Howard agreed and explained it is no different if the dealer is sloppy and exposes her hole card. He reasoned that it was up to the pit boss or dealer to protect the games.

I understood his argument, but one question still bothered me—how far would you go to be able to see that hole card? For most front-loaders, you had to practically be in a wheelchair or lay your chin on the felt. Other dealers were much easier to read, and you might even see them flash their hole card while you were standing up. So there seemed to be a direct correlation between the lowering of your ethics and how far you were willing to sink into your chair.

I finally put my nagging doubts aside and joined the party at the

Pioneer. The edge was huge and the potential returns staggering. I went back to this money machine by the Colorado River a few more times over the next year. Howard hadn't made a complete believer out of me—I still had some reservations and didn't jump in with both feet, but I was definitely getting wet.

In the end, I never fully embraced the practice of hole-card play. I continued to play blackjack primarily as a card counter while occasionally taking advantage of a sloppy dealer when I found one. Eventually, I drifted away from the practice altogether and decided it wasn't for me. However, along the way I introduced the technique to two other card counters and their paths in life changed dramatically from their involvement in hole-card play. I told them that I still had some ethical concerns about the practice, but I no longer considered it immoral. However, if I was wrong and it was indeed a sin, then one of the friends I introduced to hole-card play ended up paying a high price for the transgression.

THE INCIDENT

Like me, Allan Brown had a religious background, and expressed some reservations about hole-card play when I first mentioned it to him. So before diving into this gray area, he wisely consulted an attorney. His lawyer told him that a legal precedent had been established with an earlier court case and that hole-card play was lawful. This gave Allan the green light, and he decided to add this technique to his blackjack arsenal.

He did quite well exploiting sloppy dealers throughout Nevada— until one fateful day at Binion's Horseshoe in Las Vegas, a club with nervous pit bosses that never took losing very well. The incident began not much differently than the normal barring many other card counters had experienced. Allan Brown received the typical tap on the shoulder and was asked to go to the back room. Since Allan clearly knew his rights, he politely stated that he wasn't required to go to the back room and that he had done nothing illegal.

However, this is where the story veered far off the usual path. Rather than respecting Allan Brown's legal rights, a burly security guard grabbed Allan in a headlock, then literally yanked him out of his chair and dragged him off in front of gasping onlookers. Once in the privacy of the back room, the casino manager ordered the security guards to beat up Allan and his associate. The guards pummeled them, not only with their fists, but also with numerous kicks from hard cowboy boots as Allan and his friend lay in agony on the floor.

Then casino personnel confiscated all their chips. As a final indignity, the security guards tossed them outside, like two bags of trash, into the alley. Another member of Allan's team found them there. Eventually, an ambulance took Allan to the hospital. Allan Brown had ten broken ribs, a ruptured spleen, and contusions of the kidney.

Amazingly, this wasn't the first time the Horseshoe had beaten up winning players. The state of Nevada had previously received several reports of similar incidents. So after this brutal beating occurred, the attorney general contacted Allan Brown to pursue criminal action against the casino.

Binion's Horseshoe quickly realized the deep trouble it was in and offered to settle for the full amount Allan Brown sought in civil damages, if he would agree to drop the criminal charges. Allan refused, yet he still won the full amount in the civil suit (the actual figure is sealed by terms of the settlement). However, the criminal trial took a few unexpected turns. Even though the jury found three of the defendants from the casino guilty, the judge incredibly overturned its verdict because he considered Allan Brown to be just another card cheat. At least that was the official reason, but many believed the strange ruling came because the judge was a personal friend of Benny Binion, the owner of the Horseshoe. (Since then, the casino has changed ownership and several of the people involved in this case are now deceased.)

The Nevada deputy attorney general was livid and filed to retry the case. However, in a bizarre twist of events, the court reporter from the previous trial mysteriously disappeared, along with all the court records. Without those, there could be no retrial and the case was dropped.

Now, this scary account is not included to disparage casinos or to paint them all as evil in the same broad strokes. The Horseshoe was an aberration. It viewed winning blackjack players like a mob-run casino would have in the 1950s. Yet every casino will take it very seriously when you violate the first commandment of gambling and threaten to beat them at their own game. They may not break your legs anymore, but you still need to watch your back.

THE MONEY TREE

Alex Strickland was a solid card counter. He never had a spectacular career, but he was sharp enough to always get the best of the house. However, he didn't care much for the wild fluctuations that resulted from the slim edge of card counting. He wanted the type of job in which he would rarely have a losing day. So I thought he'd like hole-card play, since the bigger advantage yielded far more winning sessions. I was right. Alex took to the game like a cat to tuna— he couldn't get enough.

Once he learned the ropes, he never looked back and seldom did any more traditional card counting. Instead, he moved to Reno and pounded an assortment of clubs, each with their own leak. He particularly hammered the MGM with the technique known as first-basing—a surprising fact since the MGM easily had the sharpest pit and surveillance staff in all of Reno. Yet Alex Strickland and his partner Kris practically punched the company time clock there, going in nearly every day at 10:00 a.m. and systematically playing the same two dealers. Both could be read from first base when they checked under their face cards for blackjacks. Alex is fairly tall, and this proved to be beneficial—he could consistently catch a glimpse of the dealer's hole card over the top of her outstretched hand.

Today, few casinos still manually check for blackjacks (it is now commonly done with optical readers), but Alex Strickland made his living exploiting weak dealers for several years. Since he stuck to smaller stakes, he never really got a lot of heat until he tried his hand at the most questionable hole-card practice.

SPOOKING

When discussing the ethics of hole-card play, the near-unanimous consensus of blackjack experts is that front-loading and first-basing are acceptable methods, but the technique called spooking crosses over the line between right and wrong.

The reason few players feel comfortable with spooking is the extent to which one must go to get the desired information. In front-loading or first-basing, the hole card can be seen by anyone standing or sitting at the table (if they are in the right spot or have the correct angle). Some dealers are so loose that tourists next to me have started talking openly at the table with their friends about seeing the dealer's hole card.

However, spooking is an entirely different animal. This technique involves positioning an associate on the opposite end of the pit from you. He then finds the perfect viewing angle to see the dealer's hole card (at your table) when your dealer checks for black-jacks. Then your partner signals the value of the dealer's hole card across the pit to you.

This is why spooking is so widely frowned upon. In essence, you are getting a friend to walk around behind the dealer and pass information back to you. Could you even imagine trying that at the poker table with your friends? This is the reason most blackjack players consider it cheating. I know only a few people who ever spooked. One was Alex Strickland. He tried it a couple of times at the Peppermill casino in Reno. The odd layout there lent itself to provide some perfect windows of vision across each pit. However, after a few sessions, the always paranoid pit suspected something was up. They called in the Griffin Agency, and both Alex and his partner were backroomed and photographed. That incident made Alex unwelcome at most casinos and it became difficult to play anywhere in Reno from that day forward.

SHUFFLE-TRACKING

Another nontraditional way to beat the game of blackjack is a technique called *shuffle-tracking*. This is a derivative of card counting, and it involves following slugs of cards throughout the shuffling process. Here is a simplified example: Suppose you were playing a six-deck game at Harrah's. You had a great count throughout the shoe, but unfortunately the paint never came out. When the shoe finished, you still had a +14 running count. Obviously, a lot of face cards got stuck in the one deck remaining behind the cut card. If you were somehow able to track that highly positive one-deck slug throughout the shuffle process, you could gain a big advantage during the next shoe.

There are several variations of this, but the main principle is to look for fairly simple shuffles (so the slug of high cards doesn't get too diluted) and then bet differently depending on where that positive pack ends up in the next shoe. This can produce a very strong edge if done properly, but it can be extremely difficult to master this technique. Alex Strickland tried his hand with me at some simple one-pass shuffles at a casino on an Indian reservation in the Midwest. We practiced specifically for that game for a couple of weeks beforehand, then played it for thirty straight days. I won quite a bit, but still finished slightly below my EV. However, Alex had a much rougher time and ended up losing overall for the month of play, which was obviously way below EV.

Now, it is theoretically possible for a good player like Alex to put in over two hundred hours at a great game and still end up behind. But more likely the poor results were related to the inherent difficulty of shuffle-tracking. The mental gymnastics required to properly follow the shuffling process can be demanding, even for accomplished card counters. Consequently, it is much easier to make mistakes, and a few errors can quickly dissolve your strong edge.

Another problem that makes shuffle-tracking such a complex discipline to master is how little information is available on the subject. Compared to card counting, there is probably less than 1 percent as much written about shuffle-tracking. A good resource if you are interested in learning this complicated technique is the Casino Vérité Blackjack software package. With this program, you can practice on your computer and make certain you aren't making too many blunders before you attempt to try it in the casinos.

Speaking of computers, there is a far easier way to master shuffle-tracking. You can track virtually any casino shuffle with a concealed blackjack computer. However, I would never recommend anyone try it for one simple reason—they are illegal. Yet there was a time, back when Russia was still the Evil Empire, when these devices were not outlawed.

SUPER CHIPS

Keith Taft was the first person to develop a concealed blackjack computer, which enabled operators to play each hand perfectly, squeezing out a much stronger edge than traditional card counting, especially in any deeply dealt blackjack games. Mickey Weinberg built upon Taft's innovative work and designed his own shuffle-tracking program. Mickey's sophisticated software not only tracked the slugs of big cards in the freshly shuffled shoe, it was also able to locate individual aces and key cards. The ace-tracking process was very elaborate and involved entering into the computer's memory every single card played, including its suit and denomination. This allowed the operator to predict when certain cards were about to be played in the subsequent shoe. This information generated some dramatic shifts in betting and playing, depending on the probability of what the next card might be. Knowing that an ace could show up next created some highly profitable betting situations and often meant spreading to a few hands to ensure the players received the valuable ace rather than the dealer. Conversely, hit or stand decisions became much more optimal if you knew that the next card had a greater chance of being a face card than normal.

This technology turned previously poor games into potentially very profitable ones. The power of these devices inspired two of the most successful blackjack teams to join forces and attack Atlantic

City. When this powerhouse team asked me to join, my initial reaction was similar to my response to hole-card play—I thought it smacked of dishonesty and I balked. However, Mickey convinced me that computers were perfectly legal, and since the whole affair did sound like the ultimate adventure, I eventually signed on.

Despite numerous glitches, the chips worked just as powerfully as Mickey predicted. The reason the team chose Atlantic City was because casinos in New Jersey couldn't kick anyone out for card counting. So theoretically we could play with impunity. However, it wasn't long before the clubs recognized something was amiss and the heat began descending on our happy little team.

I soon became one of the very first persons to be caught using a computer in Atlantic City. However, Mickey was correct about the legality—casino officials quickly released me after examining the device and concluding that I wasn't doing anything unlawful. Despite that exoneration, I never felt comfortable using computers. It seemed like cheating, even if technically it wasn't. A few months later, one of the wires on my computer caught fire while strapped to my leg and singed a few mementos into my skin. That made me decide to pack away my blackjack computer, and the expensive device has been collecting dust in my attic ever since.

Shortly thereafter, the laws changed on concealed blackjack computers, and they are now illegal in virtually every jurisdiction. However, some people still use them, but I think they are making a colossal mistake. Risking an offense that can be punished as a felony is never a smart decision, despite the potential gain.

The common denominator between hole-card play and concealed blackjack computers is that these two techniques both sound illegal or unethical. I have included them in this chapter to show how difficult it can be to make scrupulous decisions regarding a business in which your livelihood depends on beating the house out of every chip you can. In such a setting, it is often easy to do almost anything to win. Even though many players begin blackjack with the intention of conquering the game using only their intellect, some soon discover the question has changed from "Is it legal?" to "Will I get caught?"

HARD CHOICES

It is surprisingly easy to slip past the point of no return in your battles at the blackjack tables. Winning becomes everything, and the compelling desire to succeed can drive card counters over the line. There are many temptations facing skilled blackjack players, and the *impulse* to cheat eventually rears its ugly head with everyone. This may manifest itself in several forms, such as the simple act of wanting to cap your bet on a winning hand or trying to put extra money out on the double downs to the blatant premeditated step of marking cards. Despite the high scruples you may bring with you to the tables, the cutthroat nature of the business will at least make you *think* about such acts at some point in your career. The critical question is how you *respond* to these seductive urges.

I have been approached with many types of scams over the years. One was extremely sophisticated, involving the use of a tiny concealed video camera in a belt buckle to view the dealer's hole card. The video image was relayed to a person outside the casino and then signaled back to the BP.

CHEATING

Other scams are more basic and may constitute not much more than a smash-and-grab scheme, such as using a diversion to switch cards with a friend at the table to create a winning hand on big bets. There are a number of common cheating techniques in addition to the well-known practice of marking cards. One is called card mucking. This involves taking cards out of play (at some point during the game) and then bringing them back in later. A good example of this would be removing a king from play on one round and then switching it with a 5 on a later hand. This ploy can turn an ugly 15 into a pat 20. This technique is much more difficult than just switching cards with another player at the table (which is considered an amateur move), and you have to be an expert to perform mucking.

Another cheating technique is card bending. This is generally done to aces or face cards, and will create a small warp. Consequently, these cards will bow upward and create a slight convex appearance when they are on the top of the deck. Knowing that your next card is an ace is particularly strong for betting and can get you a 50-percent edge.

It is surprisingly easy to bend aces, since every time you are dealt a blackjack, it looks fairly natural to happily slap the hand down on the felt. If this is done in the right manner, it can create a small bend in the ace. This, combined with proper deck-cutting or card-dropping techniques, can bring an ace to your hand on the first round of every single-deck game after the shuffle. This is similar to the method magicians use to cut to the exact card in a deck—they slightly bend the specific card they desire ahead of time.

Card bending in a casino may sound like the type of scam no reputable player would ever consider. However, a couple of very well respected blackjack experts, who were certainly capable of beating the house with just their brains, were arrested in Reno once for card bending. The point of all of these dark side stories is to show just how easy it is for one's character to get bent.

PLAYING WITH THE HELP

The most common form of cheating involves some form of collusion between a dealer and a player. "Collusion" means that someone on the inside is working with you. Dealers face the same temptations as players, and working with stacks of chips each day is too strong an enticement for some. The desire to dip their fingers into this pie has caused many dealers to strike an alliance with a friend or associate on the outside and attempt to perpetrate some type of fraud on the casino.

It is for this reason that surveillance has to also watch their own help very closely. When Bill Zender was the pit manager at Bally's Casino in Las Vegas, he noticed a young man buying in for almost $10,000 in cash. What struck Bill as odd was that the player didn't even sit down—he stood behind the table. Normally, when someone purchases such a large amount of chips, they plan on playing for a while. Instead, this guy played only two hands and walked—without cashing out his chips.

To Bill Zender, something in this picture looked suspicious, and he reported it as a JDLR (just doesn't look right) at the end of his day. Later that night on the graveyard shift, two associates of the young man slipped into Bally's and used the same chips for a high-stakes play at a private table. The casino ended up getting burned badly—a crooked dealer had set up a special *cooler* shoe for this cheating team and the whole episode cost Bally's $110,000.

THE SURE THING

If you play long enough, it is inevitable that some unusual opportunity will come along and offer you the chance to make some quick and easy money. It may look like a sure thing, and you may be beguiled by its attraction. But it is wisest to analyze any possible scheme from two perspectives: the first is whether the activity is legal, and the second is whether you can have a clear conscience doing it. My advice is to quickly pass on anything that plainly violates the law. However, if the opportunity is so tempting that you find your ethics eroding faster than a career politician's, then I suggest you also consider another very good reason to pass—risk versus return. To put it quite simply, the price is too high and the risk (possible jail time, humiliation, etc.) looms much larger than any potential gain. So be careful not to get so caught up in the chase that you end up cheating to achieve your success.

CHAPTER FIFTEEN

International Blackjack

Opportunities

Every card counter should frequent only casinos that offer the very best blackjack conditions. But sometimes there are fantastic games that may not be the wisest choice to play. The financial return may be great, but the risk of playing blackjack in some foreign casinos can be too high.

Risk is often a relative term. To someone not very brave or adventuresome, it may be a risk to eat at any restaurant in Latin America, but traveling abroad to play blackjack poses far greater pitfalls than just getting Montezuma's revenge. The more important question in some exotic casinos is not *how much should I expect to win*, but rather *what are my odds of returning alive*? In a few of these places, it's best to bring your wife in case the local police need someone to identify the body.

Not everyone will be interested in trekking to the far ends of the earth just to find slightly better odds and squeeze out a few more dollars in expected value. But in this chapter I'll highlight some of the foreign casinos I visited and explain why I picked their flag out of the hat. This will further illustrate the guidelines I use to find the best blackjack games and also show how other factors can sometimes make even the greatest games not worth the risk.

CASH IN THE CARIBBEAN

The Dominican Republic is very close to America geographically, but it is a world away culturally. The long drive from the antiquated airport to the bustling city of Santo Domingo bombards your senses with striking images of squalor along every mile of the road. Nothing anywhere in the United States can come close to preparing you for the poverty of its barrios. Situated on a beautiful island in the Caribbean, the Dominican Republic should be a tourist haven. It does have an abundant supply of gorgeous beaches, but the entire land and people seem to have been stained by decades of corruption and neglect.

I visited the Dominican Republic many times over several years because it had a couple of the larger casinos in the Caribbean. Most of the gamblers came from other Spanish-speaking countries like oil-rich Venezuela. I saw very few Americans in any of the clubs during my frequent trips to this island and never once saw another card counter. This surprised me, because the Dominican casinos offered some of the most favorable rules in the world.

They stood on soft 17 and players could double down on any two cards, similar to Las Vegas, but there were a few additional perks. Several clubs allowed surrender, including early surrender against a ten, which made the odds nearly even off the top, a rarity for shoe games. Plus a few places offered some unusual bonus rules to make it even sweeter. One casino mixed a joker in with the six decks. Whenever a player received it, he got paid a bonus of $25.

I quickly figured out the odds and realized that if I played at a private table against the dealer, I would get the joker about once every thirty minutes, adding an extra fifty bucks to my bottom line every hour. That's not the kind of money to make you filthy rich, but it really adds up, especially when you're already playing a strong game.

Another advantage of playing in the Dominican Republic is that the early surrender rule tremendously reduces fluctuation. Throwing in all those ugly-looking stiffs and losing only half your bet takes a lot of the erratic swings out of play, making each day's work a little more consistent and less like a roller coaster.

THE PERILS OF PARADISE

The combination of sun, sand, and smiling dealers should have made this island nation a veritable blackjack utopia. But even paradise has a downside. Few casinos had safety deposit boxes, so I often had to keep all my cash on me—all the time. There's a strange feeling that accompanies a day at the beach when you're forced to clench both hands in a death grip over the $30,000 stuffed into your fanny pack. And it certainly cuts down on the usual water sports.

However, there were a few exceptions. One casino put me up in a gorgeous oceanfront suite with a private cabana. The setting was beautiful, and fortunately the casino even had a safety deposit box. This allowed me the freedom to get outside and enjoy the exquisite setting of white sand and swaying palm trees. On my first day there I took advantage of this opportunity and did a hard morning run along a deserted beach during a torrential downpour. There wasn't a soul to be seen for miles, and the pounding surf from the tropical storm provided an inspiring cadence for my strides.

The next day, the sun came out, and so did the European tourists. Getting my heart rate up took on a whole new meaning as I jogged past hundreds of topless women from across the Atlantic.

You may wonder why I'm including this in the negatives, but most women in the real world don't resemble movie stars or supermodels. There is something extremely unsettling about getting a close-up and personal view of a seventy-five-year-old bare-chested German Frau before breakfast. It might take years of therapy to get the image of those two sun-dried melons out of my brain.

One last note—if you do stumble across this beach, keep it to yourself. For some reason, wives tend to start questioning the real purpose of your job if you share too much information, and your future gambling trips may be in jeopardy.

LIFE AND DEATH

There are some very real hazards one faces when gambling outside the United States. Some third-world countries pose serious health risks. Diseases are much more common, and tuberculosis is particularly rampant in the Dominican Republic. I tried to do a good deed once and took my cabdriver to lunch. He kept coughing, so I asked him if he had a cold. He didn't—it was TB. I stared silently at my salad, which was directly in the firing line, and quickly lost my appetite.

There can also be some very substantial financial risks when you choose to gamble in a foreign country. Aside from the obvious concern about getting robbed, the chance of getting cheated also increases. Many overseas casinos have no gaming commissions, and traditional American ethics of right and wrong can be dramatically different in other cultures.

For example, I won a ton of money at one casino in Puerto Plata, a quiet resort community on the northern coast of the Dominican Republic. During the first few days the employees were among the friendliest I'd ever met in a casino. But on the fourth day, the atmosphere in the pit suddenly changed, and I sensed a growing hostility. In most places, I would simply have been asked to leave—told I was too good for their blackjack tables and shown the door. However, the casino personnel at this club began acting strangely. The shift manager asked me how much I had won, then walked off to the side and had an animated discussion with an older man who appeared to be the owner. I couldn't make out much of the Spanish, but every dealer in the place glared at me with frozen, stony faces. Without hesitation, I collected all my chips and cashed out. Then I quickly cleaned out my hotel room. In less than five minutes, I had thrown everything into my car and was on the highway.

Maybe I overreacted, but I feared they were going to confiscate my winnings and perhaps even all the rest of my money. Using your brain to beat blackjack certainly isn't a crime, but sometimes people on the other side of the table (especially in a foreign culture) don't see it that way, so I didn't want to take any chances.

I didn't realize how late it was until I'd already started driving south to Santo Domingo. A glance at my watch showed it was just after midnight. I was about to embark on the most surrealistic ride of my life. There were people and animals constantly in the road, even at 1:00 a.m. I soon concluded that the chicken population of the Dominican Republic greatly outnumbered humans. The heat of the day causes many creatures to come alive during the night. There are virtually no streetlights, and I nearly hit a stray pig and a pair of amorous donkeys.

I got lost numerous times and nervously had to stop and ask shady-looking characters for directions, some of whom probably would have killed me if they had any inkling of how much cash I carried. I had consulted a map before leaving and estimated the trip would take about two hours, but the highway hardly compared to an American interstate, and I drove six hours before I saw the first sign for Santo Domingo.

A violent storm blew in from the mountains and flashes of lightning provided an eerie picture of the darkened countryside. The road was in terrible condition, and my little tin box of a rental car shook intensely on every pothole. The battered auto finally limped into Santo Domingo just before dawn and just before running out of gas. It certainly was an ill-advised trip, and looking back today, I feel very lucky to have survived.

So there can be a downside to exotic locales. Did the great rules and table conditions make up for the risk? In retrospect, I'm not so sure I would do it again. But earlier in my career I was much younger, hungrier, and more adventuresome. Let me recount a couple of more memorable trips I took abroad and let you decide if they were wise, unwise, or otherwise.

ASIA

A number of tremendous gaming opportunities arose in the Orient during the 1970s and 1980s. For some reason Asian gamblers hated to hit their stiffs and often openly ridiculed players who violated this cultural taboo. It was so deeply ingrained that it seemed like part of some vow they had to take as infants. Their playing style led to some highly unusual rules in the Orient, which created several profitable situations for card counters. A few countries offered a version of five-card Charlie, a popular variation used in friendly home games but one you'd never find in Vegas.

Since the majority of their Asian customers didn't hit their stiffs and rarely played their hands correctly, this rule cost these casinos very little. However, calculations by blackjack whiz Stanford Wong showed that this little rule could yield huge profits to skilled players. His research resulted in several big-money card counters and blackjack teams hitting Malaysia, Macao, and Korea over a number of years.

I made a trip to Asia with my good friend Mickey to take advantage of these great rules, but unfortunately we arrived toward the end of the party. The games were still good, but the pit bosses tended to look at any Caucasian with deep suspicion. Very few American tourists chanced upon their games, and most who did were pros.

The strategy to best exploit this five-card rule was fairly complicated. Since Wong formulated matrix numbers for only the Hi-Lo count, Mickey and I each had to switch from the multilevel systems we normally played and learn Hi-Lo just for that one trip. And there were many variations to consider, since a three-card 13 or a four-card 15 required a different strategy than its two-card relative.

Learning how to beat the game ended up being the least of our problems. We killed every casino in the entire country. Our wins sounded outlandish, since they easily ran over a *million* a day. The only problem was that it was a million in *Korean* currency. Still, it felt great to tuck 5 million into your pocket, even if it only translated into a few thousand dollars.

We'd gotten some helpful tips from players who'd already blazed the trail ahead of us. One of the biggest problems they encountered involved getting their winnings out of the country. Korea had very restrictive laws to keep its citizens from salting their money away abroad, rather than at home.

We were told that visitors could not leave with more money than they had declared when they entered Korea. This obviously created big problems for big winners and forced most experts to choose which end they wanted to put their butt on the line—either coming or going. Some of them overdeclared the amount they brought in, which caused a big flap if the customs agents decided to count your money upon arrival. Others hid cash in their shoes and available crevices when they left, which would be a disaster if they were searched.

Both of these tactics seemed like unnecessary risks to me. So I came up with a rather clever solution of creative accounting. In addition to the cash on me when entering Korea, I also brought a bogus check from Publisher's Clearing House made out for $50,000. It wasn't any good; if used, it would bounce higher than a Steve Nash dribble. But it gave me a large cushion for potential winnings, so I figured as long as we didn't go crazy and try to clean out the entire country, we would be fine when it was time to leave.

The entry part of the plan worked smoothly. However, even though our profits stayed under the $50,000 buffer, the exit strategy hit a few snags. First, one of the casinos didn't take losing very well and paid off our winnings with counterfeit bills. So we lost quite a bit there. Also, it ended up being a big hassle to convert our Korean money back into dollars at the end of the trip, and we weren't able to get everything changed. At the time, neither Mickey nor I thought this presented any problems. We guessed we might lose more on the exchange at our bank back in the States, but we didn't expect it to be a very significant amount.

Unfortunately, we had been misinformed about Korean money laws. We thought the only restriction was that you couldn't leave with more cash than you brought in. However, there also was a law that no one could take more than a small amount of Korean currency out of the country, which came into play when it was time to leave.

The Seoul airport was an absolute zoo when we tried to catch our scheduled return flight home to the United States. A strike had been going on for a couple of days, and thousands of people were stranded, frantically trying to squeeze onto the few outbound flights. It was a scene of chaos as normally polite businesspeople pushed and shoved while attempting to get to the front of long lines. Mickey and I initially failed in our efforts to get onto a plane, but finally we succeeded when Mickey offered a nice picture of Ben Franklin to an appreciative airline official, who evidently collected fine American art.

You can probably guess which one of us had thousands in local currency tucked into his fanny pack as we triumphantly strolled toward our gate. Mickey had already cleared customs and was just boarding the jet when two uniformed officials asked me what I had in my fanny pack. I innocently said that it contained money. I knew that the amount was far less than what I had entered the country with, so I didn't have anything to fear.

Or so I thought.

The next question was whether I had any Korean currency. I quickly responded yes, and they asked to see it. I pulled out all the cash and naively placed it on the counter. The reaction of the authorities would have been humorous if it hadn't been so frightening. Most SWAT teams don't surround a suspect as fast as the four armed policemen encircled me.

Whatever the legal infraction was, they took it very seriously. Mickey, to his credit, got off the airplane and came back to help. We explained how we had won the money gambling and weren't aware of the prohibitions on taking Korean currency abroad. The situation looked pretty bleak, but in the end, I think the fact that I wasn't trying to hide the money convinced them it was an honest mistake. They finally released me after a long and nerve-racking ordeal, which caused us to miss our flight home. It then took two more days to get out of a country we were fast beginning to hate.

SIDE TRIPS

The trip wasn't entirely without laughs. At the Olympos casino in Inchon, Mickey and I were the only players in the entire club. The place was deader than a funeral parlor—no music played, no slot machines jingled. There was no noise, period. You could have fired a cannon in the casino and nobody would have been hurt.

We had entered the casino separately, but only a few minutes apart. The strategy was to act like we were strangers to reduce heat. Both of us got a positive shoe right off the bat and just started pounding the blackjack tables.

A pit boss with thick glasses paced nervously and watched as two young high rollers just a few feet apart bet the casino maximum while pretending not to know each other. We only lasted three shoes before he stepped over to my table and said, "Please leave casino and take your American friend with you."

Another humorous incident happened at a casino on the idyllic island of Cheju. Other expert players had advised us to take very few bathroom breaks in Korea. The reason was because the pit bosses were so polite that they seldom barred card counters at the table. Instead, they preferred to wait until you stepped away to avoid embarrassing anyone else in the casino.

I adjusted accordingly and put in a grueling marathon session at the blackjack tables. After a long day of nature calling, I finally answered and went off to the bathroom. Sure enough, on the way back a very apologetic supervisor met me. He told me that I could no longer play blackjack at his casino, which didn't surprise me, but then he said something that did. He offered to return all the money I had lost during the day. Now, it wasn't a large amount (only about a hundred bucks in American currency), but the offer totally shocked me. Never before or since has that happened to me.

Aside from the adventure of traveling to Asia, it's only fair to analyze whether it was worth it. Let me give one more example of a great game and then we can do the math.

EUROPE

Belgium is a small country with a long history, but I didn't fly all the away across the Atlantic for the crepes or the culture—I wanted to attack the casinos. A couple of them offered the rare and seldom seen full-fledged version of early surrender—a tremendous option that made many early counters like the Czech team rich in Atlantic City before the casinos changed the rules.

I didn't experience any life-threatening situations in Belgium, but I did have some problems that are fairly common if you choose to play abroad. This trip is a good example of some of the subtle changes you encounter when you step away from the familiar sights and sounds of home.

The biggest drawback to foreign travel is the expense. Typically, you have to fork out at least $500 for the plane ticket. Another disadvantage is that comps are either nonexistent or much less prevalent outside the States. In Belgium and Korea, I had to pay for my hotel room and most of my meals. In Nevada, I *never* paid for either.

So right away the expectation to have a positive trip is much dicier since you need to win about a thousand just to break even. The time zone can also play havoc with your senses. When I first arrived in Belgium, the nine-hour difference made the normal job of counting a much more difficult undertaking. I didn't sleep well, especially with the thin walls in many of the old hotels. One night I got stuck staying at an old inn, where my tiny room was only two floors above a lively tavern. There was evidently a German polka convention downstairs, and the noise ravaged my sleep until the wee hours of the morning, when mercifully the beer finally ran out.

Surprisingly, another problem is just getting inside the casino. First of all, European casinos are much harder to find. There are no glitzy lights and huge billboards pointing the way. It's difficult enough driving on the congested European roads, but it is an extra burden when you have to practically be an Eagle Scout to locate your destination.

The first casino I played in Belgium was in the seaside community of Ostend. After a few wrong turns, I finally found the club in a seedy part of town, right next to the red-light district. Its style and decor fell far below the superior elegance of Vegas casinos, yet I still wasn't allowed to enter because, despite its appearance, the management somehow considered it a classy joint. No one was allowed inside without wearing a coat and proper dress shoes, and not until paying an entry fee.

This ticked me off on several levels. First, I never paid to get inside a casino before, and this struck me as a very dumb marketing ploy. The whole concept of gambling revolves around getting the suckers—I mean customers—in the door. Second, I never dressed up. Ever since my basketball days I've always wore sneakers.

Even though I was soon to become the biggest bettor in the entire casino, I was still turned away. In the States, many places would let you play in your pajamas if you flashed enough money. I eventually gave in to the casino's silly little rules and trudged off to buy a pair of cheap shoes. I saved a little money by accepting the casino's offer of a loaner coat, even though it was about two sizes too big.

Next, I had to exchange money at the cage before I even played a hand. This was a hassle and expensive, since there was a small premium to pay every time you bought chips with American currency. Consequently, it was very difficult to guess how much I might need to convert for that evening's session. Playing in denominations of francs rather than dollars also presented a huge challenge. Already suffering from jet lag, it taxed every cell in my brain to not only figure out the true counts and play correctly with the unusual rules, but to also convert my bets from dollars to francs.

The games in foreign countries are often slow and tedious. One reason for this is back betting. The casino I played had nine spots instead of the maximum of seven in the States. And that still wasn't enough to handle all the traffic. Many gamblers had to stand behind the table and place their bets on top of other players' spots. This created a lot of confusion and often brought games to a halt when former friends started arguing over how much each had originally bet in the spot.

CUSTOMS

I didn't last long at most clubs in Belgium because the combination of being both a big bettor and an American quickly raised suspicions. Still, it was a great trip financially, and thankfully there were none of the harrowing events that I'd experienced in the Dominican Republic and Korea. At least until I returned home.

When I flew into New York, I had to clear customs before switching to a different plane for the rest of the trip. Everyone is required to declare whether they have over $10,000 in cash in their possession when entering the country. There's nothing illegal with carrying that much, but the government just wants to keep an eye on the lowlifes and money launderers.

Being an upright and honest citizen, I dutifully filled out the form and declared all of my cash, which weighed in at just under $40,000. The amount must have surprised them because everybody started going ballistic. Before I could board my next flight, a pair of special customs agents arrived and wanted to count the money again. That day the term "breezeway" took on a whole new meaning, because I had to drop my pants while they searched for additional stashes. For a while, I thought they planned to do a full cavity search. And I don't mean the kind that requires a dentist.

Fortunately, the matter got resolved without anyone having to climb up my butt with a flashlight. Still, it put a damper on the whole trip. It's extremely frustrating to be treated like a criminal by your own country simply because you are in a line of work that requires large amounts of cash.

RISK VERSUS RETURN

Now let's analyze these three trips (the Dominican Republic, Korea, and Belgium) and see if they were worth all the additional hassle and effort. I gained about an extra .3 percent on average from those foreign casinos over typical games in the United States. Although the table limits did vary, a rough comparison showed my yield to be about $225 an hour in average shoe games Stateside (based on my $100,000 bankroll) and about $300 per hour in the stronger games overseas.

On longer trips like these, I hoped to get in at least fifty hours of play. Otherwise, the time and cost of the journey is hardly worthwhile. So I expected to win about an extra three grand (after deducting the travel expenses) over a comparable play in Vegas.

However, the example above is a very loose approximation and doesn't consider all factors, one of which is the additional time (often a few days) needed to fly to Europe or Asia. The other component to consider is the potentially higher risk. Most trips I took abroad were much more mundane than the ones I cited in this chapter. Rarely did I feel like the hammer was about to fall; in fact, all of the previous stories were shared precisely because of their *unusual* nature.

Yet traveling abroad with large amounts of cash can easily become a lethal mix. There is always going to be an added element of jeopardy for serious players who embark for foreign lands. Though most trips will go smoothly and without mishap, there are very real concerns to mull over before you hop on the next plane to Beirut just because you heard that the casinos there have single-deck blackjack.

PUERTO RICO

Let me end this chapter with the flip side of the coin. I imagine all of you can understand the logic of traveling overseas to increase your odds. But what if instead of heading off to faraway spots in search of better games, you left the country to play inferior games?

I'm sure you're wondering why anyone would do such a stupid thing. The reason is that some trips are intended primarily for vacation and to take in the sun rather than to search for riches. A good example of this would be several trips I took to the lush island of Puerto Rico. I played blackjack there for only one reason—to get comps and reduce the overall cost of my tropical beach getaway.

Some of the casinos in Puerto Rico were exceptionally generous, and I not only received free room and meals, but also got my airfare comped up front. However, the rules were bad. Players could only double on 9, 10, or 11 and weren't allowed to resplit pairs. These restrictions cost me about .25 percent over the average shoe game I normally played back in the States.

Was gambling in Puerto Rico worth it just to get a tan? It's a tough call. I played about twenty hours on each trip, so my expected return was reduced by about a thousand bucks because of the inferior rules. Yet I did get several thousand dollars in free benefits (ocean-view suite, gourmet meals, and cute drinks with pink umbrellas).

My advice is this—if you're already planning a vacation to a hot beach spot like Aruba or the Bahamas, then playing some blackjack can be a very smart move. The downside is that when the cards go bad, it can really put a damper on your family vacation. Losing is never fun, but it's especially aggravating when you're dumping money like crazy in a game that you'd normally not even play back home.

I had two particularly brutal beatings at the blackjack tables in Puerto Rico. One ended up as the worst day I'd ever had gambling, and it came just before Christmas. The joy of spending the holidays festively in the islands with loved ones quickly evaporated into questioning the wisdom of mixing business with pleasure.

Of course, there were many other trips during which I won big and still got free waffles every morning for my kids. Those are the fun times that make it seem worthwhile. But a general principle is this—you are usually better off playing only the best games and taking your vacations away from the green felt jungle to some place like Hawaii.

THE BOTTOM LINE

However, you still should incorporate foreign casinos into your schedule. The best games are almost always at places that lie off the beaten path. By traveling frequently, serious blackjack players greatly increase their odds of finding that rare gem that will fatten their bankroll—especially if they can milk the game before some big-money team discovers the game and burns it out.

I have had the good fortune of unearthing several gold mines over the years, one of which was a small casino in the Dominican Republic that no other card counter ever stumbled across (at least while the fantastic conditions were in place). Other adventuresome counters I know have also found riches by going the extra mile. One player won over a million dollars in Malaysia before the casino pulled the plug. And the Czech team found many incredible opportunities, including a French casino that dealt *every* card in the six-deck shoe. So I'm convinced the potential rewards outweigh the risks and difficulties of playing blackjack abroad.

CHAPTER SIXTEEN

Promotions

Promotions have been the heart and soul of most casino marketing strategies ever since King Tut gave away free camels on opening night. And sometimes the suits in charge of marketing concoct a new gimmick to create traffic that inadvertently offers a tremendous edge to players. Remarkably, this type of blunder occurs in both large and small clubs, but because there are so many promotions to weed through, the difficulty comes in distinguishing the wheat from the chaff. Most of the time this is fairly easy, because the typical promotion adds very little extra value for gamblers. However, occasionally you find a rare nugget that makes up for all the rest.

There are few things in life quite as attractive as free money. Yet casinos routinely give away thousands of dollars every day. The best deals are the ones that require no risk whatsoever. These are commonly called a *free roll*. A simple example of this might be standing in line for a free chance to win $1,000. This is a legitimate opportunity with a positive edge, but is often inefficient because of the time involved and the long odds.

Fortunately, free money also comes in larger denominations and more practical situations. If you get on a mailing list as a preferred customer, some clubs will send you *bounce-back* vouchers. These are cash inducements to speed up your return to the casino. I have received many of these over the years, but one clearly stands out over the rest. A large casino in Reno sent me an offer of $300 in free money once a year for three straight years. There were some restrictions, and the $300 came in the form of special tokens that could only be used on slots; moreover, all the coins had to be played through the machines at least once before you could cash out.

The first year I ended up with $270 and the second year $240. Not bad considering there was zero risk. But on the third year, I hit the jackpot when I snapped off a royal flush for $4,600. The fact that I picked up a little over five grand in free money from this club was even more amazing since I had previously been kicked out of it for card counting. Evidently, communication between the blackjack pit and casino marketing was virtually nonexistent, and I somehow remained on their most-valued-customer list.

PROFITABLE EXTRAS

The next best thing to no risk is low risk. This comes in several sizes and shapes. Some casinos offer what are called gambler spree programs. The basic premise of these is that if you gamble so many hours at a specific bet level, you will receive cash back at the end of your trip. Several foreign casinos use these incentives or rebate a percentage of your losses back to you in cash.

Another variation is getting a bonus in nonnegotiable chips. For example, the Hilton and Harrah's properties used to give an extra 10 percent on a player's initial buy-in (under a special junket program), so $1,000 could become $1,100. This is still free money, but since you have to play through the entire amount (at least once), there can be some fluctuation. Consequently, you may actually lose, but this is still a great deal, assuming the blackjack game is worth playing in the first place.

COUPONS

Another version of free money comes in match-play coupons, such as the lucky buck coupons. Typically, these are only for small amounts ($2 to $5 max), and although they carry a strong edge (often close to 50 percent), the low limits discourage all but the most frugal gamblers. However, I have occasionally seen match-play coupons acceptable for bets up to $500, and a few casinos have offered a "first card is an ace" coupon for larger dollar amounts.

The best coupon I ever found was in a fun book given out free to customers at the Lady Luck Casino in Vegas. Most coupons were only marginally worthwhile, but one offered a free insurance bet for one hand. It was probably a mistake by marketing, but the coupon had no maximum amount printed on it. So if you strategically waited for a big bet opportunity, you could use the coupon instead of your own money—a strong enough edge to get me sifting through garbage cans looking for extra fun books.

SIDE BETS

Every now and then some bright bulb in casino marketing thinks of a new angle for an old game. Blackjack has seen a number of these during the past two decades, and often they come in the form of side bets. Some of the more recent innovations are Super Sevens, Lucky Ladies, Royal Match, Over/Under 13, and Red/Black.

The trick lies in figuring out which (if any) of these are potentially profitable and which will always favor the house, regardless of the strategy. Most of the time when a new game is introduced, like Spanish 21 or 6–5 blackjack, there is no realistic way to win. However, occasionally a juicy opportunity slips through the cracks and makes it to the tables. One of these was Double Exposure, a game in which the house won on all ties, but compensated by allowing players to see the normally hidden dealer's hole card. This was a very strong game to count, but eventually they modified the rules (after being pounded by me and a number of other experts).

BLACKJACK PROMOTIONS

Perhaps the most popular (and simplest to beat) promotion is when a casino pays 2 to 1 instead of 3 to 2 on blackjacks. This deal is usually restricted to a very short time frame, but the edge is so strong that flocks of eager card counters always show up whenever it is offered. The advantage for this promotion is normally close to 2 percent, and you don't even have to count to beat the game. Basic strategy alone is sufficient to win.

If you hear about a casino offering one of these deals, you need to do two things. First, make sure it is actually 2 to 1 on *all* black-jacks. It is much more common for a casino to offer this deal *only* on suited blackjacks, which greatly reduces the edge, making it only marginally better than a normal game. If it is indeed the real McCoy, the second thing you need to do is get on the phone and call me, because I love free money.

UNUSUAL RULES

Quirky rules are not only hard to play; they can also be hard to evaluate. A small casino in Wendover once allowed players to split any 16s (e.g., 9-7 or 10-6). At first glance, this variation didn't appear overly valuable, but Stanford Wong intuitively saw its potential and calculated that the bizarre rule actually yielded a hefty 1.2 percent advantage. I didn't play that game because the maximum bet was only $50. However, sometimes casinos offer great rules with higher limits.

My personal all-time favorite was when the Ramada Express of-fered a couple of promotions each month to draw more traffic to their dying casino. Most of those were virtually worthless (like three 7s paid an extra $25), but one particular promotion caught my attention. Any five-card hand was an automatic winner. This yielded a monster 1.4 percent edge and was even better than the Korean five-card rule. I beat them for $22,400 on the first day of the promotion. It was supposed to run again later in the month; instead, they quickly shut it down after just a few hands when the same smiling faces showed up at the blackjack tables.

ALL FOR NOTHING

Not all promotions you find will match up to the great deals highlighted in this chapter. Sometimes you may go to great lengths for little or no gain. I once drove all night with Alex Strickland from Chicago to Vicksburg, Mississippi, when we heard about a 2 to 1 blackjack promotion at the Isle of Capri Casino. Since their sister property (the Isle of Capri in Biloxi) had previously barred me, I decided to dye my hair jet black and get a perm so that I would have a new suave look before joining the party. Unfortunately, I picked the world's worst hairstylist. One hour and fifty wasted dollars later, I looked more like Don King than Don Juan.

My sagging spirits quickly rose when I entered the casino and saw two big stacks of chips in front of Alex Strickland. I anticipated a big payday that would more than make up for my having the ugliest hairdo in the entire Midwest. I quickly found an empty seat, played one spot at table max, lost the hand, and then got kicked out. To top off the miserable day, on the long return drive back to Chicago, a cop nailed me with a speeding ticket.

Blair Rodman and Anthony Curtis had a similar experience (without the visit to the medieval barber) at a Native American casino in California. Curtis caught wind of an unbelievable 3 to 1 blackjack promotion scheduled to take place at the Casino Morongo. Since this incredible rule gave players one of the biggest edges in the history of blackjack, they left Vegas at 5:00 a.m. to make sure they secured seats. Unfortunately, everyone else had heard about the fabulous deal, too, and over a hundred pros showed up at the small club. Every table was jam-packed, forcing Anthony and Blair to spend hours trying to find an open spot. Through a great deal of scrambling and the charms of Blair's beautiful wife, they finally snagged some seats shortly before the start of the promotion at 6:00 p.m. However, the Casino Morongo pulled the plug and cancelled the promotion before it even began, dealing a bitter blow to everyone present (some of whom had flown in from across the country).

HOW TO STRIKE PAY DIRT

The Morongo fiasco illustrates the old saying "Loose lips sink ships." When a great deal like that gets publicized on the Internet, the chance for success rapidly diminishes. However, there are times when it pays to network and share secrets with other pros. I have done so in numerous situations, and owe a lot to Alex Strickland for finding some of the better deals.

If you don't have friends scattered in casino towns across the country, you can greatly increase your odds of striking the mother lode by subscribing to the *Las Vegas Advisor*, a publication dedicated to finding the best deals for value-conscious gamblers. Its founder, Anthony Curtis, has done a tremendous job over the years of exposing the most profitable gaming opportunities. It is a great resource for every blackjack player, from the low roller who wants to pinch pennies and maximize coupons to the big hitters who want the inside scoop on the best deals in town.

CHAPTER SEVENTEEN

Internet Gambling

There are two easy ways to make $50,000 a year. The first is to live in Bill Gates's neighborhood and trick-or-treat at his house every Halloween, and the other is by playing blackjack on the Internet. Although the gravy train may be running out, Internet casinos historically have offered some of the greatest promotions ever seen.

Internet gambling has some strong advantages over land-based casinos. One is in the convenience of being able to play blackjack anytime, anywhere, dressed any way you want. If your dream is to gamble bare-chested while wearing only your boxers, then your ship has come in. Internet casinos are open around the clock and you can freely smoke, drink, or belch without bothering anyone else at the table.

However, a much bigger benefit than just the casual dress code is available to advantage players looking for an edge. Imagine this scenario: it is your very first visit to Atlantic City. You stroll around the opulent casino for a while, then plunk down a C-note at an empty blackjack table. Donald Trump himself walks over to greet you. When he finds out you've never played at his casino before, he tells the dealer to give you an extra hundred bucks, and you receive $200 in chips for your $100 buy-in. Just the Donald's way of welcoming you to his club.

While this story may seem far-fetched, those are the types of deals that happen every day online. Why? Stiff competition. Every casino wants your business, and many are willing to give away free money just to get you in the door. They can afford to do this because their expenses are incredibly low.

A typical bricks-and-mortar casino is saddled with a very high overhead. It usually has to pay top dollar to buy premium land in a high traffic area, then spend millions to construct an ornate palace to attract the gaming public. City, state, and federal taxes can also pinch the bottom line, not to mention the casino having to pay its dealers, pit bosses, manager, cocktail waitresses, and countless other workers every payday.

The casinos in cyberspace incur only a fraction of these costs. They have few employees, can operate out of a small office or even a closet, and often are based in tax-free Caribbean countries. Therefore, their profit margin can be astronomically high on each gambling dollar. This provides incentive for them to grab as big a piece of the pie as possible. And it is very big. Conservative estimates showed Internet casinos raking in $5.7 billion in 2003, and that figure is projected to more than double by 2006.

Not all of these profits need to end up in the pockets of casino operators. You can also get your fingers into this tasty pie and rake in some fairly easy money by gambling online. But it is not done in the traditional way. Most blackjack games on the Internet are immune from the normal methods a pro would use to attack them. The table rules aren't bad (typically no worse than 0.5 percent against the players), but they usually shuffle the cards after every hand, so regular card counting is fruitless. So it would seem like online blackjack is a losing proposition, since you will still be a net loser even with perfect basic strategy. However, smart players can gain an incredible advantage in the generous promotions available online. Since there are well over a thousand Internet casinos, there is intense competition to attract new customers, and the most common way to do this is with liberal bonus offers. And since Internet casinos give away cash rather than comps, these benefits can really add up.

THE GOOD

There are several different types of bonuses. Some are fairly normal, such as the match-play bonuses, which are worth approximately one-half the face value and are taken after each hand whether you won or lost. Others are downright weird, such as the sticky bonuses, which can never be withdrawn and can only be used for wagering. A much better deal is found in the bonuses that have fewer strings attached. These mainly come in two forms—free money and a percentage bonus of your deposit.

Surprisingly, a few Internet casinos offer free cash without any risk. At these clubs you either don't have to make any deposit to claim your bonus, or they will give you all your money back if you lose within the first twenty-four hours. Unfortunately, most of these can't-lose deals are restricted to very small dollar amounts (typically a maximum of $50 to $100). Still, it is unwise to look a gift horse in the mouth, and there is little reason to hesitate when free cash is laid on the table. But the more rewarding offer is the percentage bonus. These are primarily for first-time customers and can vary widely depending on the casino and the size of the initial deposit. A small deposit of $50 might qualify for a fantastic 200 percent bonus, while a larger amount such as $1,000 might only get 10 percent. Notice, however, that both of these deals yield the same result—a free $100. Which is better? Obviously, the $50 deal is a much higher advantage play, but aside from the fluctuation and increased risk, there will actually be little difference in the end result.

Some Internet casinos also offer ongoing bonuses. Many will have special deals and gimmicks, such as free money on your birthday, or an extra bonus for repeat deposits. This last one can add up quite fast, and getting a hefty bonus on *every* new deposit would put you on the fast track to wealth.

Another deal that some casinos offer is to give a small bonus each and every month (typically $20 to $80). Not much, but enough so you can buy pizza and beer for all your buddies on bowling nights. It is also possible to make money off these same friends (which has to be one of the greatest perks of capitalism). Many Internet casinos will deposit free cash into your account for every warm-blooded body you refer to their site.

Also, it never hurts to ask. If you find a casino you'd like to play, but its bonus is below average, ask if it is willing to give you a better deal or perhaps match some competitor. If that doesn't work, get on its mailing list and you might receive a good offer down the road.

A while back I decided to take advantage of these extraordinary opportunities and make some extra money on the Internet. My original plan was to simply grab a few of the more lucrative and low-risk bonuses for small money plays. However, after dipping my toes into the water, I quickly recognized that the percentage bonuses were potentially far more rewarding. So I decided to up the ante. Soon I began depositing thousands of dollars at a pop.

Most of the deals I pursued yielded very strong edges—often 20 to 30 percent over the house. And despite my initial reluctance to send large sums of money to Internet casinos, I ended up a big winner overall. In a little over half a year, I cleared $73,000. Although I made less per hour online than I did at land-based casinos, this was still a tremendous result for what was at most a part-time job (usually no more than two or three hours a day). And the fact that I didn't have to travel all over the world to play blackjack made it very appealing—especially with the greatly reduced fluctuations inherent in the juicy bonus offers.

However, despite the fact that I love making easy money, there was also a downside to this business, and I eventually quit Internet gambling. I will explain the rationale for my decision in the next few pages to help you decide whether to add cybercasinos to your list of potential playing targets.

THE BAD

Despite the twin benefits of convenience (24/7 gambling from any-where in the world) and profitable bonuses, there are a number of negatives associated with cybercasinos. Most of these revolve around two key questions.

Do Internet casinos cheat?

Will I get paid if I win?

In established places like Las Vegas, these issues should never come up. The games are well regulated and paying off big winners isn't a problem. While the vast majority of Internet casinos are rep-utable and honest, few can compare to solid established clubs like Caesars that have been in business for decades. An alarming num-ber of cybercasinos come and go almost as fast as the circus blows through town. And another disturbing fact is the dubious own-ership. Perhaps you've never been a fan of big-money casino moguls like Steve Wynn, but he is practically a canonized saint compared to some Internet casino operators, a few of whom simply crossed over from the pornography industry, hoping to further pad their bank accounts in the second-most-profitable business model on the Internet.

With such a potentially seedy background, the questions regard-ing cheating and getting paid are valid concerns with Internet casi-nos. Consequently, many blackjack players become paranoid about gambling online. It is a natural tendency whenever you lose to *think* you might have been cheated. This apprehension is fairly common at the tables in regular land-based casinos, but it is truly a serious fear when playing online, where it doesn't seem at all preposterous to envision some sinister software programmer willing to manipu-late results to increase profits.

However, while there is no question some cheating has hap-pened at Internet casinos, the consensus of most experts is that cheating is not very widespread. How should you respond? To play or not to play—that is the question.

There is no doubt in my mind that a couple of casinos cheated me during my short Internet career. Normally, that would be enough to pull the plug, and the logical reaction would be to end this chapter right here. Losing money at the tables is bad enough, but nobody likes to get swindled out of their hard-earned cash. But surprisingly, I think Internet casinos are still worth a look. If the rest of the picture is pretty enough, occasionally getting cheated may just have to be an acceptable part of doing business.

The other concern about online gambling is actually more daunting. If there is a good chance the Internet casino will never pay you, it almost doesn't matter whether you win or lose or get cheated. And not being able to collect your winnings certainly takes the fun out of playing. This is possibly the biggest issue facing anyone trying to reap bonuses. While land-based casinos will happily and immediately pay up, some Internet casinos take a much more confrontational stance. Rather than treat winners with a smile, they scowl, stonewall, and do everything possible to deny your bonus. At various times they will refuse to pay, confiscate your winnings, freeze your account, or make you wait for months while they go through a litany of excuses and claim the check is in the mail. This ordeal is draining and time consuming. It forced me to wear several other vocational hats—I also had to be a meticulous accountant and a persistent bill collector if I wanted to retrieve what was rightfully mine.

Most places eventually paid up, although it was agonizing to wait months for that big check to arrive (when it should have taken days). However, there were four clubs that never paid me at all. Despite my repeated letters, phone calls, and e-mails, I ended up with nothing—losing not only my winnings, but also my initial deposits.

The reason some Internet casinos drag their feet so much is because they are severely underfinanced and rely on new deposits to pay previous winners. So the longer they can string out your payment, the more time it gives them to bring in fresh capital. But even if they are legitimate and honest casinos, one really big winner could potentially wipe out these smaller operations and leave everyone else who is owed money holding the bag (or the laptop, if that is easier to throw when you're mad).

THE UGLY

"Addiction" is one of the most loaded words in our language and conjures up images of desperation and ruin. Almost everyone is affected either directly or indirectly by some addiction. The consequences are often catastrophic (drugs or alcohol, for example), and gambling is one of the vices in which it rages in its absolute worst form. Many lives and families have been destroyed by this all-consuming fire. Although most true pros never succumb to this pervasive element, I've seen cases where seemingly normal players go ballistic and desperately dance on the razor's edge.

The subject of addiction is always the elephant in the room nobody wants to talks about in gambling. Playing cards for a living can be gut-wrenching and emotionally draining, and if you feel a propensity to go on tilt and chase your losses, this is not the business for you. The oft-repeated advice is certainly applicable here—if you can't afford to gamble, don't.

However, as bad as this vice is, any weakness a player may have is multiplied by a factor of 10 when gambling online. There are many reasons why it is far easier to enter the danger zone of addiction on the Internet than in a land-based casino. *The usual restraints are gone. Nobody is watching you when you go crazy. The money no longer looks real.* With a few clicks of the mouse, you can literally blow thousands of dollars and leave your financial world shattered.

It is primarily because of this insidious danger that many elected officials have tried to regulate Internet gambling, but this is a difficult task and several versions of "anti-Internet gambling" bills have failed to pass. However, there is precedent for this action, and our government retains the right to protect its citizens from any areas that impact their health, safety, or welfare. A few places (Louisiana and South Dakota, for example) have already moved to outlaw Internet gambling in their states. MasterCard and Visa have also taken steps to prohibit credit card use for online gambling transactions.

Many feel that drastic steps are necessary to combat the powerful addiction of Internet gambling. But it is not solely out of concern for our well-being that so many diverse forces have banded together to stop the Internet casino menace. Our government receives no tax revenue from online gambling. Instead, they see American money flowing away overseas. And the credit card companies stand to lose thousands of dollars from people who rack up huge gambling bills and are either unable or unwilling to pay. Some of these cases have gone to litigation; a California couple recently won their lawsuit and avoided paying $115,000 they had lost gambling online.

Hopefully, the legal issues of Internet gambling will soon be resolved. Right now the antiquated Interstate Wire Act from the RICO racketeering laws of the 1960s leaves the entire field in a hazy, gray area. And that leads to potentially the worst-case scenario for Internet gambling. Even if you successfully navigate through all the possible pitfalls—slow pay, cheating casinos, and addiction—you could still get arrested for illegal gambling. Though this is highly unlikely to happen, it could become a possibility, depending on how the law is clarified in the future. I've included an article by attorney Robert Loeb in Appendix 3 to give a greater legal perspective on this complex issue.

LOG ON OR LOG OUT?

Given the long list of obstacles, many players assume Internet gambling is just not worth the hassle. It is indeed a tough call to make. I finally quit playing for a couple of reasons, such as constantly being lied to about when I could expect to receive my check, but the deciding factor for me became the shifting legislative winds in Washington. When I first started playing online, I was convinced the activity was perfectly legal. However, Congress started pushing hard to outlaw it. Now, while I (like Robert Loeb) consider it highly unlikely any individual American bettor will be prosecuted, I didn't want to take that chance, and I decided to move on from Internet gambling before the laws changed and possibly made it a crime.

Now, in retrospect, I probably overreacted. A few years have passed since then and the government still hasn't clarified this law. Yet with the high-profile explosion of poker on the Internet (such as Chris Moneymaker winning millions at the 2003 World Series of Poker after qualifying in an online tournament), I think Internet gambling is only going to become more common and accepted. His unprecedented success actually encouraged many other poker players to go online to sharpen their skills and win money. The year after Moneymaker's amazing Cinderella story, several players from an Internet poker site made the World Series of Poker's final table, and the winner once again originated from an online tournament.

So, for better or worse, it looks like Internet gambling is here to stay, and it could grab a huge share of the gambling market in the future (assuming any lingering legal issues are resolved). And despite their drawbacks, these cybercasinos certainly offer many benefits. Novice blackjack players don't have to worry about making mistakes, since they can keep a basic strategy chart right on the desk or even use a popup one (available at www.casinosage.com) while playing online. Experienced card-counting warriors can ply their trade from the comfort of home rather than traveling to every remote casino on the face of the planet, searching for new games.

However, the main attraction is still the money. The bonuses are so generous they more than make up for the occasional cheating or deadbeat casino. There may not be another legitimate business in the world in which you can potentially turn $1,000 into six figures. The fat bonuses available online are especially ideal for a beginning player starting out on a shoestring bankroll, since Internet casinos offer the best chance to make any serious money for those limited to only small bets.

PARAMETERS

The bevy of bonuses available on the Internet is almost endless. The difficulty comes in sorting through all the offers and determining which are really worthwhile and which should get sent to the trash. First, keep in mind the old axiom—*if it looks too good to be true, it probably is.* Whenever an Internet casino is giving away the farm with simply incredible promotions, it should cause concern. It may be running a Ponzi scheme, and your money might end up on the wrong end of the pyramid. This doesn't mean you should pass on the best deals, but you should definitely be more suspicious. Here is an example: I received an unsolicited e-mail yesterday from an Internet casino promising a 50 percent bonus on deposits up to $5,000. Now, getting $2,500 in free money is a tremendous deal, but such a generous offer could be financial suicide for the casino. It might be worth the risk, but there's a good chance the balloon will pop before you get paid, or the bonus could get rescinded. Losing $1,000 to claim a $2,500 bonus that never materializes can quickly wipe the smile off your face.

The main criteria for evaluating these opportunities are risk and time. Always carefully read the fine print and make sure you fully understand all the conditions necessary to qualify for a bonus. Usually, there are a fixed number of play-through requirements. Here is an example from the highly respected InterCasino. It gives its customers up to $80 in free money each and every month. To qualify, you need to play through this bonus at least twenty five times. To evaluate this deal, you first figure out the total amount of action required (25 × $80 = $2,000 in wagers). InterCasino's blackjack game has a disadvantage of approximately 0.5 percent, so you would lose about $10 over the course of your play. This leaves an average profit of $70.

Fortunately, the games are very fast on the Internet and flat betting $10 a hand creates $2,000 in action in less than one hour at most casinos. So your EV is about $70 an hour. This is oversimplified and doesn't take all the other tasks into consideration (correspondence, bookkeeping, begging to get paid, etc.), but is a reasonable way to judge whether a particular deal is worth your time. Of course, you can dramatically increase the hourly wage by betting more—at $20 per hand, you would take only thirty minutes to qualify, and $100 a pop would require less than ten minutes of your time, all for the same $70 profit, but with a great deal more fluctuation.

WHERE TO PLAY

With so many portals to explore, it's difficult to decide where to take your gambling dollars. A number of Web sites try to bridge this gap and condense the information overload into practical advice for the online gaming community. A few of the more popular sites are www.casinomeister.com, www.winneronline.com, the www.wizard ofodds.com, www.casinocity.com, www.gamemasteronline.com, and www.gonegambling.com. Topics covered at these places are casino reviews, message boards, sites to be avoided, payment problems, and current bonus offers. A few other well-visited spots are www.gambling grumbles.com, which resolves disputes; www.bonusrating.com, which lists various promotions; and www.fairbet.com, which independently tests casino software for fairness.

These sites contain many helpful tips, but they are not always impartial. Their judgment in rating Internet casinos can easily be clouded, since they carry ads from some of the same casinos they review. This is often their only source of revenue, so it is understandable that they might hesitate to bite the hand that feeds them and blacklist a casino that is one of their biggest advertisers.

A good rule of thumb is to stick to the places that use established software. Some of the bigger providers for Internet casinos are CryptoLogic, Boss Media, and Microgaming. Also, it is much less likely you will have problems if you deal with Internet casinos in established countries where they are well regulated. Australia and Great Britain have taken a more realistic approach than the United States and have licensed online gambling, rather than try to prohibit it. They maintain high standards, and it is extremely doubtful operations in these two countries will fold up for lack of funds. Another wise precaution is to patronize Internet casinos that are audited by an independent company. An example of this is VIP Casino, whose payout rates are reviewed by PricewaterhouseCoopers.

However, you still need to make sure it is legal for you to play. The casino may be properly set up and perfectly legal in the country where it originates, but citizens of other countries might be excluded from being able to play there. Some cybercasinos will refuse action from citizens of Canada or the United States (for legal reasons), from residents of Denmark (bonus abuse), or from any comrades in Russia (fear of not being able to collect).

HOW TO PURCHASE CHIPS

One of the biggest questions regarding Internet gambling is "Are the financial transactions secure?" The only thing worse than losing two grand shooting dice on your laptop would be if the casino manager stole your credit card number and bought a new Rolex for his girlfriend in Zurich. Fortunately, the industry has gone to great lengths to protect your funds and outright theft is rare.

However, it can be difficult to get your money into play. At your friendly local casino, this is a simple process. You just grab the money in your wallet and slap it down on the felt. Yet there is no way to physically hand over cash to your Internet blackjack dealer, so other methods must be used. Credit cards and PayPal used to be the most common, but both have backed away from online gambling. Many other options have been developed to fill this void. The best known is NETELLER (an online account that can be funded by electronic bank-transfer, credit card, or certain bank deposits). Other methods are ACH (a direct bank-transfer mechanism), money orders, checks (sent by mail), wire transfers, and FirePay (a Web-based account).

NUTS AND BOLTS

The first step in getting started is to choose an Internet casino and download its software. If you only plan on playing blackjack, then you can usually opt for a condensed edition, rather than the full-fledged version that contains every casino game. A broadband connection is optimal for this task, because each casino is normally saved to your hard drive. It can always be deleted later if you never play at that site again.

A critical component to plundering Internet casinos is keeping good records. One reason for this is to see if your overall results mirror those of land-based casinos, but the more important reason is to keep track of your money. Once you start playing at multiple casinos, the maze of deposits, bonuses, and withdrawals can get very confusing, very fast. If you are proficient with database software, setting up the bookkeeping is a snap. It's best to have all this info on your computer, where you can access it quickly anytime, even while you are playing. But if you haven't been able to open up Excel since your son went off to college, then an old-fashioned pencil and ledger book will also do the job. You will need to keep track of several different categories. Here are the bare minimum:

1. Name of casino
2. Mailing and Web site address
3. Telephone number
4. E-mail address
5. User name and password
6. Date and amount of all deposits
7. Time played and ending balance
8. Bonuses (when requested and when received)
9. Payment (when requested and when received)
10. Profit or Loss

This list gives the basic structure for making money online, but for anyone wanting more details on Internet gambling, I recommend *Crushing the Internet Casinos*, by Barry Meadow.

FINE POINTS

Here are a couple of final tips to help you succeed. Getting paid is usually the biggest headache of gambling online. A number of places will offer every lame excuse in the book to either avoid paying or to deny the bonus. Sometimes these denials are technically legitimate—perhaps you didn't meet some obscure detail of the promotion, such as only playing during a full moon. But others are just plain bogus. Either way, a lot of these problems can be avoided by going the extra mile. If you vary your bets, play over several days, and leave your money in the account for a while, you will look more like a normal gambler and much less like a smash-and-grab bonus hustler. Just make sure doing so will not violate any of the terms and conditions of the bonus you sought in the first place. Also keep in mind that online blackjack is a losing game without the bonuses. So you are giving away a small percentage on every extra hand you play over the minimum requirements.

Another big problem is that the transactions (deposits and withdrawals) are difficult to trace. Most Internet casinos use generic names, and if two different places each owed you the same amount, it's hard to tell which one has paid and which one is still shining you on. Therefore, it is helpful to deposit odd amounts ($510 instead of $500, for example). This can greatly aid in tracing the flow of money and keep you from sending angry e-mails to the wrong company.

I also suggest you start out conservatively in relation to your blackjack bankroll. The Internet gambling industry is unregulated, and there is little recourse if you have a beef with any casino. Many have gone out of business or simply folded up shop and opened elsewhere under a new name. It is bad enough to lose your money with the click of a mouse, but even more aggravating to win, then still end up losing because some offshore casino absconded with your cash. A case in point is a friend of mine who deposited $100,000 at one Internet casino that subsequently went under and recovered only a very small portion of his money. But despite the risks, I still feel Internet gambling has great potential and may represent the future for blackjack players looking for an edge.

Online gambling may not be legal in certain jurisdictions. Make sure to consult with the appropriate authorities in your area before you play for money online.

CHAPTER EIGHTEEN

♣ ♠ ♥ ♦

The Final Hand

Many of you began this book wondering, "Can I become a pro?" By now you're knowledgeable enough to see what it takes and whether it is something you want to try. Just don't miss the forest for the trees. I know one blackjack player who made over $100,000 a year on slot machine promotions in Laughlin, so don't be afraid to look beyond the obvious. This is why I discussed a few other techniques other than traditional card counting (blackjack tournaments, Internet casinos, etc.) that can give you an edge over the casinos.

However, I am still a purist. I made my mark in the gambling world the old-fashioned way, one deck at a time. And I believe card counting is the most viable way to beat the house. It's not easy, but discipline, drive, and determination will help you navigate the labyrinth of casino traps. When a job needs to be done, there are generally two types of people: those who jump in and help move the piano, and those who quickly offer to move the stool. If you're the type always looking for the easy way out, your chance of succeeding in blackjack is greatly diminished. However, the skills and techniques needed to become a winning blackjack player can be mastered by nearly anyone willing to put in the work.

THE REAL WINNERS

I wrote about the danger of addiction in chapter 17. But this weakness is not just limited to losing money or the family farm. Part of the appeal of playing blackjack for a living is the adrenaline rush it offers. There are few professions in the world that can match the "workplace environment" of action-packed casinos. It is all too easy to get caught up in this excitement. And it is very possible to win at blackjack, but still lose at life.

I certainly have nothing against making money. My main regret after each trip is that I didn't win more. But gambling is an industry that can really warp your perspective and values. It certainly affected me, and I spent too much time and energy pursuing the almighty dollar and too little pursuing truly important matters.

Blaise Pascal stands out as one of history's most intriguing individuals. He was an outstanding philosopher, a brilliant theologian, and a gifted mathematician. He also did some of the earliest work on gambling probability. This unusual combination of rare genius in so many different fields gave him a rather unique perspective on life, and his most famous quote touched on the theme of gambling and God. He postulated that the ultimate wager had to do with our existence and eternal destiny, rather than cards or chips.

Therefore, I think it's important to find balance and make sure your life is meaningful. Many people believe that all gamblers will eventually die broke. That saying is at least half-true. We do all die. There is an old Italian proverb that says, "When the game is over, the pawns, rooks, kings, and queens all go back into the same box." When I've cashed in my last chips and they lower my casket into the ground, a few friends and my loved ones will toss in a little dirt, then express their final thoughts. I hope they will remember me as more than just someone who made a lot of money at blackjack.

ROLLER COASTER

Hopefully, this book not only showed you what it takes to be a pro, but what it doesn't take. Success isn't restricted to math geniuses or those who possess a phenomenal memory. If you're willing to work hard, the odds are good that you will become a winning player. However, to do it for a living does require a sizable bankroll— I would recommend at least $50,000 for a full-time player. This would yield over $100 an hour, enough to make your time worthwhile and earn you plenty of comps to keep travel costs to a minimum. Not many other jobs offer such high pay along with the chance to eat free in gourmet restaurants every day and stay in fancy suites every night.

Yet, while there is certainly a great deal of mystique and appeal that comes with being a professional blackjack player, there are also drawbacks. At times it can be an awfully hard way to make easy money. The wild fluctuations can be brutal, and unless you are well financed, they can play havoc with your psyche. For some it is the dream job, but for others it can easily become a nightmare. I compare it to being on the ocean. Some people can't take the waves and spend much of the cruise leaning over the rail. Blackjack is similar to that. Some counters casually accept losing as part of the game while others spend all night tossing restlessly in bed after a tough day at the tables. But until you get in the boat, you will probably never know how well you can handle the stormy swings.

One solution may be to look at blackjack as the perfect part-time vocation—a great supplement on top of your regular job. This is probably the wisest course to follow, especially for anyone just starting out in blackjack. There is value in having a career with security, a regular paycheck, and health benefits. When you rely on blackjack to pay the rent every month, it can be a roller-coaster existence that's hard to stomach.

However, don't get me wrong. Making card counting your business can be a smart financial decision for the right person and a very enriching experience. My card-counting career took me far from my small hometown in Maine to places I never dreamed of visiting—aboard cruise ships and to foreign lands where I was the only Caucasian in the entire casino. I've eaten foods I never thought I'd try, like frog legs, escargot, oysters, and caviar; and some dishes I'd like to forget, like the time in Korea when I gagged on a dinner that featured dog meat as the main ingredient. I've visited all fifty states and twenty-seven countries and walked on cobblestone streets in Santo Domingo dating back to the time of Columbus and played in the world's oldest casino in Belgium. I've watched spectacular sunsets at Lake Tahoe and slowly sipped Dom Pérignon champagne after a big win. I've also trudged wearily along the Jersey shore, fighting off a bitter cold wind, while mumbling to myself after another disastrous day at the tables. I've been wined and dined like a king, and I've also been treated like a criminal.

Was it all worth it? In the end, each of us will march to the beat of our own drummer, and you have to decide how high you want to climb. Over 99 percent of the players at a blackjack table will lose in the long run. They are like salmon trying to buck the odds and swim upstream.

Personally, I have never liked losing, and I feel it is far better to be the fisherman than the fish. I've given you enough ammunition to turn the tables on the casinos and beat them at their own game. So the choice is yours. I hope you will choose to play blackjack like the pros.

APPENDIX 1

A Sample Log

Here is a sample log. The dates, places, names, and numbers have all been changed.

Mandalay Bay Casino

Date	Shift	Name	Hours	Result	Comments
Sept 24–27 (Sa–Tu)	S	Kevin Blackwood	8	L 23,100	RFB Parlor Suite[1]
Nov 1–3 (Fr–Su)	S	Kevin Blackwood	5	W 14,400	Lots of heat Sunday, from PB Mike Edsall
Dec 14–16 (We–Fr)	D	Jered Souder	4	W 5,550	I wore glasses and Pit was cool

Hilton Casino

Date	Shift	Name	Hours	Result	Comments
Feb 16–17 (Mo–Tu)	G	Dr. Casey Martin	2	W 15,200	Massive heat
April 18 (Th)	S	No Name	1	L 6,400	Nervous Pit
June 22 (Sa)	D	Jim Hill	1	W 2,900	86'd by shift manager[2]

Now let's break down each category. Dates are important to keep for several reasons. It's important to space out your visits to specific casinos or towns. I rarely returned to the same club more frequently than every other month. Otherwise you face the problem of getting too well known. There were occasions when I bent this rule—such as when incredible profitable situations occurred that I didn't think would last long—but for the most part I tried to minimize my exposure in any one place. You might also notice I included the days of the week. These are important for your log because pit bosses work different schedules. A club that is difficult to play on a Friday might be totally relaxed on a Tuesday, when the regular paranoid shift manager is off.

Playing under a pseudonym is a gray area that many people are uncomfortable with. Unfortunately, it becomes the only option for many high-stakes pros once their identity is burned. Giving out your real name, even to a new casino, often will bring an immediate barring if you are already on a widely distributed undesirable list. Consequently, in order to survive at the blackjack tables, most serious card counters are forced to go undercover and take on a new persona and name. You will see from the above examples that I switched to a new name after getting heat during my November visit to Mandalay Bay. And after extreme scrutiny at the Hilton, I chose to not give any name for my play on April 18. If you do resort to using pseudonyms, it is critical to keep good records. Otherwise you will end up getting very confused about who you are and where you live.

The next category lists which of the three shifts I played. Most casinos are open twenty-four hours and operate three separate full-time shifts (day = D, swing = S, and graveyard = G). Just as the days of the week can change the mood of the club you are playing, so can the shifts. For example, it is not uncommon for a casino to be virtually unplayable for card counters on swing, but relaxed on graveyard.

The next two categories are hours played and win/loss. I didn't always keep track of the exact hours I played at each individual club, but it is helpful to record this data to keep from overplaying a particular casino. The win/loss is a far more important item to watch, because cumulative wins over time can draw a lot of attention. So even if you are not getting any scrutiny at a casino, it is wise to be cautious if you have previously taken a lot of money from their tables.

The last category covers comments on how the casino viewed my action. This is probably the most important item to enter into the log. If you play and travel a lot, it is easy to forget who to watch out for or where to be more careful. Also, this is the category where you should list any disguises you might have used. I personally didn't resort to any extravagant disguises (like getting a wig and a leather miniskirt, trying to pass as Tina Turner), but I did routinely vary some basic components of my appearance. I played with and without different types of glasses and would shave my beard or change my hairstyle, especially after getting a lot of heat.

The above examples contain only the basic information, but I've flagged two entries to expand on. Here is the additional data I recorded for the entry marked number 1: "Casino host Linda Urness loved my action and offered me comped tickets for a future Eagles concert at the Mandalay Bay. She is a big rock music fan, and I need to remember to bring her a *Hotel California* CD next visit as a thank-you gift."

The reason I included these details is because your most significant trips to the casinos are when you either win big or lose big. When I suffer through a financial bath like I did at the Mandalay Bay, I want to be able to take advantage of it since losing that much money should buy me a lot of future play. So I definitely try to get on the casino host's good side. One of the best ways to do that is to find out whatever you can about that person and try to cultivate that relationship.

The flip side is shown in the entry flagged as number 2. There I received immediate heat from the always vigilant Hilton pit and eventually got barred. Whenever these adverse events occur, it is critical to record as many details as possible about the casino personnel who detected your skillful play. Here is my entry from that event: "86'd by day shift manager, Kerry Livgren, a sharp-looking no-nonsense man in early fifties with blonde hair and bushy mustache."

The above sample log doesn't include the year along with the dates, but yours should. It is also mandatory to keep track of your overall win/loss. This is primarily to comply with IRS requirements, but also to give yourself an accurate read on how you are doing as a card counter. Many players fool themselves into thinking they are net winners when they are actually losing. Other items you might want to add would be what type of games you played and your bet spread. For example, many clubs will have a variety of options at the blackjack tables: on some trips I might have played their shoe games, while the next visit I attacked their single or double decks.

card counter. Man

APPENDIX 2

Hi-Opt II Matrix

I believe Hi-Opt II is the best all-around system to use for card counting. However, many players are scared off by its complexity and stiff learning curve. Therefore, I have simplified the index numbers in the following chart to lessen the difficulty in memorization. I did this by rounding *most* of the actual matrix numbers to the nearest multiple of 5 (5, 10, 15, and 20). While these approximations will reduce some of your accuracy, it greatly diminishes the chance for errors, as these numbers are much easier to recall in the heat of battle.

This simplified strategy will still squeeze out most of your edge and is generic enough to use for different conditions (rule changes or varying number of decks). This chart contains only numbers for the more important hands and assumes you will use basic strategy for all other situations.

S = stand, H = hit, D = double down, P = pair split

Player's Hand	DEALER'S UPCARD									
	2	3	4	5	6	7	8	9	10	A
16	S	S	S	S	S	15	15	10	0	10
15	S	S	S	S	S	20	15	15	5	20
14	−5	−5	S	S	S	H	H	20	10	20
13	−2	−2	−5	−5	−5	H	H	H	H	H
12	5	2	0	−2	−2	H	H	H	H	H
11	D	D	D	D	D	D	D	−5	−5	2
10	D	D	D	D	D	D	−5	−2	5	5
9	2	−2	−5	D	D	5	15	H	H	H
8	H	15	10	5	5	H	H	H	H	H
10-10	S	15	10	10	10	S	S	S	S	S
A-9	S	15	15	10	10	S	S	S	S	S
A-8	15	5	5	2	2	S	S	S	S	S
A-7	2	−5	D	D	D	S	S	H	H	H
A-6	2	−5	D	D	D	H	H	H	H	H
A-5	H	10	0	D	D	H	H	H	H	H
A-4	H	10	0	−5	D	H	H	H	H	H
A-3	H	10	5	−5	0	H	H	H	H	H
A-2	H	10	5	0	0	H	H	H	H	H

The correct way to use this chart is to alter your play (from basic strategy) whenever the true count equals or exceeds the matrix number. For example, normally you hit a hard 12 versus a 2 upcard, but if the true count is +5 or greater, then the proper play is to stand. Conversely, you stand on a 12 versus a 6 if the true count is greater than −2 (−3, −4, etc.). You also should take insurance anytime the true count reaches +4 or higher.

APPENDIX 3

Legal Issues

Is Blackjack Card Counting Illegal?

By Henry Tamburin, author of *Blackjack: Take the Money and Run*, popular columnist for *Casino Player*, and publisher of *Blackjack Insider*.

"How do casinos get away with excluding card counters from playing blackjack?"

As long as a card counter is only using his brains to decide how to play his hand, then the act of card counting is not illegal. Yet the Nevada courts have allowed casinos to exclude card counters because technically the casino is private property. Many players and lawyers believe that barring skillful players from playing blackjack is an unconstitutional form of discrimination. However, the Supreme Court prohibits discrimination only against persons who are members of "suspect classifications" based on race, creed, sex, national origin, age, or physical disability. Therefore, until a law is passed or blackjack players bring a challenge, casinos will continue the practice of barring card counters.

In Atlantic City casinos, the late Ken Uston won the right in the New Jersey courts for card counters to count cards there. Essentially, the New Jersey Supreme Court told the Atlantic City casinos that they could not bar card counters unless the New Jersey Casino Control Commission issued a rule saying that counters could be barred.

"Can the casinos legally 'backroom' a card counter?"

"Backrooming" is a word that has come to denote the practice of detaining or harassing a player who is barred. Usually, the casino will ask to see some form of identification and take the player's picture. Under common law and the laws of most states, it is illegal for a business establishment to detain a person, unless the customer has committed a crime and the business is holding the person while awaiting the arrival of police. Therefore, when a casino security agent asks if a player will accompany him to the office, the player has the right to refuse, unless he is being held for a crime. In Nevada, a casino has the right to question and detain any person suspected of cheating. New Jersey, however, made the point that card counting is not a crime and therefore it is not permissible for a casino to detain and question a person suspected of being a card counter. The casino also does not have the right to demand identification because it is ejecting someone for card counting. A player should not have to provide his name upon request of the casino, but it could conceivably be considered obstruction of justice to refuse to provide one's name upon the request of the police. A player also cannot be forced to pose for a photograph.

"Can a casino have a card counter arrested for trespassing if he returns and plays blackjack in a casino in which he was previously barred from playing?"

Most states have trespassing statutes that makes it a misdemeanor for a person to remain on or return to a property after receiving notice from the owner that the person is not allowed on the premises. When barring a card counter, most casinos will tell that person "not to return." However, the barred player usually does not face arrest and prosecution if he does return.

Internet Gambling: The Land of No Enforcement

By Robert A. Loeb, attorney and coauthor of *Blackjack and the Law*

Who Can Regulate or Prohibit Internet Gambling?

1. United States Government

The federal Wire Act (18 U.S.C. § 1084) is the primary federal law that can be, and has been, used to prosecute individuals and companies involved in the business of Internet gambling activities across state lines. In addition, the Travel Act (which outlaws crossing state lines to commit various crimes, and definitely can include gambling) and the Illegal Gambling Business Act (which basically makes it a federal crime to operate a continuing gambling business that is illegal in the state where it operates and involves five people) have been used to prosecute gambling entities that take bets over the telephone, and arguably could be used to prosecute federal Internet gambling cases.

The applicability of the Wire Act to Internet gambling is the subject of great confusion and debate. Even before gambling made its way to the Internet, it was unclear whether the Wire Act applies only to sports betting or to all gambling. Another issue is that the Wire Act covers "transmission of a wire communication." The law has not answered whether that applies to the Internet, and especially does not answer whether it covers a wireless connection to the Internet. Nevertheless, the federal government has rarely had trouble extending its jurisdiction, and even if the bettor maintains a wireless connection, almost all Internet communications are dependent on some form of wired communication for routing or other purposes.

The Wire Act has been used to obtain a federal conviction in the case of Jay Cohen. Cohen was one of the operators of an offshore betting service, which was being charged with federal crimes for illegal gambling. Perhaps he thought that the law would vindicate him, but in any event, Cohen made the mistake of returning to the United States from the Caribbean. It was only when he arrived here that he could be arrested and prosecuted. He was convicted in 2000, and that conviction has been upheld.

I have not been able to find any prosecution of bettors for Internet gambling. Many lawyers feel that the Wire Act does not cover individual bettors. I wouldn't go that far, because an individual bettor could theoretically be charged for aiding and abetting, or for conspiracy to engage in Internet betting. In fact, I know that some prosecutors in the U.S. Justice Department take that very position.

Since the advent of Internet gambling, there has always been legislation pending in Congress to prohibit Internet casinos, or make them impossible to operate. I think I've seen at least a hundred articles in different publications about the possible passage of bills that would ban Internet casinos or discourage them into oblivion. The Kyl, Goodlatte, and Leach bills have not yet been passed because of competing legislative interests. I would predict that eventually a watered-down compromise version of one of these bills will pass, with enough loopholes and exemptions that will make enforcement, already a difficult undertaking, impossible. These bills get caught up in politics, with various competing special interests, including the gaming industry, banks, Native Americans, antigambling organizations, Internet corporations, and legislators who don't understand the issues but are sensitive to the direction of political winds. It may well be that any legislation that gets passed is irrelevant.

The biggest obstacle to the effectiveness of any legislation is enforcement. In the legal field, the key word is jurisdiction. First, the government needs physical jurisdiction over the person or company it seeks to regulate in any way. Obviously, it is difficult to arrest, or serve a summons on, a person or an entity that is not located in a given state, and is not even physically in this country. It's just as difficult to fine or jail a person or entity that has never physically been in this country. And even if the federal government, or a state government, won a case against such an entity, how could you get at their assets, which are similarly not even in this country? In addition, the government needs what lawyers call subject matter jurisdiction over a dispute. Basically, this means that there has to be a clear law in place to govern Internet gambling, and there has to be sufficient activity within the United States to govern a particular transaction. Obviously, the government cannot force people from other countries to submit to the law of the United States, to come to the United States to face trial, and so on.

However, the regulatory power of the U.S. government is so great that it is the major force behind the decisions of MasterCard and Visa to restrict the use of their cards and accounts for Internet gambling. Similarly, domestic companies that finance Internet Gambling, develop software, and advertise Internet gambling, as well as, Internet service providers and land-based gambling corporations that might diversify onto the Internet, are all vulnerable to governmental regulation and "persuasion" to keep them from becoming involved with Internet casinos.

2. World Trade Organization

Early in 2004, a panel of the World Trade Organization (WTO) found that federal prohibitions against Internet gambling are an unfair trade barrier. The WTO would have the United States allow its citizens to gamble on the Internet, a privilege citizens of many other countries enjoy. On the one hand, there are American legislators who are reluctant to flaunt the WTO (because they urge other countries to follow WTO rulings on other subjects), and will be motivated to legalize Internet gambling in the United States, albeit with certain regulation and restrictions. On the other hand, there are other legislators who care little for the international community, and won't like to be told what to do by outsiders.

3. State Governments

Some states have enacted specific statutes to criminalize Internet gambling, while a majority of states claim that they would rely on already existing general gambling laws to prevent the legalization of Internet gambling, even without the specific prohibition on gambling on the Internet.

As of early 2002, five states (Illinois, Louisiana, Nevada, Oregon, and South Dakota) have specifically prohibited Internet gambling, according to the General Accounting Office. Kentucky, Minnesota, New York, and perhaps most other states have general gambling prohibitions under which officials are claiming that Internet gambling is implicitly outlawed.

4. The Verdict

There are few, if any, laws that specifically make Internet gambling illegal. But most prosecutors think Internet gambling is against the law, even for bettors. To my knowledge, only one bettor has been charged with gambling on the Internet (in Minnesota). But knowing how federal prosecutors work, it is inevitable that they will bring charges against some bettors in the future. That won't be not because they will be targeting the bettors, but because they will target the "bookies"—that is, the Internet casino owners or other facilitators of online betting. The prosecutors will want to get witnesses who have done business with the Internet casinos to testify about the Internet gambling companies. How will they induce the bettors to "cooperate" with the investigation? They'll do it by squeezing bettors, by threatening bettors with aiding and abetting an illegal operation. In fact, they won't merely threaten prosecution of the bettors; they will also get the bettors to admit to aiding and abetting, and they will get the bettors to testify against the Internet casinos, or others, in exchange for a promise of leniency. This may seem like a long shot, but some bettors will be the long-shot victims of these tactics.

GLOSSARY

ace-neutralized A multiparameter system that counts aces as zero to increase playing efficiency.

ace-reckoned A system that incorporates aces into its primary count to simplify betting.

action The total amount wagered over a period of time.

back-counting Counting the cards without playing, usually with the intent of signaling in a Big Player.

backed off A milder form of barring, without being trespassed from the property.

balanced count Any counting system in which the respective card count values balance out to zero.

bankroll Total amount of funds available for gambling.

barred Permanently prohibited from playing blackjack at a casino.

basic strategy The optimal way to play each hand of blackjack.

bet The player's wager on a particular hand.

bet sizing Optimally betting in relationship to your advantage.

bet spread The ratio between a player's minimum and maximum bets.

Big Player (BP) Big bettor for a blackjack team.

black book A book listing the individuals who are barred from entering casinos.

blackjack   The game of twenty-one, also an ace and a ten dealt on the first two cards.

blacks   Chips in the $100 denomination are commonly colored black.

burn card   After the shuffle and cut, one card is normally removed from play, and is called the burn card.

bust   Whenever the total of any hand exceeds 21, the hand loses.

bust card   The individual card that brings the hand's total over 21.

buy-in   The transfer of cash for chips at the table.

card counting   A system used to keep track of the cards that have been played that will give players an advantage over the house.

cashier's cage   The money transaction area in each casino where chips are cashed out.

casino manager   The top casino executive on duty.

chips   The tokens, unique to each casino, that are used for making wagers.

chip tray   The rack that drops into the blackjack table to hold the various rows of chips for the dealer to distribute to the rare players who win.

comp   Complimentary room, food, beverage, events, or shows that are offered by the casino to qualified players.

cooler   A prearranged stacked deck or shoe used in cheating.

CTR   A Currency Transaction Report, mandatory for any cash transactions totaling $10,000 or more in a twenty-four-hour period.

dealer   The casino employee who deals the cards.

discard rack   A clear plastic device screwed into the table to hold the used cards after play.

double down   Doubling the original bet and receiving only one additional card—typically done on a total of 10 or 11.

draws the paint   Receiving a ten-valued card when hitting.

eighty-six   Bar an individual from playing in the casino.

EV   The player's *expected value*, expressed in terms of win/loss.

exposed   Turning over a card so that its value can be seen.

face cards   Any ten-valued card (jack, queen, or king).

first base   The first seat at the blackjack table to the dealer's left.

first-basing   Seeing the dealer's hole card from the first-base position.

floorman   A casino executive who supervises part of a pit.

free roll   A situation in which there is absolutely no risk.

front-loading   Seeing the dealer's hole card from the front of the table as she tucks it in under her upcard.

Griffin Agency   Detective agency hired by many casinos to identify potential threats to the casino vaults.

handheld game   A blackjack game in which the dealer holds the cards in her hand rather than in a shoe.

hard hand Any blackjack hand not counting an ace as 11.

heads-up Playing alone against the dealer.

heat Whenever a card counter has his play scrutinized closely.

Hi-Lo One of the simplest and most popular counts in the world.

hit When a player scratches or signals the dealer for an extra card for his hand.

hole card The dealer's down card.

hole-card play Taking advantage of sloppy dealers who unknowingly show their hole card.

host A casino employee who caters to higher-betting customers.

house money Winnings over and above what you brought to the casino.

Illustrious 18 The eighteen most important matrix numbers for varying your play from basic strategy.

insurance If a dealer shows an ace up, any player can take insurance if he thinks the dealer might have blackjack and will get paid 2 to 1 on any winning bet.

junket Short gambling trips subsidized by the participating casino.

Kelly system betting A method for optimally betting in relationship to your perceived edge on any given hand.

loaded deck A deck (or decks) that has extra cards deliberately placed or removed to distort the correct proportion.

Martingale system Best known of the progressive betting systems where you double your bet after each loss.

matrix A mathematical chart of index numbers showing the correct number at which to deviate from basic strategy for card counters.

multilevel count Any system in which the count values are higher than plus or minus one.

multiparameter system A counting system that keeps track of at least two separate counts, usually a main count and a side count of aces.

natural Another term for a two-card 21, or blackjack.

nickels Chips in the $5 denomination.

pack The deck, or any undealt portion thereof.

paint Any picture card.

pair Any two cards of the same rank, including all 10s and face cards.

pat A hand that is 17 or higher and doesn't need a hit.

pays the table Usually means the dealer has busted and every player at the table wins.

penetration How deeply the cards are dealt before shuffling.

pit boss A supervisor for table games.

positive count A situation in which the remaining decks contain more high cards than low cards and favors the players rather than the house.

preferential shuffling   When a dealer consistently shuffles away most positive counts.

press   During a hot streak, many gamblers increase or "press" their bets.

progressive betting systems   Nonscientific and bogus methods to gain an edge over the house without counting cards, by changing your bets in a fixed manner.

push   A hand that ends in a tie and in which no money changes hands.

quarters   Chips in the $25 denomination.

RC   The running count. Overall count, unadjusted to decks remaining

reds   Chips in the $5 denomination are generally colored red.

RFB   Complimentary room, food, and beverage.

round   Each complete hand of play for everyone at the table.

ROR   Risk of ruin—the mathematical risk of losing every last dollar in your bankroll.

SD   The *standard deviation* from the expected result.

selective memory   Affliction that distorts an accurate recollection of previous results.

shift   Casinos are usually open twenty-four hours, with three separate eight-hour shifts (day, swing, and graveyard).

shift boss   Casino employee who supervises all of the pit bosses on a particular shift.

shoe   The device positioned to the left of the dealer that is used to hold multiple decks of cards.

shuffle-tracking   Following cards through the shuffle process to determine their approximate location in the next shoe.

silver   One-dollar chips are often silver-colored metallic tokens, evoking the days when actual silver dollars were used in the casinos.

six-deck shoe   Most common version of blackjack today with six decks dealt from a shoe.

snapper   Slang for a blackjack—when the first two cards consist of an ace and a ten.

soft hand   Any blackjack hand that counts an ace as 11.

split   Players (but not dealers) have the option to split any two equal-valued cards by matching their original bet. Then each hand is played separately.

spooking   Spying the dealer's hole card from across the pit.

spotter   A teammate who counts down a shoe for the Big Player.

stand   The decision to receive no more cards from the dealer.

steaming   Betting higher than normal to chase losses.

stiff   A hard hand totaling 12 to 16—a common sight for this author.

suits   Casino executives.

surrender   A rule that allows you to forfeit half your bet by throwing in your hand.

TC true count (RC ÷ remaining decks). Number derived when the RC is divided by number of remaining decks.

third base The playing position to the extreme right of the dealer.

toke A tip for the dealer.

unbalanced count Any counting system in which the card count values are unbalanced and do not add up to zero.

undersirables Advantage players who are not welcomed by casinos.

upcard The upcard is the card in the dealer's hand that is face up.

wonging Placing bets only during positive counts (named after Stanford Wong).

W2-G A tax form given out to casino slot patrons when they hit a jackpot over $1,200.

RESOURCES

Blackjack Library

Blackjack Attack, by Don Schlesinger
Blackjack for Blood, by Bryce Carlson
Burning the Tables in Las Vegas, by Ian Andersen
Casino Tournament Strategy, by Stanford Wong
Comp City, by Max Rubin
Million Dollar Blackjack, by Ken Uston
Professional Blackjack, by Stanford Wong
Theory of Blackjack, by Peter Griffin

Training Tools

Blackjack 6-7-8 Strategy Cards (www.stickysoft.com)
Casino Vérité Blackjack, by Norm Wattenberger (www.qfit.com)
Gamemaster's Blackjack School (www.bjrnet.com/gamemasters)

Magazines and Newsletters

Blackjack Insider Newsletter
Casino Player
Las Vegas Advisor
Midwest Gaming and Travel

Web Sites

AdvantagePlayer.com
BlackjackInfo (www.blackjackinfo.com)
BlackjackInsider (www.bjinsider.com)
Blackjack Review Network (www.bjrnet.com)
BlackjackTournaments.com
Bj21.com
CardCounter.com
CasinoCity.com

Table Conditions

"Current Blackjack News" (www.bj21.com)
Trackjack (www.trackjack.com)

ACKNOWLEDGMENTS

I am especially indebted to Mickey Weinberg and Howard Grossman for their willingness to read large parts of my manuscript and provide valuable feedback. Several illustrations and examples in this book came from insights provided by Howard and Mickey.

Stanford Wong also read large sections of my rough draft and offered excellent advice.

I greatly appreciate the willingness of authors Henry Tamburin and Robert Loeb to contribute their expertise on the complex legal issues involving gambling for my appendix. I also used two examples in chapter 4 from a great article Henry Tamburin wrote for *Casino Player Magazine* (the starting hands that yield 70 percent of your win or 85 percent of your loss).

Credit must also be extended to Don Schlesinger. Much of the criteria smart blackjack players use to evaluate good games stems from his classic work *Blackjack Attack*. Several sections in this book were influenced by his instrumental writing and his helpful suggestions.

Norm Wattenberger also deserves recognition for his powerful software package, Casino Vérité Blackjack, which gives players the tools to tap into the complex mathematical formulas unearthed by Schlesinger and others. All the computer simulations in this book were done using his software.

I am very grateful to the numerous other experts who graciously gave of their time and allowed me to interview them for this book. These include the following:

Bill Zender for chapters 10, 11, and 14
Rick Blaine for chapter 12
Allan Brown for chapters 12, 13, 14, and 17
Alex Strickland for chapters 12, 14, and 16
Blair Rodman for chapters 13 and 16
Anthony Curtis for chapters 13 and 16
Eddie Rhoades for chapter 13
Kenneth Smith for chapter 13

Many other authors either influenced this book directly or affected my card-counting career and deserve credit, most notably the late great Kenny Uston, whose inspiration can be seen throughout this book. Other influences include Bryce Carlson, Arnold Snyder, Lawrence Revere, Peter Griffin, Lance Humble, Edward Thorp, Julian Braun, Fred Renzey, Barry Meadow, Ian Andersen, and the incomparable George C.

I am extremely grateful to both Greg Dinkin and Frank Scatoni at Venture Literary and to Matthew Benjamin at HarperCollins for their vision and energy in putting this project together.

Special thanks also go out to the following:
Walt Fox and Steve C., for critiquing the first four chapters
Al Rogers for providing excellent feedback on chapters 6 and 7
Robert Parker for his helpful suggestions to improve chapter 11
Karl Keska, Greg Whiteley, and Mike Bilyeu for their input on chapter 12
Bob Welch for his insights on chapter 18
Rod Wood for his research on blackjack training tools

Michael Dalton for his contributions to the Resources

Rob Wiser for suggesting a more humorous way to explain comps

Dan Pegoda for helping me revise some rough spots

Justin Wood and Tim Wood for their work on the graphs and tables

Dr. Eliot Jacobson for allowing me to use his Hi-Opt I and Hi-Lo index charts

Olaf Vancura and Ken Fuchs for allowing me to use material from *Knock-Out Blackjack*

Stanford Wong for allowing me to use material from *Casino Tournament Strategy*

And finally, heartfelt thanks to my wonderful wife, and also to Tony and Cindy Favreau for their tireless work in reading and critiquing my manuscript. This book is markedly better because of their help.

INDEX